F. T
edic
ns of plans
umer durable, as ex
odic consumer antici
main purp
gthen the pr   f
ntentions in ...   y ap-
te revisions of sa   size.
rocedures, and better sp
ecasting equations.

ECONOMIC FORECASTS AND EXPECTATIONS

NATIONAL BUREAU OF ECONOMIC RESEARCH
Studies in Business Cycles

Economic Forecasts and Expectations

ANALYSES OF FORECASTING

BEHAVIOR AND PERFORMANCE

JACOB MINCER

Editor

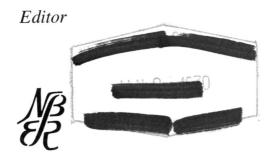

NATIONAL BUREAU OF ECONOMIC RESEARCH

New York 1969

Distributed by COLUMBIA UNIVERSITY PRESS

NEW YORK AND LONDON

NATIONAL BUREAU OF ECONOMIC RESEARCH

RELATION OF THE DIRECTORS TO THE WORK AND PUBLICATIONS OF THE NATIONAL BUREAU OF ECONOMIC RESEARCH

1. The object of the National Bureau of Economic Research is to ascertain and to present to the public important economic facts and their interpretation in a scientific and impartial manner. The Board of Directors is charged with the responsibility of ensuring that the work of the National Bureau is carried on in strict conformity with this object.

2. The President of the National Bureau shall submit to the Board of Directors, or to its Executive Committee, for their formal adoption all specific proposals for research to be instituted.

3. No research report shall be published until the President shall have submitted to each member of the Board the manuscript proposed for publication, and such information as will, in his opinion and in the opinion of the author, serve to determine the suitability of the report for publication in accordance with the principles of the National Bureau. Each manuscript shall contain a summary drawing attention to the nature and treatment of the problem studied, the character of the data and their utilization in the report, and the main conclusions reached.

4. For each manuscript so submitted, a special committee of the Board shall be appointed by majority agreement of the President and Vice Presidents (or by the Executive Committee in case of inability to decide on the part of the President and Vice Presidents), consisting of three directors selected as nearly as may be one from each general division of the Board. The names of the special manuscript committee shall be stated to each Director when the manuscript is submitted to him. It shall be the duty of each member of the special manuscript committee to read the manuscript. If each member of the manuscript committee signifies his approval within thirty days of the transmittal of the manuscript, the report may be published. If at the end of that period any member of the manuscript committee withholds his approval, the President shall then notify each member of the Board, requesting approval or disapproval of publication, and thirty days additional shall be granted for this purpose. The manuscript shall then not be published unless at least a majority of the entire Board who shall have voted on the proposal within the time fixed for the receipt of votes shall have approved.

5. No manuscript may be published, though approved by each member of the special manuscript committee, until forty-five days have elapsed from the transmittal of the report in manuscript form. The interval is allowed for the receipt of any memorandum of dissent or reservation, together with a brief statement of his reasons, that any member may wish to express; and such memorandum of dissent or reservation shall be published with the manuscript if he so desires. Publication does not, however, imply that each member of the Board has read the manuscript, or that either members of the Board in general or the special committee have passed on its validity in every detail.

6. Publications of the National Bureau issued for informational purposes concerning the work of the Bureau and its staff, or issued to inform the public of activities of Bureau staff, and volumes issued as a result of various conferences involving the National Bureau shall contain a specific disclaimer noting that such publication has not passed through the normal review procedures required in this resolution. The Executive Committee of the Board is charged with review of all such publications from time to time to ensure that they do not take on the character of formal research reports of the National Bureau, requiring formal Board approval.

7. Unless otherwise determined by the Board or exempted by the terms of paragraph 6, a copy of this resolution shall be printed in each National Bureau publication.

(Resolution adopted October 25, 1926, and revised February 6, 1933, February 24, 1941, and April 20, 1968)

CONTENTS

TABLES

CHARTS

FOREWORD

The basic motivation of the studies collected in this volume is the belief that a proper understanding of how the economy functions is not possible without knowledge of how economic expectations are formed and how accurate they are. In contrast to the usual research conditions in which expectational data are not available, these essays deal with recorded expectational or forecasting data. The data provide an opportunity for substantive and methodological inquiry into the basic questions concerning the formation and accuracy of economic expectations. The essays complement one another in focussing on various aspects of these questions.

The following is a brief guide to the contents of the studies in the order in which they are presented. More detailed summaries are provided in the text of each essay.

The first essay, by Jacob Mincer and Victor Zarnowitz, is an exposition and development of methods for assessing the predictive accuracy of forecasts. Accuracy is evaluated first by means of statistical measures of the closeness with which predictions approximate realizations. Accuracy analysis in this absolute sense is followed by a comparative analysis, in which predictive performance is evaluated by comparisons of actual forecast errors with errors resulting from alternative or "benchmark" extrapolations of the series. The margin of superiority of forecasts over such extrapolations can be viewed as a measure of substantive forecasting effectiveness.

The testing of forecasts against benchmark extrapolations is an extension of "naive model" procedures. It is proposed as an optimal naive model test. The optimal benchmark extrapolation is one in which parameters (weights) to be applied to past data in projecting the future are not simply assumed but, rather, are estimated from the data so as to yield the smallest prediction error. Optimal benchmarks of this sort are approximated in practice by linear autoregressions.

Extrapolations not only serve as benchmarks for the evaluation of forecasting performance but may also be viewed as ingredients in the formulation of forecasts. Methods are presented to decompose forecasts and forecast errors into extrapolative and nonextrapolative (autonomous) components. The analysis is extended to multiperiod forecasting, and illustrated by applications to a sample of macroeconomic forecasts compiled in the National Bureau's study of short-term economic forecasting.

One element of forecast error arises from errors in current and past data which constitute the base for projecting the future. In the second study, Rosanne Cole attempts to estimate to what degree forecasting accuracy might be impaired by the existence of these measurement or data errors. Her analysis distinguishes between effects of data errors on systematic (bias) and random components of forecast errors, and between effects arising from errors in variables and from errors in estimated relationships among variables.

Using successive revisions of provisional GNP estimates as a measure of GNP data errors, and simulating both extrapolative and econometric forecasting methods, Cole estimates that over one-third of the observed average forecast error is likely to have been induced by data errors.

Questions about forecasting behavior, rather than accuracy, are the central focus of the essay by Jacob Mincer. One of the questions is: Can we learn from data on actual forecasts how the forecasts were generated? Specifically, can we learn something about the nature of the forecasting procedure, at least insofar as the extrapolative part of forecasting is concerned? Within limits, positive answers are obtained for linear extrapolation.

These results are based upon a theoretical analysis of properties and implications of different forms of linear extrapolation. The analysis shows that adaptive or "error-learning" behavior is not restricted to the exponential form (geometrically declining weights applied to past observations) but can be ascribed to all forms of linear extrapolation. Moreover, a frequently observed or postulated phenomenon, known as regressivity in forecasting, is associated with a particular type of nonexponential extrapolation, termed "convex." Convex forecasting is adaptive, in the sense that forecast revisions are a fraction of the currently observed forecast error, but the fraction is smaller for longer-term than for near-term forecasts.

The analysis developed in Mincer's paper is extended and applied by Stanley Diller to an exploration of the term structure of interest rates. Diller starts with the question: If the forward rates implicit in the term structure can be viewed as market forecasts of future spot rates, what is the form and what are the properties of the implicit forecasting function? Earlier investigators have inferred two seemingly independent properties of forecasting behavior from data on the term structure: adaptivity — revisions of future forecasts based on discrepancies between past forecasts and current realizations, and regressivity — the prediction that future values will tend to move toward normal or trend levels. To these, Diller adds a third: extrapolation — if the forward rates are forecasts, they must be in part expressible as an extrapolation of past spot rates. Diller shows that all three properties are satisfied by a forecasting scheme with a convex extrapolative component.

In ascertaining the empirical consistency of such a scheme with several sets of data, Diller adduces support for the Hicks-Meiselman-Kessel formulations of the expectations hypothesis. He also provides further insights and leads for future research by empirically implementing several alternative decompositions of forecasts (forward rates) into extrapolative and other components, and by exploring their accuracy as predictors of subsequent spot rates.

The last essay, by Thomas Juster, is an analysis of the predictive performance of intentions or plans to buy consumer durables, as expressed in periodic consumer anticipations surveys. Juster compares the predictive contribution of consumer buying intentions data to that of other variables, such as income, income change, and expressed attitudes of optimism or pessimism regarding near-term economic prospects. He finds that intentions data were superior predictors of future purchases by different groups of consumers (cross sections), but performed rather weakly in past efforts to forecast changes in purchases by the population as a whole over time.

Juster's main purpose in this study is to strengthen the predictive power of buying intentions in time series by appropriate revisions of sample size, sampling procedures, and better specifications of forecasting equations.

The proposed reformulation is a logical implication of the notion that expressed intentions represent imperfect information on the subjective purchase probabilities held by consumers. With such reformulation, Juster arrives at the following tentative conclusions, based on accuracy analyses of admittedly short time series: When used in conjunction with such variables as income and income change, the anticipations variables typically exert a dominant influence in predictive efficiency. Forecasting equations incorporating anticipations generate much more accurate predictions than autoregressive extrapolation. Forecasting models containing both consumer attitudes and consumer buying intentions perform best, provided properly measured intentions data are available.

This volume is the fourth in the series of research reports of the National Bureau's study of short-term economic forecasting.[1] The first two essays in this volume were conceived as methodological frameworks for the statistical analysis of forecasting data compiled by the study. In addition to serving this purpose, the formulations and their applications to the empirical materials stimulated additional related research in expectational economics. This research is embodied in the third and fourth essays. The fifth essay has its independent origin in continued analyses of surveys of consumer anticipations conducted at the National Bureau. Efforts to improve the forecasting efficiency of these surveys have been greatly strengthened by the cooperation of the U.S. Census Bureau.

The National Bureau's study of short-term economic forecasting is supported by grants from Whirlpool Corporation, General Electric Company, Ford Motor Company Fund, Relm Foundation, and U.S. Steel Corporation, as well as by other funds of the National Bureau. A grant of electronic computer time to the National Bureau by the International Business Machines Corporation was used for some of the statistical analyses in this volume. Juster's study of consumer anticipations was supported, in part, by the National Science Foundation.

We are indebted to the Bureau staff reading committees, which included Gary Becker, Phillip Cagan, Milton Friedman, John Kendrick, and Julius Shiskin; and to the Board reading committee, which in-

[1] The three reports thus far published are: Geoffrey H. Moore and Julius Shiskin, *Indicators of Business Expansions and Contractions,* New York, NBER, 1967; Victor Zarnowitz, *An Appraisal of Short-Term Economic Forecasts,* New York, NBER, 1967; Rendigs Fels and C. Elton Hinshaw, *Forecasting and Recognizing Business Cycle Turning Points,* New York, NBER, 1968. Scheduled for publication is R. Cole, "Errors in Estimates of Gross National Product."

cluded Emilio G. Collado, Henri Theil, and the late A. G. Abramson. Helpful comments and suggestions were also received from Gregory Chow, Franklin Fisher, Zvi Griliches, Albert Hart, George Katona, Reuben Kessel, Michael Lowell, E. Scott Maynes, Anna Schwartz, and Lester Telser. Geoffrey H. Moore's interest in forecasting behavior and performance and his influence on the substance of this volume predated the initiation of the studies and continued through their development. Finally, the volume represents a largely cooperative effort: The intellectual debt of each author to the co-authors is self-evident.

We are grateful for highly competent research assistance to: Martha Calaghan Bergsten, Avrohn Eisenstein, Dorothy Finger, Veronica Lavitola, Paul Wachtel, and Cecilia Weidemann. The charts were expertly drawn by H. Irving Forman and the manuscript was edited by Sharon Rasmussen.

JACOB MINCER

ECONOMIC FORECASTS AND EXPECTATIONS

ONE

The Evaluation
of Economic Forecasts

JACOB MINCER AND VICTOR ZARNOWITZ

INTRODUCTION

An economic forecast may be called "scientific" if it is formulated as
a verifiable prediction by means of an explicitly stated method which
can be reproduced and checked.[1] Comparisons of such predictions and
the realizations to which they pertain provide tests of the validity and
predictive power of the economic model which produced the forecasts.
Such empirical tests are an indispensable basis for further scientific
progress. Conversely, as knowledge accumulates and the models improve, the reliability of forecasts, viewed as information about the
future, is likely to improve.

Forecasts of future economic magnitudes, unaccompanied by an
explicit specification of a forecasting method, are not scientific in the
above sense. The analysis of such forecasts, which we shall call "business forecasts," is nevertheless of interest.[2] There are a number of
reasons for this interest in business forecasts:

NOTE: Numbers in brackets refer to bibliographic references at the end of each
chapter.

[1] The definition is borrowed from Henri Theil [7, pp. 10 ff.].

[2] In practice, sharp contrasts between scientific economic model forecasts and business forecasts are seldom found; more often, the relevant differences are in the *degree*

1. To the extent that the predictions are accurate, they provide information about the future.

2. Business forecasts are relatively informative if their accuracy is not inferior to the accuracy of forecasts arrived at scientifically, particularly if the latter are more costly to obtain.

3. Conversely, the margin of inferiority (or superiority) of business forecasts relative to scientific forecasts serves as a yardstick of progress in the scientific area.

4. Regardless of the predictive performance ascertainable in the future, business forecasts represent a sample of the currently prevailing climate of opinion. They are, therefore, a datum of some importance in understanding current economic behavior.

5. Even though the methods which produce the forecasts are not specified by the forecasters, it is possible to gain some understanding of the genesis of forecasts by relating the predictions to other available data.

In this paper we are concerned with the analysis of business forecasts for some of these purposes. Specifically, we are interested in methods of assessing the degree of accuracy of business forecasts both in an absolute and in a relative sense. In the Absolute Accuracy Analysis (Section I) we measure the closeness with which predictions approximate their realizations. In the Relative Accuracy Analysis (Section II) we assess the net contributions, if any, of business forecasts to the information about the future available from alternative, relatively quick and cheap methods. The particular alternative or benchmark method singled out here for analysis is extrapolation of the past history of the series which is being predicted. The motivation for this choice of benchmark is spelled out in Section II. It will be apparent, however, that our relative accuracy analysis is suitable for comparisons of any two forecast methods.

The treatment of extrapolations as benchmarks against which the predictive power of business forecasts is measured does not imply

---

to which the predictions are explicit about their methods, and are reproducible. Information on the methods is not wholly lacking for the business forecasts, nor is it always fully specified for econometric model predictions. Note also that distinctions between unconditional and conditional forecasting, or between point and interval forecasts are not the same as between scientific and nonscientific forecasts. The latter are usually unconditional point predictions, but so can "scientific" forecasts be. [Cf. 7, p. 4.]

that business forecasts and extrapolations constitute mutually exclusive methods of prediction. It is rather plausible to assume that most forecasts rely to some degree on extrapolation. If so, forecast errors are partly due to extrapolation errors. Hence, an analysis of the predictive performance of extrapolations can contribute to the understanding and assessment of the quality of business forecasts. Accordingly, we proceed in Section III to inquire into the relative importance of extrapolations in generating business forecasts, and to study the effects of extrapolation error on forecasting error.[3]

All analysts of economic forecasting owe a large intellectual debt to Henri Theil, who pioneered in the field of forecast evaluation. A part of the Absolute Accuracy Analysis section in this paper is an expansion and direct extension of Theil's ideas formulated in [8]. Our treatment, indeed, parallels some of the further developments which Theil recently published.[4] However, while the starting point is similar, we are led in different directions, partly by the nature of our empirical materials, and partly by a different emphasis in the conceptual framework. The novel elements include our treatment of explicit benchmark schemes for forecast evaluation, which goes beyond the familiar naive models to autoregressive methods; our attempt to distinguish the extrapolative and the autonomous components of the forecasts; and our analysis of multiperiod or variable-span forecasts and extrapolations.

The empirical materials used in this paper consist of eight different sets of business forecasts, denoted by eight capital letters, A through H. These forecasts are produced by groups of business economists, economic departments of large corporations, banks, and financial magazines. Most use is made here, for illustrative purposes, of a subgroup of three sets of forecasts, E, F, and G, which represent a large opinion poll and small teams of business analysts and financial experts. The data for all eight sets summarize the records of several hundred forecasts, all of which have been processed in the NBER study of short-term economic forecasting.[5] It is worth noting that our substantive conclusions in this paper are broadly consistent with the evidence

---

[3] For an analysis of a particular extrapolation method, known as "adaptive forecasting," see Jacob Mincer, "Models of Adaptive Forecasting," Chapter 3 in this volume.

[4] Theil [7, Chapter 2, especially pp. 33–36].

[5] For a detailed description of data and of findings, see [13].

based on the complete record. A summary of the analyses and of the findings is appended for the benefit of the impatient reader.

I. ABSOLUTE ACCURACY ANALYSIS

ERRORS IN PREDICTIONS OF LEVELS

At the outset, it will be helpful to state a few notations and definitions: A_{t+k} represents the magnitude of the realization at time $(t + k)$; and $_{t+k}P_t$, the prediction of A_{t+k} at time t. The left-hand subscript of P is the target date, the right-hand subscript is the base date of the forecast; and k is the time interval between forecast and realization, also called the forecast span.

Although the terms "forecast" and "prediction" are synonyms in general usage, we shall reserve the former to describe a set of predictions produced by a given forecaster or forecasting method, and pertaining to the set of realizations of a given time series A. Single predictions $_{t+k}P_t$ are elements in the set, or in the forecast P, just as single realizations A_{t+k} are elements in the time series A. Different forecasts (methods or forecasters) may apply to the same set of realizations, but not conversely.[6]

Consider a population of constant-span (say, $k = 1$) predictions and realizations of a time series A. The analytical problem is to devise comparisons between forecasts $_tP_{t-1}$ and realizations A_t which will yield useful descriptions of sizes and characteristics of forecasting errors $u_t = (A_t - {}_tP_{t-1})$.

A simple and useful graphic comparison is obtained in a scatter diagram relating predictions to realizations.[7] As Figure 1 indicates, a perfect prediction ($u_t = 0$) is represented by a point on the 45° line through the origin, the line of perfect forecasts (LPF). Clearly, the smaller the dispersion around LPF the more accurate is the forecast. A measure of dispersion around LPF can, therefore, serve as a measure of forecast accuracy. One such measure, the variance around LPF, is known as the *mean square error of forecast*. We will denote it by

---

[6] For some purposes, not considered in this paper, the converse may be admissible. A forecaster may be evaluated by the performance of a number of forecasts he produced, each set of predictions pertaining to different sets of realizations.

[7] The "prediction-realization diagram" was first introduced by Theil in [8, pp. 30 ff.].

M_P. Its definition is:

(1) $$M_P = E(A - P)^2,$$

where E denotes expected value. Preference for this measure as a measure of forecast accuracy is based on the same considerations as the preference for the variance as a measure of dispersion in conventional statistical analysis: This is its mathematical and statistical tractability. We note, of course, that this measure gives more than

FIGURE 1-1. The Prediction-Realization Diagram

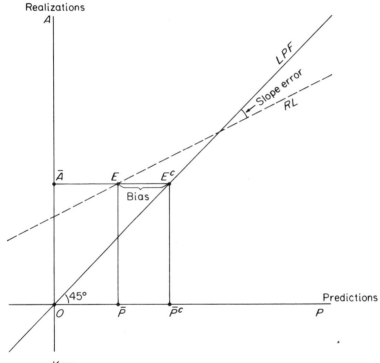

Key:
LPF – Line of perfect forecasts
RL   – Regression line
$\bar{A}$ – Mean realization
$\bar{P}$ – Mean prediction
$\bar{P}^c$ – Mean corrected prediction
E   – Mean point
E^c – Corrected mean point

proportionate weight to large errors, an assumption which is not particularly inappropriate in economic forecasting.[8]

The square root of M_P measures the average size of forecast error, expressed in the same units as the realizations. The expression $M_P = 0$ represents the unattainable case of perfection, when all points in the prediction-realization diagram lie on LPF. In general, most points are off LPF. However, special interest attaches to the location of the *mean point,* defined by $[E(A), E(P)]$. The forecast is *unbiased* if that point lies on LPF, that is if $E(P) = E(A)$. The difference $E(A) - E(P) = E(u)$ measures the size of bias. The forecast systematically underestimates or overestimates levels of realizations, if the sign of the bias is positive or negative, respectively.

Unbiasedness is a desirable characteristic of forecasting, but it does not, by itself, imply anything about forecast accuracy. Biased forecasts may have a smaller M_P than unbiased ones. However, other things being equal, the smaller the bias, the greater the accuracy of the forecast. The "other things" are the distances between the points of the scatter diagram: Given that $E(P) \neq E(A)$, a translation of the axes to a position where the new LPF passes through the mean point will produce a mean square error, M'_P, which is smaller than the original M_P. This is because the variance around the mean is smaller than the variance around any other value.

Formally, we have:

(2) $$M_P = E(A - P)^2 = E(u^2) = [E(u)]^2 + \sigma^2(u)$$

and

$$M'_P = \sigma^2(u).$$

The presence of bias augments the mean square error by the mean component $[E(u)]^2$. The other component of M_P, the variance of the error around its mean, $\sigma^2(u)$, is an (inverse) measure of forecasting *efficiency.*

Further consideration of the prediction-realization scatter diagram yields additional insights into characteristics of forecast errors. Thus nonlinearity of the scatter indicates different (on average) degrees of

---

[8] From a decision point of view, this measure is optimal under a quadratic loss criterion. For an extensive treatment of this criterion see Theil [9].

over- or underprediction at different ranges of values. Its heteroscedasticity reflects differential accuracy at different ranges of values.

These properties of the scatter are difficult to ascertain in small samples. Of greater interest, therefore, is the inspection of a least-squares straight-line fit to the scatter diagram. The mean point is one point on the least-squares regression line. Just as it is desirable for the mean point to lie on the line of perfect forecasts, so it would seem intuitively to be as desirable for all other points. In other words, the whole regression line should coincide with LPF. If the forecast is unbiased, but the regression line does not coincide with LPF, it must intersect it at the mean point. At ranges below the mean, realizations are, on average, under- or overpredicted, with the opposite tendency above the mean. The greater the divergence of the regression line from LPF, the stronger this type of error. In other words, the larger the deviation of the regression slope from unity, the less efficient the forecast: It is intuitively clear that rotation of the axes until LPF coincides with the regression line will reduce the size of $\sigma^2(u)$.

Before the argument is expressed rigorously, one matter must be decided: As is well known, two different regression lines can be fitted in the same scatter, depending on which variable is treated as predictor and which is predictand. Because, by definition, the forecasts are predictors, and because they are available before the realizations, we choose P as the independent and A as the dependent variable.

While

$$(3) \qquad\qquad A_t \equiv P_t + u_t$$

is an identity, a least-squares regression of A_t on P_t produces, generally:

$$(4) \qquad\qquad A_t = \alpha + \beta P_t + v_t.$$

Only when the forecast error u_t is uncorrelated with the forecast values P_t is the regression slope β equal to unity. In this case, the residual variance in the regression $\sigma^2(v)$ is equal to the variance of the forecast error $\sigma^2(u)$. Otherwise, $\sigma^2(u) > \sigma^2(v)$. Henceforth, we call forecasts *efficient* when $\sigma^2(u) = \sigma^2(v)$. If the forecast is also unbiased, $\alpha = 0$, $\sigma^2(v) = \sigma^2(u) = M_P$.

To illustrate the argument, consider a forecaster who underestimated the level of the predicted variable repeatedly over a succession of time periods. His forecasts would have been more accurate if they were all raised by some constant amount, i.e., the historically observed average error. Other things being equal—specifically, assuming that the process generating the predicted series remains basically unchanged as does the forecasting method used—such an adjustment would also reduce the error of the forecaster's future predictions. Now suppose that the forecaster generally underestimates high values and overestimates low values of the series, so that his forecasts can be said to be inefficient. Under analogous assumptions, he could reduce this type of error by raising his forecasts of high values and lowering those of low values by appropriate amounts.

Since, generally, $M_P \geqq \sigma^2(u) \geqq \sigma^2(v)$, a forecast which is unbiased and efficient is desirable. In the general case of biased and/or inefficient forecasts, we can think of regression (4) as a method of correcting the forecast P_t to improve its accuracy.[9]

The corrected forecast is $P^c = \alpha + \beta P_t$ and the resulting mean square error equals $M_P^c = \sigma^2(v) \leqq \sigma^2(u) \leqq M_P$. We can visualize this linear correction as being achieved in two steps: (1) A parallel shift of the regression line to the right until the mean point is on the 45° diagonal in Figure 1. This eliminates the bias and reduces the mean square error M_P to $\sigma^2(u)$, in equation 2. (2) A rotation of the regression line around the mean point ($E = E^c$) until it coincides with LPF (i.e., $\beta = 1$). This further reduces the M_P to $\sigma^2(v)$.

We can express the successive reductions as components of the mean square error:

$$(5) \quad M_P = E(u)^2 = [E(u)]^2 + \sigma^2(u) = [E(u)]^2 + [\sigma^2(u) - \sigma^2(v)] + \sigma^2(v).$$

---

[9] Theil calls it the "optimal linear correction," [7, p. 33, ff.].

It might be tempting to call optimal those forecasts which are both unbiased and efficient. We refrain from this terminology for the following reason: The regression model (4), in which we regress A on P rather than conversely, can also be interpreted by viewing realizations (A_t) as consisting of a stochastic component ϵ_t and a nonstochastic part $\tilde{A}_t$ [cf. 7, Ch. 2], (4a) $A_t = \tilde{A}_t + \epsilon_t$, with $E(\epsilon_t) = 0$, and $E(\tilde{A}_t \epsilon_t) = 0$.

The stochastic component ϵ_t can be viewed as a "random shock" representing the outcome of forces which make future events ultimately unpredictable. The forecaster does his best trying to predict A_t attaining ϵ_t as the smallest, irreducible forecast error. Thus, we prefer to reserve the notion of *optimality* to forecasts $P_t = \tilde{A}_t$ whose M_P is minimal, namely $M_P = \sigma^2(\epsilon_t)$. It is clear, from this formulation, that optimal forecasts are unbiased and efficient, but the converse need not be true. Questions of optimality are not directly considered in the present study.

The concept of "rational forecasting," as defined by J. F. Muth [5, pp. 315–335], implies unbiased and efficient forecasts utilizing all available information.

If ρ_{AP}^2 denotes the coefficient of determination in the regression of A on P, then $\sigma^2(v) = (1 - \rho_{AP}^2)\sigma^2(A)$. Also,[10] $\sigma^2(u) - \sigma^2(v) = (1 - \beta)^2\sigma^2(P)$. Hence, the decomposition of the mean square error is:

$$(5a) \qquad M_P = [E(u)]^2 + (1 - \beta)^2\sigma^2(P) + (1 - \rho_{AP}^2)\sigma^2(A).$$

We call the first component on the right the mean component (MC), the second the slope component (SC), and the third the residual component (RC) of the mean square error. In the unbiased case, MC vanishes; in the efficient case SC vanishes. In forecasts which are both unbiased and efficient both MC and SC vanish, and the mean square error equals the residual variance (RC) in (4).

Thus far we have analyzed the relation between predictions and realizations in terms of population parameters. However, in empirical analyses we deal with limited samples of predictions and realizations. The calculated mean square errors, their components, and the regression statistics of (4) are all subject to sampling variation. Thus, even if the predictions are unbiased and efficient in the population, the sample results will show unequal means of predictions and realizations, a nonzero intercept in the regression of A on P, a slope of that regression different from unity, and nonzero mean and slope components of the mean square error. To ascertain whether the forecasts are unbiased and/or efficient, tests of sampling significance are required.

Expressing the statistics for a sample of predictions and realizations, regression (4) becomes:

$$(6) \qquad A_t = a + bP_t + \hat{v}_t$$

and, corresponding to (5a), the decomposition of the sample mean square error, M_P, is:

$$(7) \qquad M_P = \sum_{t=1}^{n} (A_t - P_t)^2 = (\bar{A} - \bar{P})^2 + (1 - b)^2 S_P^2 + (1 - r_{AP}^2)S_A^2.$$

The test that P is both unbiased and efficient is the test of the joint null hypothesis $\alpha = 0$ and $\beta = 1$ in (4). If the joint hypothesis is rejected, separate tests for bias and efficiency are indicated. The respective null hypotheses are $E(u) = 0$ and $\beta = 1$.

[10] $\sigma^2(u) = \sigma^2(A) + \sigma^2(P) - 2\,Cov\,(A, P) = \sigma^2(A) + \sigma^2(P) - 2\beta\sigma^2(P)$
$\sigma^2(v) = \sigma^2(A) - \beta^2\sigma^2(P)$.
Subtracting, $\sigma^2(u) - \sigma^2(v) = \sigma^2(P) - 2\beta\sigma^2(P) + \beta^2\sigma^2(P) = (1 - \beta)^2\sigma^2(P)$.

TABLE 1-1. Accuracy Statistics for Selected Forecasts of Annual Levels of Four Aggregative Variables, 1953–63

		A. Summary Statistics for Predictions (P), Realizations (A), and Errors						
				Standard	Root Mean	Percentage of M_P Accounted for by		
	Code and	Mean		Deviation	Square Error	Mean Component	Slope Component	Residual Variance
Line	Type of Forecast [a]	$\bar{A}$ [b] (1)	$\bar{P}$ (2)	S_A (3) S_P (4)	$\sqrt{M_P}$ (5)	(MC) (6)	(SC) (7)	(RV) (8)
		Gross National Product (GNP) (billion dollars)						
1	E (11)	458.1	447.3	76.4 79.3	16.7	39.4	5.4	55.2
2	F (11)	458.1	453.2	76.4 79.5	8.8	28.1	14.0	57.9
3	G (11)	458.1	459.9	76.4 82.3	7.9	4.6	54.8	40.6
		Personal Consumption Expenditures (PC) (billion dollars)						
4	E (11)	296.4	287.6	49.0 52.6	5.5	76.2	12.2	11.7
5	F (11)	296.4	293.4	49.0 52.1	10.0	27.7	27.8	44.5
		Plant and Equipment Outlays (PE) (billion dollars)						
6	E (10)	32.6	32.0	3.8 5.2	2.9	4.2	44.1	51.7
		Index of Industrial Production (IP) (index points, 1947–49 = 100)						
7	E (11)	149.6	148.8	21.6 21.9	6.0	1.7	3.1	95.1
8	F (11)	149.6	150.4	21.6 21.8	4.6	2.6	2.0	95.4
9	G (11)	149.6	152.1	21.6 23.3	4.8	24.2	17.0	58.7

(continued)

Table 1-1 presents accuracy statistics for several sets of business forecasts of GNP, consumption, plant and equipment outlays, and industrial production. Part A shows means and variances of predictions and realizations, as well as the mean square error and its components expressed as proportions of the total. Part B shows the regression and test statistics for the hypotheses of unbiasedness and efficiency.

The statistical tests in most cases reject the joint hypothesis of unbiasedness and efficiency. This is accounted for largely by bias, and the preponderant bias is an underestimation of consumption and of

TABLE 1-1 (concluded)

		B. Regression and Test Statistics					
Line	Code and Type of Forecast [a]	a (1)	b (2)	r^2_{AP} (3)	F-Ratio for ($\alpha = 0$, $\beta = 1$) (4)	t-Test for $E(A) = E(P)$ (5)	t-Test for $\beta = 1$ (6)
		Gross National Product (GNP)					
10	E (11)	33.252	.950	.972	3.85 *	−2.68 *	.93
11	F (11)	24.357	.957	.992	2.45 **	−2.07 *	1.47 **
12	G (11)	32.531	.925	.995	7.99 *	.73	3.49 *
		Personal Consumption Expenditures (PC)					
13	E (11)	28.753	.931	.995	40.04 *	−5.94 *	3.25 *
14	F (11)	20.893	.939	.994	68.20 *	−2.07 *	2.61 *
		Plant and Equipment Outlays (PE)					
15	E (10)	13.256	.605	.667	3.70 *	−.66	2.61 *
		Index of Industrial Production (IP)					
16	E (11)	8.771	.950	.918	.14	−.44	.53
17	F (11)	3.968	.968	.952	.24	.54	.43
18	G (11)	10.989	.912	.968	3.10 *	1.87 *	1.62 **

[a] Number of years covered is given in brackets. All forecasts refer to the period 1953–63, except the plant and equipment forecasts E (line 6), which cover the years 1953–62.
[b] The realizations (A) are the first annual estimates of the given variable reported by the compiling agency.
* Significant at the 10 per cent level.
** Significant at the 25 per cent level.

GNP. Most of the forecasts seem inefficient. However, the degree of inefficiency is relatively minor, as the regression slopes are close to unity, though they are consistently below unity (Part B, column 2).

The decomposition of the mean square error in Part A of Table 1-1 suggests that the residual variance component is by far the most important component of error, and the slope component rather negligible. The mean component often accounts for as much as one-fourth of the total mean square error.

The correlations between forecasts and realizations are all positive and very high (their squares are shown in Part B, column 3). This is to be expected in series dominated by strong trends. Where trend domination is weaker, as in the plant and equipment series, the correlation is lower. These coefficients do not constitute measures or components of absolute forecasting accuracy. They are shown here merely for the sake of completeness and conventional usage. The coefficient of determination is, at best, a possible measure of relative accuracy. It specifically relates the mean square error of a linearly corrected forecast to the variance of realization [see Section III, equation (18), note 28]. This is not a generally useful measure of forecasting accuracy.

ERRORS IN PREDICTIONS OF CHANGES

Economic forecasts may be intended and expressed as predictions of changes rather than of future levels. The accuracy analysis of levels can also be applied to comparisons of predicted changes $(P_t - \mathring{A}_{t-1})$ with realized changes $(A_t - A_{t-1})$. A complicating factor in this analysis of changes are base errors, due to the fact that the value of A_{t-1} was not fully known at the time the forecast was made.[11] This is why the base is denoted by $\mathring{A}_{t-1}$.

If the forecast base were measured without error, the accuracy statistics for changes would be almost identical with those for levels. Clearly, the forecast error u_t and, hence, the mean square error would be the same since:

$$(A_t - A_{t-1}) - (P_t - A_{t-1}) = A_t - P_t = u_t.$$

By the same token, the mean and variance components of the mean square error would be identical. The only difference would emerge in the decomposition of the variance into slope and residual components. This is because the regression of $(A_t - A_{t-1})$ on $(P_t - A_{t-1})$ differs from the regression of A_t on P_t.

Denote the regression slope in this case by

$$\beta_\Delta = \frac{\text{Cov}\,(A_t - A_{t-1}, P_t - A_{t-1})}{\sigma^2(P_t - A_{t-1})};$$

from which it follows that:

---

[11] Though we excluded them in the preceding section, base errors also tend to obscure somewhat the analysis of forecast errors in predictions of levels. For an intensive analysis of the effects of base errors on forecasting accuracy, see Rosanne Cole, "Data Errors and Forecasting Accuracy," in this volume.

(8) $$1 - \beta_\Delta = \frac{\text{Cov } (u_t, A_{t-1}) - \text{Cov } (u_t, P_t)}{\sigma^2(P_t - A_{t-1})}.$$

Assume that the level forecast is efficient in the sense that $\beta = 1$, because Cov $(u_t, P_t) = 0$. Then $\beta_\Delta = 1$ only if Cov $(u_t, A_{t-1}) = 0$. The additional requirement that Cov $(u_t, A_{t-1}) = 0$ for the efficiency of fore- casts of changes [12] is an additional aspect of efficiency in forecasts of levels. It indicates that forecast errors cannot be reduced by taking account of past values of realizations or, put in other words, the extrap- olative value of the base (A_{t-1}) has already been incorporated in the forecast.

In Table 1-2 the same accuracy statistics are shown for forecasts of changes as were shown for forecasts of levels in Table 1-1. We note that, while the regression slopes b in Table 1-1 were close to unity, here they are substantially smaller. It appears that this is explainable largely by a positive Cov (u_t, A_{t-1}) in equation (8) and also as an effect of base errors.[13] Not surprisingly, the correlations between forecasts and realization (Part B, column 3) are weaker here than they are for predictions of levels.

UNDERESTIMATION OF CHANGES

A systematic and repeatedly observed property of forecasts is the tendency to underestimate changes. Comparisons of predicted and observed changes permit the detection of such tendencies. We search for their presence also in our data.

In order to understand better the empirical results, it is useful to define clearly the existence of such tendencies and to inquire into their possible sources.[14] Underestimation of change takes place whenever the predicted change $(P_t - A_{t-1})$ is of the same sign but of smaller size

[12] $\beta_\Delta = 1$ also when Cov $(u_t, A_{t-1}) = $ Cov $(u_t, P_t) \neq 0$. However, in that case both level and change forecasts are inefficient, since M_P is larger when Cov $(u_t, P_t) \neq 0$ than when it is zero.

[13] See Rosanne Cole's essay, pp. 64–70 of this volume. It might seem that the base errors which bias the regression slopes downward in Table 1-2 would also increase the mean square errors of predicted changes compared to the mean square error in levels. This is not necessarily true, however, and Table 1-2, in fact, shows mean square errors smaller than in Table 1-1. According to Rosanne Cole's analysis, the explanation, again, lies in the way base errors affect forecasts.

[14] For a different and more extensive discussion of this issue, see Theil [8, especially Chapter V].

TABLE 1-2. Accuracy Statistics for Selected Forecasts of Annual Changes in Four Aggregative Variables, 1953–63

A. Summary Statistics for Predictions (P_Δ), Realizations (ΔA), and Errors

Line	Code and Type of Forecast [a]	Mean $\Delta\bar{A}$ [b] (1)	Mean $\bar{P}_\Delta$ (2)	Standard Deviation $S_{\Delta A}$ (3)	Standard Deviation S_{P_Δ} (4)	Root Mean Square Error $\sqrt{M_P}$ (5)	Mean Component (MC) (6)	Slope Component (SC) (7)	Residual Variance (RV) (8)
							Percentage of M_P Accounted for by		
		Gross National Product (GNP) (billion dollars)							
1	E (11)	19.8	11.3	14.1	13.4	14.0	34.7	9.0	56.3
2	F (11)	19.8	17.5	14.1	17.0	7.5	8.8	29.7	61.5
3	G (11)	19.8	22.8	14.1	16.2	7.9	13.4	21.2	65.4
		Personal Consumption Expenditures (PC) (billion dollars)							
4	E (11)	12.9	6.5	4.9	6.5	4.6	63.1	16.0	20.9
5	F (11)	12.9	11.2	4.9	8.3	7.9	12.3	67.2	20.5
		Plant and Equipment Outlays (PE) (billion dollars)							
6	E (10)	1.1	.3	3.5	2.2	2.9	7.3	1.0	91.7
		Index of Industrial Production (IP) (index points, 1947–49 = 100)							
7	E (11)	5.2	2.4	8.6	5.0	6.3	18.5	5.9	75.6
8	F (11)	5.2	4.5	8.6	9.5	3.6	3.4	17.3	79.3
9	G (11)	5.2	7.1	8.6	8.9	4.3	17.8	7.3	74.9

(continued)

than actual change ($A_t - A_{t-1}$). Graphically, it occurs whenever a point in the predictions—realizations diagram (as in Figure 1, but relating changes rather than levels) is located above the LPF in the first quadrant or below LPF in the third quadrant. A *tendency* toward underestimation exists when most points in the scatter are so located. In terms of a single parameter, such a tendency may be presumed when the mean point of the scatter is located in that area.

Algebraically, we detect a tendency toward underestimation of

TABLE 1-2 (concluded)

				B. Regression and Test Statistics			
Line	Code and Type of Forecast [a]	a (1)	b (2)	$r^2_{\Delta AP_\Delta}$ (3)	F-Ratio for $\alpha = 0, \beta = 1$ (4)	t-Test for $E(\Delta A) =$ $E(P_\Delta)$ (5)	t-Test for $\beta = 1$ (6)	$r_{E_t E_{t-1}}$ (7)
				Gross National Product (GNP)				
10	E (11)	12.160	.676	.412	3.77 *	−2.42 *	1.20	−.5706 **
11	F (11)	6.728	.749	.814	2.95 **	−1.60 **	2.10 *	−.3950
12	G (11)	2.324	.766	.778	2.48 **	1.31 **	1.71 **	.3323
				Personal Consumption Expenditures (PC)				
13	E (11)	9.600	.501	.442	18.85 *	−4.43 *	2.68 *	.1094
14	F (11)	6.973	.526	.808	18.27 *	−1.24 **	5.53 *	−.0212
				Plant and Equipment Outlays (PE)				
15	E (10)	.874	.832	.292	.43	−.89	.36	.2580
				Index of Industrial Production (IP)				
16	E (11)	2.073	1.300	.567	1.24	−1.58 **	.79	−.1537
17	F (11)	1.449	.834	.846	1.96 **	−.62	1.40 **	−.4020
18	G (11)	−0.924	.865	.799	1.61	1.54 **	.94	.1865

See notes to Table 1-1.

changes by:

$$(9) \qquad E|P_t - A_{t-1}| < E|A_t - A_{t-1}|,$$

provided $E(P_t - A_{t-1})$ is of the same sign as $E(A_t - A_{t-1})$.

Or, what is almost equivalent, and analytically more tractable:

$$(10) \qquad E(P_t - A_{t-1})^2 < E(A_t - A_{t-1})^2,$$

with the same proviso.

Inequality (10) is highly suggestive of the sources of tendencies toward underestimation of changes. The left-hand side is the mean square error in predicting forecasts P_t by means of the past values A_{t-1}; the right-hand side is the mean square error in predicting realizations A_t by means of the past values A_{t-1}. The inequality can be broadly interpreted to mean that underestimation arises when past events bear a closer (and positive) relation to the formation of forecasts than to future realizations. This is very plausible. Forecasts differ from realizations because information is incomplete. To the extent that some elements of information are lacking, the effect is likely to be produced.

Now, decomposing (10), we get:

(11)
$$[E(P_t) - E(A_{t-1})]^2 + \sigma^2(P_t - A_{t-1}) < [E(A_t) - E(A_{t-1})]^2 + \sigma^2(A_t - A_{t-1}).$$

According to (11), underestimation of changes occurs because:

(12a) $E(P_t) < E(A_t),$

when both A_t and P_t are greater than A_{t-1}, or

(12b) $E(P_t) > E(A_t),$

when both A_t and P_t are less than A_{t-1}, and/or because

(13) $\sigma^2(P_t - A_{t-1}) < \sigma^2(A_t - A_{t-1}).$

It is important to note that condition (13) necessarily holds when predictions of changes are efficient, i.e., when $\beta_\Delta = 1$, because, in that case: $\sigma^2(A_t - A_{t-1}) = \sigma^2(P_t - A_{t-1}) + \sigma^2(u_t).$[15] Thus, *underestimation of changes is a property of unbiased and efficient forecasts of changes,* or, what is equivalent, of unbiased and efficient forecasts of levels in which all of the extrapolative information contained in the base (A_{t-1}) has been exploited.[16] But, as the analysis shows, it can also arise in biased or incorrect forecasting.

In Table 1-2, the actual forecast base $\mathring{A}_{t-1}$ contains errors. These, as we noted, tend to bias the regression slopes downward. They may therefore contribute to the observed reversal of inequality (13). As comparisons of columns 3 and 4, Part A, show, $S^2(P_t - \mathring{A}_{t-1}) > S^2(A_t - A_{t-1})$ in six of the nine recorded cases. Whether a better agreement with the inequality in (13) would obtain in the absence of base errors

[15] Since $A_t - A_{t-1} = P_t - A_{t-1} + u_t$, it follows that var $(A_t - A_{t-1}) =$ var $(P_t - A_{t-1}) +$ var $(u_t) + 2$ cov $(P_t - A_{t-1}, u_t)$. But the last term in the above vanishes under the assumed conditions, since, for efficient forecasts with $\beta_\Delta = 1$, cov $(u_{t-1}, A_{t-1}) =$ cov $(u_t, P_t) = 0$ (see note 12).

[16] A fortiori, underestimation of changes is a property of "rational" forecasting in the sense of Muth [5, p. 334].

is not clear. It depends, in part, on the effects past errors exert on the forecast levels P_t.[17]

Where the variance of predicted change *exceeds* the variance of actual change in Table 1-2, the source of underestimation of changes in our data must lie in the underestimation of levels (12). This characteristic is observed in Table 1-1. Changes are, indeed, underestimated in all these forecasts where levels were underestimated, and overestimated in those few forecasts where levels were overestimated. (Compare Part A, columns 1 and 2, of Tables 1-1 and 1-2.)

The tendency to underestimate changes is explored in greater detail in Table 1-3. Here each of the individual predictions of change is classified as an under- or overestimate. We find that two-thirds of the increases in GNP were underestimated, and one-third overestimated. But of the decreases, which were relatively few and shallow, half were missed and barely one-fourth underestimated. For consumption, no year-to-year decreases are recorded, and underpredictions of increases represent nearly two-thirds of all observations. It seems unlikely that such high proportions could be due to chance.

At the same time, in series with weaker growth but stronger cyclical and irregular movements, underestimates of increases, while frequent, are not dominant. Table 1-3 shows this clearly for the forecasts of gross private domestic investment and plant and equipment outlays. For industrial production, the situation is similar, though the proportion of underestimates for the *decreases* may be significant.[18]

We conclude that the underestimation of changes reflects mainly a conservative prediction of growth rates in series with upward trends. This implies, in turn, that the levels of such series must also be underestimated, a fact already noted. To what extent the purported generality of underestimation of changes is true beyond the conservative underestimation of increases remains an open question.

[17] The reader is referred again to Rosanne Cole's essay. Here we may note that to the extent that base errors are incorporated in P_t, $S^2(P_t)$ is augmented. This may explain the observation in Table 1-1 where $S^2(P_t) > S^2(A_t)$ in all cases (columns 3 and 4, Part A).

[18] It should be noted that Table 1-3 includes all forecast sets that have thus far been analyzed in the NBER study and is thus based on much broader evidence than Table 1-1. In particular, the representation of investment forecasts is greatly strengthened here by the inclusion of gross private domestic investment forecasts (GNP component) along with those of plant and equipment outlays (OBE-SEC definition).

TABLE 1-3. Forecasts of Annual Changes in Five Comprehensive Series, Distribution by Type of Error, 1953–63

Predicted Variable and Type of Change [a]	Forecast of Annual Changes [b]				Probability of as Many or More Under-estimates [c]
	Total Number (1)	Under-estimates (2)	Over-estimates (3)	Turning Point Errors (4)	(5)
Gross national product (8)					
Increases	64	43	21	0	.004
Decreases	14	3	4	7	.756
Personal consumption expenditure (5)					
Increases [d]	45	29	13	3	.010
Gross private domestic investment (4)					
Increases	22	10	9	3	.500
Decreases	12	5	4	3	.500
Plant and equipment outlays (2)					
Increases	12 [e]	5	4	2	.500
Decreases	5	2	3	0	.812
Industrial production (7)					
Increases	57	28	23	6	.288
Decreases	13	9	3	1	.073

[a] The number of forecast sets covered is given in parentheses. Increases and decreases refer to the direction of changes in the actual values (first estimates for the given series).

[b] Underestimates indicate that predicted change is less than the actual change; overestimates, that predicted change exceeds actual change; turning point errors, that the sign of the predicted change differs from the sign of the actual change.

[c] Based on the proportion of all observations, other than those with turning point errors, accounted for by the underestimates (i.e., column 2 divided by the difference between column 1 and column 4). Probabilities taken from Harvard Computation Laboratory, *Tests of the Cumulative Binomial Probability Distribution,* Cambridge, Mass., 1955.

[d] All observed changes are increases.

[e] Includes one perfect forecast (hence the total of observations in columns 2–4 in this line is 11).

II. RELATIVE ACCURACY ANALYSIS

The quality of forecasting performance is not fully described by the size and characteristics of forecasting error as analyzed in Section I. Sizes of forecasting errors cannot even be compared when sets of predictions differ in target dates or in the economic variables to be predicted. Theil goes beyond the matter of comparability in suggesting that a sharp distinction must be made between *size* of forecasting error and *consequences* of forecasting error. According to him, "the quality of a forecast is determined by the quality of the decision to which it leads." [19]

This emphasis on consequences can be further generalized by relating, incrementally, the gains obtainable from reducing forecast errors which the particular forecasting method accomplishes relative to an alternative, to the cost of producing such reductions. In principle, such a rate-of-return criterion is a ratio of imputed dollar values, in which numerator and denominator provide for comparability and for an economically unambiguous ranking of forecasting performance regardless of target dates and variables.

In this part of our analysis, we suggest a criterion for the appraisal of forecasting quality which derives from this economic concept but is necessarily more limited. In the absence of a gain function (for the numerator) and of an investment cost function (for the denominator), we measure the payoff only in terms of the reduction in forecasting error obtained by the forecast (P) compared with an alternative, less costly, "benchmark" method (B). The benchmark we propose is the extrapolation of the past own history of the target series. Our proposed index of forecasting quality is the ratio of the mean square error of forecast M_P to the mean square error of extrapolation M_X. The ratio represents the *relative* reduction in forecasting error. It ranks the quality of forecasting performance the same way as a rate-of-return index, in which the return (numerator) is inversely proportional to the mean square error of forecast, and the cost (denominator) inversely proportional [20] to the mean square error of extrapolation, the latter representing the difficulties encountered in forecasting a given series.

Benchmarks other than extrapolations could be used when the comparison is considered relevant. In this sense, our procedure is general and the particular benchmark illustrative. However, the justification for the extrapolative benchmark is that it is a relatively simple, quick, and accessible alternative; at least the recent history of a variable to be forecast is usually available to the forecaster. Trend projection is an old and commonly used method of forecasting, and naive extrapo-

---

[19] Theil [7, p. 15].

[20] With proportionality coefficients fixed across forecasts.

lation models have already acquired a traditional role as benchmarks in forecast evaluation.[21]

It should be noted that the generally used naive extrapolation benchmarks do not depend on the statistical structure of the time series and require no more than knowledge of the forecast base. This knowledge, moreover, is not utilized optimally.[22] In contrast, our B assumes, in principle, that all the available information on past values has been utilized optimally for prediction; a best extrapolation being defined as one which produces a minimal forecast error.

Optimal extrapolations are not easy to construct. In this paper we use autoregressive extrapolations (to be labeled X) as comparatively simple substitutes.[23] The regression estimates used in producing these benchmarks are derived from values of realizations which are available to the forecaster in the base period. In this respect, the practical forecasting situation is reasonably well simulated, including the limited knowledge that the forecaster has of current and of more recent data, which are typically preliminary.

THE RELATIVE MEAN SQUARE ERROR AND ITS DECOMPOSITION

We shall call our index of forecasting quality, which is a ratio of the mean square error of forecast to the mean square error of extrapolation, the *relative mean square error,* and denote it by RM. If "good" forecasts are those that are superior to extrapolation, the relative mean square error provides a natural scale for them: $0 < RM < 1$. If $RM > 1$, the forecast is, *prima facie,* inferior.

Since each of the mean square errors entering RM can be decomposed into mean, slope, and residual components, it is useful to inquire how the components affect the size of RM. Denoting the "linearly corrected" mean square errors (or residual components) by M_P^c and M_X^c, and the remainders by U_P and U_X, we have:

---

[21] An early application of a naive model test is found in [4]. See also Carl Christ in [2] and Milton Friedman, "Comment" in the same volume, pp. 56–57, 69, 108–111. More recently, Arthur M. Okun has applied such tests to selected business forecasts in [6, pp. 199–211]. Furthermore, our index can be seen as a generalization of Theil's "inequality index," where B is the "most naive," "no-change" extrapolation [7, p. 28].

[22] For recent references from a large and growing mathematical literature which addresses itself to optimality defined by the mean square error criterion, see P. Whittle [11] and A. M. Yaglom [12].

[23] For a description and evaluation of these models, see Section III below.

$$(14) \qquad RM = \frac{M_P}{M_X} = \frac{1 - \dfrac{U_X}{M_X}}{1 - \dfrac{U_P}{M_P}} \cdot \frac{M_P^c}{M_X^c} = g \cdot RM^c.$$

If X is a best extrapolation, it must be unbiased and efficient. In that case, we would expect $M_X^c = M_X$, and $g = \dfrac{M_P}{M_P^c} \geq 1$, and, therefore, $RM^c \leq RM$.

The autoregressive extrapolations used in our empirical illustrations may be far from optimal. Moreover, sampling fluctuations tend to obscure expected relations. Nonetheless, we find in Table 1-4 that $RM^c < RM$ in twelve out of eighteen cases. The instances in which $RM^c > RM$ are concentrated in forecasts of industrial production, where the extrapolations used are apparently well below the envisaged standard. Similar results are obtained below for predictions with varying spans in quarterly and semiannual units (Table 1-8, columns 3 and 4).

Judging by the size of RM, most forecasts (six out of nine) studied in Table 1-4 are superior to autoregressive extrapolations, and all but one set (this one predicting plant and equipment outlays) of corrected forecasts are superior. The margin of superiority in the corrected forecasts is substantial: Most RM^c are less than half. Note that some forecasts, which would seem inferior on the basis of $RM > 1$, are nevertheless relatively efficient judging by $RM^c < 1$.

It is also interesting to note that forecasts perform relatively poorly in series which are very volatile, hence very difficult to extrapolate, such as plant and equipment outlays. They also perform relatively poorly at the other extreme, where the series, being smooth, are quite easy to extrapolate, as in the case of consumption. In the former case, however, the inferiority is due mainly to inefficiency, whereas in the case of consumption, the inferiority is largely due to bias: the RM^c are small.

CONTRIBUTIONS OF EXTRAPOLATIVE AND OF AUTONOMOUS
COMPONENTS TO FORECASTING EFFICIENCY

Thus far, we have viewed extrapolation as an alternative method of forecasting. In practice, however, P and X are not mutually exclusive. Extrapolation is likely to be used in some degree by forecasters in

TABLE 1-4. Absolute and Relative Measures of Error, Selected Annual Forecasts of Four Aggregate Variables, 1953–63

Line	Code and Type of Forecast [a]	Absolute Error Measures [b]					Relative Error Measures [c]		
		Mean Square Error	Components of M		Ratios to Mean Square Error		Relative Mean Square Error	Components of RM	
		M (1)	U (2)	M^c (3)	U/M (4)	M^c/M (5)	RM (6)	g (7)	RM^c (8)
				Gross National Product (GNP)					
1	E Level	279.12	125.05	154.07	.448	.552	1.178	1.444	.816
2	Change	195.52	85.44	110.08	.437	.563	1.074	1.461	.735
3	F Level	78.15	32.90	45.25	.421	.579	.330	1.375	.240
4	Change	56.24	21.65	34.59	.385	.615	.309	1.338	.231
5	G Level	62.85	37.33	25.52	.594	.406	.265	1.963	.135
6	Change	62.55	21.64	40.91	.346	.654	.344	1.260	.273
7	X Level	236.85	48.15	188.70	.203	.797			
8	Change	181.98	32.21	149.77	.177	.823			
				Personal Consumption Expenditures (PC)					
9	E Level	100.72	88.94	11.78	.886	.117	2.855	7.613	.375
10	Change	61.84	48.92	12.92	.791	.209	2.314	3.679	.629
11	F Level	30.23	16.78	13.45	.555	.445	.857	2.002	.428
12	Change	20.70	16.46	4.24	.795	.205	.774	3.739	.207
13	X Level	35.28	3.85	31.43	.109	.891			
14	Change	26.73	6.20	20.53	.232	.768			
				Plant and Equipment Outlays (PE)					
15	E Level	8.58	.74	7.84	.086	.914	2.480	.908	2.732
16	Change	8.58	.71	7.37	.083	.917	2.124	1.095	1.939
17	X Level	3.46	.59	2.87	.171·	.829			
18	Change	4.04	.24	3.80	.059	.941			
				Index of Industrial Production (IP)					
19	E Level	36.63	1.79	34.84	.049	.951	.397	.841	.472
20	Change	39.21	9.57	29.64	.244	.756	.540	.811	.666
21	F Level	21.59	.99	20.60	.046	.954	.234	.839	.279
22	Change	13.09	2.71	10.38	.207	.793	.180	.773	.233
23	G Level	23.31	9.63	13.68	.413	.587	.252	1.362	.185
24	Change	18.37	4.61	13.76	.251	.749	.253	.819	.309
25	X Level	92.35	18.47	73.88	.200	.800			
26	Change	72.59	28.09	44.50	.387	.613			

[a] Eleven years were covered in all cases except lines 15 and 16, when only ten were covered. For more detail on the included forecasts, see Table 1-1, note a. Code X refers to autoregressive extrapolations used as benchmarks for the relative error measures (see text).

[b] Lines 1–18: billions of dollars squared; lines 19–26: index points, squared, 1947–49 = 100. In each case, $M = U + M^c$ (i.e., the numbers in column 1 equal algebraic sums of the corresponding entries in columns 2 and 3).

[c] $RM = gRM^c$. See text and equation 14.

producing P. Indeed, we can think of every forecast P as having been derived from: (a) projections from the past of the series itself, (b) analyses of relations with other series, and (c) otherwise obtained current anticipations about the future. Write $P = P_X + P_R$. The forecast P is a sum of the extrapolative component P_X and a remainder, the autonomous component P_R.

This scheme of forecast genesis leads to a further analysis of forecasting quality in terms of two questions: (a) To what extent is the predictive power of P due to the autonomous component? (b) Does P efficiently utilize all of the available extrapolative information? These questions have a bearing on the interpretation of our indexes RM.

It is clear that when $RM < 1$, useful (that is, contributing to a reduction in error) autonomous information must have been applied in the forecast P. Otherwise, the forecast can do no better than the extrapolation. We have already seen, however, that even when $RM > 1$, the forecast may well be relatively efficient, that is when $RM^c < 1$. This case again reveals the contribution of autonomous components to predictive efficiency. In other words, the corrected forecast P^c and, therefore, P may contain predictive value beyond extrapolation, even when $RM > 1$. But what if $RM^c > 1$? Do we then conclude that P contains no predictive value beyond extrapolation?

It is obvious that such a conclusion is unwarranted in the example when $RM^c = 1$. Here the mean square error of P^c and of X (assume $X^c = X$) are the same. But this does not mean that $P^c \equiv X$, unless each of the predictions produced by the two forecasts are identical. Hence, in general, so long as P^c differs from X, but $RM^c = 1$, P must contain predictive power stemming from sources other than extrapolation, while X must contain predictive power not all of which was used by P. Relating, in multiple regression, both P and X to A, the partial correlations of P and of X must be positive. Indeed, in the special case $RM^c = 1$, it is easily shown that these partials must be equal to one another. For recall the well-known correlation identities:

$$1 - R^2_{A.PX} = (1 - r^2_{AP})(1 - r^2_{AX.P}) = (1 - r^2_{AX})(1 - r^2_{AP.X}).$$

It follows that:

(15) $$RM^c = \frac{1 - r^2_{AP}}{1 - r^2_{AX}} = \frac{1 - r^2_{AP.X}}{1 - r^2_{AX.P}}.$$

For $RM^c = 1$, the equality $r^2_{AP.X} = r^2_{AX.P}$ must hold. But for $P^c \equiv X$, both partials must be equal to zero. In the general case when $RM^c \neq 1$, we see from expression (15) that $RM^c < 1$ when $r^2_{AP.X} > r^2_{AX.P}$ and $RM^c > 1$ when $r^2_{AP.X} < r^2_{AX.P}$.

The fact that $r^2_{AP.X} > 0$ means that the forecast P contains predictive power based not only on extrapolation but also on its autonomous component. Indeed, $r^2_{AP.X}$ is a measure of the net contribution of the autonomous component. At the same time, $r^2_{AX.P} > 0$ means that X contains some amount of predictive power that was not used in P. P_X, the extrapolative component of P, is not identical with X, and is indeed inferior to X in terms of predictive power. $r^2_{AX.P}$ is thus a measure of the extent to which available extrapolative predictive power was not utilized by the forecast P.

Combining (14) and (15), one can now also write:

$$(16) \qquad\qquad RM = g \cdot \frac{1 - r^2_{AP.X}}{1 - r^2_{AX.P}}.$$

The anatomy of the measure of relative accuracy and its usefulness are now fully visible. The extent to which P is better than X depends on:

a. the relative mean and slope proportions of error measured by g. This is more likely to affect adversely the performance of P than of X.

b. the relative amounts of independent [24] effective information contained within P and X (i.e., on $r^2_{AP.X}$ and $r^2_{AX.P}$).

The above analysis makes it clear that a thorough evaluation of P cannot rely merely on the size of RM, the ratio of the total mean square errors. RM may be large, indicating a poor forecast. But P may be highly efficient (its RM^c being small) and, even if it is not, it may still contain information of value, in the sense of being capable of reducing forecast errors when introduced in addition to X. This information, the net predictive value of the autonomous component of the forecast P, is measured by the partial $r^2_{AP.X}$, regardless of the sizes of the other components.

Table 1-5, columns 1-5, shows, for the selected forecasts, the elements that enter the function RM^c according to equation 15.

The predictive efficiency of P, as measured by the simple determina-

[24] Strictly speaking, uncorrelated, since the applied decomposition procedures are linear.

tion coefficients r^2_{AP} in column 4, is typically very high for the level forecasts (.910 to .995) and considerably smaller, but still significantly positive (.412 to .846) for changes. There is, however, one particularly weak set of plant and equipment forecasts of set E, for which these coefficients are much lower (.667 for levels and .282 for changes, see lines 11 and 12).

TABLE 1-5. Net and Gross Contributions of Forecasts and of Extrapolations to Predictive Efficiency [a]

Line	Code and Type of Forecast	RM^c (1)	Coefficients of Determination Partial		Simple	
			$r^2_{AP.X}$ (2)	$r^2_{AX.P}$ (3)	r^2_{AP} (4)	r^2_{AX} (5)
		Gross National Product (GNP)				
1	E Level	.816	.345	.180	.972	.965
2	Change	.736	.361	.107	.412	.179
3	F Level	.240	.804	.176	.992	.965
4	Change	.231	.789	.074	.814	.179
5	G Level	.135	.873	−.067	.995	.965
6	Change	.273	.736	.029	.778	.179
		Personal Consumption Expenditures (PC)				
7	E Level	.383	.694	−.075	.995	.986
8	Change	.617	.647	−.389	.442	.042
9	F Level	.438	.775	.427	.994	.986
10	Change	.202	.822	−.119	.808	.042
		Plant and Equipment (PE)				
11	E Level	2.732	.007	.344	.667	.783
12	Change	2.704	.038	.531	.282	.650
		Index of Industrial Production (IP)				
13	E Level	.474	.542	.044	.910	.829
14	Change	.672	.324	.001	.567	.361
15	F Level	.280	.833	.412	.952	.829
16	Change	.235	.783	.092	.846	.361
17	G Level	.186	.816	.001	.968	.829
18	Change	.312	.733	.145	.799	.361

[a] This table includes the same forecasts as those covered in Tables 1-1, 1-2, and 1-4. Eleven years are covered except for lines 11 and 12, where ten years are covered.

The correlations between A and X are, as a rule, lower than those between A and P (compare columns 4 and 5). Also, the r^2_{AX} coefficients tend to be much higher for levels than for changes (column 5). Again, the PE forecasts of set E provide some exception to those regularities. The values of r^2_{AX} are very low for changes in GNP and consumption, but significantly higher for changes in production and rather high for those in plant and equipment outlays.[25]

The partial coefficients $r^2_{AP.X}$ are lower than the simple ones r^2_{AP}, except for the forecasts of changes in consumption (compare columns 2 and 4). However, all but two of them (those for the PE outlays) are significantly positive. On the other hand, the partials $r^2_{AX.P}$ are, with four exceptions, very low and not significant. Only for the extremely poor forecasts of investment does $r^2_{AX.P}$ exceed $r^2_{AP.X}$; in all other instances, the reverse is emphatically true (columns 2 and 3).

The interpretation of these results is as follows: The included forecasts of GNP, PC, and IP are more efficient than the autoregressive extrapolations X, since they show $RM^c < 1$ (column 1). The predictive efficiency of these forecasts is attributable in large measure to (autonomous) information other than that conveyed by the extrapolations, as indicated by the relatively high coefficients $r^2_{AP.X}$ (column 2). The extrapolations contribute very little to the reduction of the residual variance of A, which was left unexplained by these forecasts, as indicated by the very low coefficients $r^2_{AX.P}$ in columns 3 (the two exceptions here are the level forecasts F for consumption and production, see lines 9 and 15). This is not to say that forecasters do not engage in extrapolation. It means, rather, that whatever extrapolative information (X) was available was already embodied in P.

For the PE forecasts of set E, the situation is almost reversed. Here $RM^c > 1$, and $r^2_{AP.X}$ is not significantly different from zero, but $r^2_{AX.P}$ is; and, for changes, r^2_{AX} is even larger than r^2_{AP} (lines 11 and 12).

To sum up the findings in Table 1-5: With the exception of PE forecasts, autonomous components significantly contribute to the predictive power of forecasts. At the same time, again with the ex-

---

[25] The coefficients r^2_{AX} for changes in GNP, in PC, and in IP are .179, .042, and .361, respectively. For PE, the coefficient r^2_{AX} is .650.

There is, of course, only one value of r^2_{AX} (or of r^2_{AP}) for any given series covered (levels or changes). For convenient comparisons, some of these values are entered more than once in column 5.

ception of PE forecasts, business forecasts P seem to exploit most of the extrapolative information available in X. Since $r^2_{AX.P}$ is small, there is an almost perfect (inverse) correlation between $r^2_{AP.X}$ and RM^c. RM^c is, therefore, a good index of the contribution of autonomous components to forecasting efficiency of P. Indeed, significant contributions of autonomous components are reflected in RM^c below unity.

III. FORECASTS AS EXTRAPOLATIONS

EXTRAPOLATIVE COMPONENTS OF FORECASTS

Table 1-5 and other evidence suggested that most of the predictive value contained in extrapolations was exploited by forecasters in P. This does not mean, however, that extrapolations necessarily are an important ingredient in business forecasting. To the extent that they are important, extrapolation errors $(A - X)$ are an important part of forecast errors $(A - P)$, and the analysis of the predictive performance of extrapolations is useful in evaluating the quality of forecasting P.

In order to establish the empirical relevance of extrapolation error in appraising forecast errors, we first inquire about the relative importance of extrapolation in generating the forecasts P. Next we proceed to a closer study of extrapolations and their forecasting properties. The conclusions are in turn applied to the analysis of forecast errors.

Since a good extrapolation is expected to be unbiased and efficient, the mean and slope components are not likely to be attributable to extrapolation errors. We, therefore, restrict our question to the role of extrapolation in generating the adjusted forecast P^c. If X is the extrapolation, the question can be answered by the coefficient of determination r^2_{PX}.[26] These coefficients are shown in column 1 of Table 1-6.

We may note that r^2_{PX} underestimates the relative importance of extrapolative ingredients in P. This is because our autoregressive

---

[26] Our statistical procedures, which measure the net contribution of the forecast to predictive efficiency by $r^2_{AP.X}$, and the importance of extrapolative components in generating the corrected forecasts P^c by r^2_{PX}, classify as extrapolative all the autonomously formulated forecasting which is collinear with extrapolation. We implicitly treat as autonomous only those elements of P_R which are uncorrelated with P_X.

benchmark X does not necessarily coincide with the extrapolative component P_X contained in P, even if it was arrived at by linear auto-regression: The implicit weights allocated to the various past values of A in formulating P_X may be different from those which determine X. Our X is the systematic component in the autoregression of A on its past values. The best estimate of P_X, however, is the systematic com-ponent of the regression of P on the past values of A:

$$(17) \qquad {}_tP_{t-1} = \alpha + \beta_1 A_{t-1} + \beta_2 A_{t-2} + \cdots + \delta_t.$$

The residual δ_t in (17) is an estimate of the autonomous component in P; the systematic part of (17) is an estimate of the extrapolative component P_X. The coefficient of determination $r^2_{PP_X}$ measures the relative importance of (autoregressive) extrapolation in generating P^c. Clearly, r^2_{PX} is an underestimate of $r^2_{PP_X}$ since P_X is a linear combi-nation of the same variables as X, but the coefficients in P_X are deter-mined by maximizing the correlation.

As a comparison of columns 1 and 2 in Table 1-6 shows, there is actually little difference between the two measures r^2_{PX} and $r^2_{PP_X}$ es-pecially in the GNP forecasts. Extrapolation is an important ingre-dient in all forecasts of levels. Trend projection is a common, simple method of forecasting. It is not surprising to find the extrapolative component of forecasting to be more important when the trend is stronger and the fluctuations around the trend in the series are less pro-nounced. As shown in Table 1-6, the relative importance of extrapo-lative components is greatest in consumption, least in industrial pro-duction and plant and equipment. And, by the same token, forecasts of change contain much less extrapolation than forecasts of levels.

Regression (17) constitutes an orthogonal decomposition of the fore-cast P into an extrapolative component P_X and autonomous com-ponent $P_R = \delta$. The net contribution of each to forecasting efficiency can, therefore, be measured by the simple coefficients of determination $r^2_{AP_X}$ and $r^2_{A\delta}$. Moreover, since $r^2_{AP_X} + r^2_{A\delta} = r^2_{AP}$, the ratios $\dfrac{r^2_{AP_X}}{r^2_{AP}}$ and $\dfrac{r^2_{A\delta}}{r^2_{AP}} = 1 - \dfrac{r^2_{AP_X}}{r^2_{AP}}$ can be used to measure the relative contribution of each com-ponent to the forecasting power of P^c.

These absolute and relative coefficients of determination are shown

TABLE 1-6. Extrapolative and Autonomous Components of Forecasts: Their Relative Importance in Forecast Genesis and in Prediction

Line	Code and Type of Forecast	r^2_{PX} (1)	$r^2_{PP_X}$ (2)	$r^2_{AP_X}$ (3)	$r^2_{A\delta}$ (4)	$\dfrac{r^2_{AP_X}}{r^2_{AP}}$ (5)	$\dfrac{r^2_{A\delta}}{r^2_{AP}}$ (6)
	Gross National Product (GNP)						
1	E Level	.983	.984	.967	.005	.995	.005
2	Change	.002	.064	.001	.411	.002	.998
3	F Level	.968	.968	.976	.016	.984	.016
4	Change	.046	.078	.097	.717	.119	.881
5	G Level	.987	.988	.978	.017	.983	.017
6	Change	.063	.091	.110	.668	.141	.859
	Personal Consumption Expenditures (PC)						
7	E Level	.991	.991	.994	.001	.999	.001
8	Change	.003	.481	.032	.410	.072	.928
9	F Level	.987	.987	.994	.000	1.000	.000
10	Change	.039	.097	.023	.785	.028	.972
	Plant and Equipment Outlays (PE)						
11	E Level	.775	.923	.481	.186	.721	.279
12	Change	.289	.289	.362	.060	.856	.143
	Index of Industrial Production (IP)						
13	E Level	.950	.968	.880	.030	.967	.033
14	Change	.143	.143	.022	.545	.039	.961
15	F Level	.851	.877	.849	.103	.892	.108
16	Change	.116	.255	.152	.694	.180	.820
17	G Level	.922	.922	.864	.104	.893	.107
18	Change	.066	.145	.242	.557	.303	.697

Note: Forecasts cover eleven years in all cases.

in columns 3 through 6 of Table 1-6. We find that wherever extrapolation is an important ingredient of forecasting (see column 2), its relative contribution (column 5) to predictive power is also very strong. Thus the importance of trend extrapolation in predicting levels dwarfs the autonomous component both as an ingredient and in its relative contribution to predictive accuracy. The relative importance of autonomous components becomes visible and strong in the (trendless and volatile) predictions of changes.

Quite reasonably, we may ascribe to forecasters a heavier reliance on extrapolation whenever it is likely to be relatively efficient.

EXTRAPOLATIVE BENCHMARKS AND NAIVE MODELS

Table 1-6 showed that linearly corrected forecasts of levels very strongly resemble extrapolations. Thus, aside from mean and slope errors, which are more properly attributable to autonomous forecasting, errors in forecasting levels consist largely of extrapolation errors. We proceed, therefore, to the analysis of the predictive properties of extrapolations.

Different kinds of extrapolation error are generated by different extrapolation models. Various models have been used in the forecasting field, either as benchmarks for evaluating forecasts or as methods of forecasting. If extrapolation is viewed as a method of forecasting, those extrapolations are best which minimize the forecasting error.[27] If extrapolative benchmarks are to represent best available extrapolative alternatives, the same criterion applies. The same naive model, therefore, cannot serve for any and all series. The optimal benchmark in each case depends on the stochastic structure of the particular series. When the assumptions about the structure of A are specified, the appropriate benchmarks and their mean square errors can be deduced.

For example, consider a series A which is entirely random. The best extrapolation is the expected value of A, and the mean square error of extrapolation is the variance of A. Our relative mean square [28] is, in this case:

$$(18) \qquad\qquad RM = \frac{M_P}{\sigma_A^2}.$$

Proceeding to the case of serially correlated realizations A, the simplest specification of the stochastic structure of A is a first order autoregression:

$$(19) \qquad\qquad A_t = \alpha + \beta A_{t-1} + \xi_t,$$

where ξ_t is uncorrelated with A_{t-1}, has mean zero, and is not serially

[27] Minimization of the mean square error is the prominent criterion in the mathematical literature (see note 22).

[28] Note that the randomness of A does not make it unpredictable by means of P. P may possibly utilize lagged values of another, related random series. Note also that $RM = r_{AP}^2$ when $P = P^c$.

correlated. Here, the mean square error of extrapolation is the variance of ξ_t, which can be expressed as:

$$(20) \qquad M_X = \sigma^2(\xi_t) = (1 - \rho^2)\sigma_A^2,$$

where ρ is the first order autocorrelation coefficient in A. The relative mean square error becomes:

$$(21) \qquad RM = \frac{M_P}{(1 - \rho^2)\sigma_A^2}.$$

It is easily seen that expression (21) holds in the more general case, with ρ as the multiple autocorrelation coefficient, when the series to be predicted has the following linear autoregressive structure:

$$(22) \qquad A_t = \alpha + \beta_1 A_{t-1} + \beta_2 A_{t-2} + \cdots + \epsilon_t.$$

Specification (22) is not necessarily the best or even a sufficiently general assumption about the stochastic nature of most economic time series. However, it can easily be generalized into a polynomial function with power terms for the various A's including time and its powers as variables.

$$(23) \qquad A_t = \sum_{i=0}^{\infty} \alpha_i t^i + \sum_{k=1}^{\infty} \sum_{j=1}^{\infty} \beta_j A_{t-j}^k + \epsilon_t.$$

The relative mean square error (21) remains of the same form in this generalized case. In all cases, RM is a criterion which takes into account the difficulty in extrapolating: The larger the variance of the series and the smaller the serial correlation in it, the more difficult it is to extrapolate. The denominator of RM, the benchmark for M_P, is precisely the product of these two factors.

It might seem that a best benchmark derived from an optimal extrapolation is too stringent a criterion of forecasting quality. Recall, however, that forecasts contain (autonomous) information in addition to extrapolation. A good forecast is one which exploits all available knowledge, not just the past history of the series A. In terms of our criterion, good forecasts should exhibit $RM < 1$, even when the benchmark is optimal.

Naive models are benchmark forecasts which have been constructed as shortcuts for purposes here under consideration. Indeed, the present discussion is an extension of the ideas underlying this construction.[29]

(N1) $$A_{t+1} = A_t + \eta_t \quad \text{and}$$

(N2) $$A_{t+1} = A_t + (A_t - A_{t-1}) + w_t.$$

The first of these models projects the last known level of the series (say, that at t) to the next period $(t + 1)$; the forecast here is simply $\hat{A}_{t+1} = A_t$. The second model projects the last known change one period forward, by adding it to the last known level; in this case, the forecast is $\hat{A}_{t+1} = A_t + \Delta A_t$. It is clear that these models are special cases of the general autoregressive model (22). For example, N1 assumes that β_1 in (23) equals one, and all other coefficients equal zero. The naive models obviously exploit only part of the information contained in the given series.

While some knowledge of the structure of the series may suggest a preference for one or the other of the two naive models,[30] it should be clear that neither is in any sense an optimal benchmark. In fact, no claim was ever made on behalf of these models that they can serve such a function. They are simply very convenient, and can serve as sufficient criteria for discarding inferior forecasts. But they cannot be used alone to determine acceptability of the forecasts, even in the restricted sense here proposed.

Table 1-7 shows that the root mean square errors of the naive models N1 and N2 are substantially greater than those of the linear autoregressive models X for each of the four variables covered in this study (compare the corresponding entries in lines 1–8 and 9–16, columns 1 and 2). The margins of superiority of X are large, except for industrial production. N1 is slightly better than N2 for plant and equipment outlays; it is worse than N2 for the other variables (compare columns 1 and 2, lines 9–16).

N1 shows substantial biases for GNP and consumption, but not for investment and industrial production (Table 1-7, column 3, lines 9–16).

---

[29] See note 21. An interesting application of a particular autoregressive model as a testing device is found in [1, pp. 402–409]. (These tests use exclusively comparisons of correlation coefficients.)

[30] If a first order autoregression holds (as in equation 19), then N1 can be shown to be more suitable than N2. If the autoregressive structure is of a higher order (with more lagged terms), N2 will likely do a better job than N1.

The bias proportions for N2 are negligible for levels but fairly large for changes in GNP, consumption, and production (only in the last case is N2 more biased than N1; see columns 3 and 4, lines 9–16 in Table 1-7). The autoregressive extrapolations, which are virtually all unbiased, are on the whole definitely better in these terms than either of the naive models.

TABLE 1-7. Accuracy Statistics for Autoregressive and Naive Model Projections of Annual Levels and Changes in Four Aggregative Variables, 1953–63

Line	Predicted Variable [a]		Root Mean Square Error ($\sqrt{M_X}$)		Proportion of Systematic Error (U_X/M_X)		Correlation with Observed Values (r_{AX})	
			Selected Model [c]	Range [d]	Selected Model [c]	Range [d]	Selected Model [c]	Range [d]
			Autoregressive Models [b]					
1	GNP	Level	15.39	15.39–18.12	.203	.07–.28	.982	.977–.982
2		Change	13.49	13.49–15.23	.177	.09–.27	.424	.018–.424
3	PC	Level	5.94	5.94– 6.40	.109	.11–.23	.993	.993
4		Change	5.17	5.17– 5.33	.232	.23–.30	.204	.204–.427
5	PE	Level	1.86	1.86– 2.32	.171	.12–.20	.885	.808–.885
6		Change	2.01	2.01– 2.42	.059	.01–.07	.806	.567–.806
7	IP	Level	9.61	9.61–11.23	.200	.09–.36	.911	.865–.911
8		Change	8.52	8.52– 9.81	.387	.14–.48	.601	.200–.601
			Naive Models [e]					
			N1	N2	N1	N2	N1	N2
9	GNP	Level	24.60	19.34	.657	.195	.981	.972
10		Change	23.96	17.46	.664	.527	0	.460
11	PC	Level	13.68	8.77	.881	.206	.995	.986
12		Change	13.67	7.64	.876	.669	0	.319
13	PE	Level	2.23	1.65	.144	.208	.824	.915
14		Change	3.46	1.66	.050	.007	0	.379
15	IP	Level	10.58	11.78	.154	.324	.883	.882
16		Change	9.75	10.36	.268	.553	0	.512

[a] GNP = gross national product; PC = personal consumption expenditures; PE = plant and equipment outlays; IP = index of industrial production.

[b] For explanation of the general form of autoregressive models, see equation (24) in the text.

[c] Five-lag models for GNP and industrial production and two-lag models for consumption and plant and equipment outlays were selected on the basis of minimum M_X. For a description of these models, see p. 34 ff.

[d] Refers to the results for models with varying numbers of lagged terms (from one to five quarters), as estimated for each of the variables covered.

[e] Naive model N1 extrapolates the last known level of the given series, N2 extrapolates the last known change. See the text below.

Finally, the highest correlations with observed values obtained for the X models exceed those for N1 and N2 in most instances, but the differences here are often small (Table 1-7, columns 5 and 6, lines 1–8, compared with lines 9–16).[31] This is not surprising, since correlations for N models are equivalent to X models with one or two lagged terms. The correlations based on levels are high for both N1 and N2 but those based on changes are, of course, always zero for the N1 model, which assumes that the change in each forecast period is identically zero.

To sum up, the differences in predictive performance between the extrapolative models reflect the differences in statistical structure of the series to which the models are applied. Thus, for series such as GNP, IP, and PC, which are fairly smooth and have persistent trends (are highly autocorrelated), N2 proves to be superior to N1. For the more cyclical and irregular series, such as PE (which are less strongly autocorrelated), N2 is, on the contrary, the inferior one.[32] But for all four series X has a better over-all record than either N1 or N2. Indeed, only one lagged term in the X model suffices to achieve superiority over N1, since in that case X is identical with a linearly corrected N1.

EMPIRICAL AUTOREGRESSIVE BENCHMARKS

In practical applications it is difficult to specify and to estimate the autoregressive extrapolation function. If specification (22) is assumed to be correct,[33] the best estimate is obtained by a linear least-squares fit of A_t to past data.[34]

(24) $A_t = a + b_1 A_{t-1} + b_2 A_{t-2} + \cdots + v_t.$

The prediction made at the end of the current year t for the next year $t + 1$ then takes the form:

(24a) $\hat{A}_{t+1} = a + b_1 A_t + b_2 A_{t-1} + \cdots + 0;$

---

[31] Large margins in favor of X are found for industrial production and changes in PE outlays only. Model N2 shows slightly higher correlations than X in two cases (GNP changes and PE levels) and N1 in one case (consumption).

[32] Note that such series have greater frequencies of turning points. It is also clear that N1 produces smaller errors than N2 at turning points.

[33] For experiments with the more general specification (23), see [3].

[34] See [10, pp. 173–220].

and

$$\hat{v}_{t+1} = (A_{t+1} - \hat{A}_{t+1}) \text{ is the extrapolation error.}$$

Given (24a) and realizations for n periods, the estimated mean square error of extrapolation is:

(21a) $$M_X = \frac{1}{n} \sum_t (A_{t+1} - \hat{A}_{t+1})^2.$$

If the extrapolation X is unbiased and efficient, the form of its mean square error is the same as the denominator in (21); since

(21b) $$M_X = (1 - r_{AX}^2) \cdot S_A^2.$$

Note, however, that r_{AX}, the correlation between A and $\hat{A}$, is not the same as the multiple correlation coefficient $\hat{\rho}$ implicit in (24). Only if specification (22) were a correct description of the population, and the sample large enough, would the value of r_{AX} approximate $\hat{\rho}$. Given, unavoidably, a less than optimal specification, $\hat{\rho}$ is likely to over-estimate, and r_{AX} to underestimate, the proper parameter ρ in the mean square error of the "ideal" (optimal) benchmark. The relative mean square errors based on (21a) constitute, therefore, less than maximally stringent benchmark criteria.

Regressions (24) were fitted to data beginning in 1947 and ending in the year preceding the forecast.[35] Quarterly, seasonally adjusted data were used to derive corresponding extrapolations. Annual extrapolative predictions were computed by averaging the extrapolations for the four quarters of the target year.[36]

The question of how many lagged terms to include in (24) in order to produce extrapolations could be answered, in principle, if we had confidence that specification (22) is, indeed, the best. In that case we could adopt the rule that we add successively more remote terms to

---

[35] That is, the period of fit for the 1953 forecast was 1947–52, and so on, ending with the forecast for 1963 based on the fit to the data covering the period 1947–62. In these computations, data on the *levels* of the given series were used; the forecasts of changes were derived from those of levels.

[36] The value of A in the last quarter of the current (base) year was also derived by extrapolation, since it is typically not known to the end-of-year forecaster. This is especially true for series available only in quarterly rather than monthly units, such as GNP and components. For the PE series, however, anticipations of the fourth quarter and the following first quarter are available from the Department of Commerce–Securities and Exchange Commission surveys, and have been used.

the right hand side of (24) until we used A_{t-k}, such that the additional set A_{t-k-1} to A_{t-n} (in our case, $t - n$ is 1947) yields no further increase in the adjusted multiple correlation coefficient $\hat{\rho}$.

In practice, again, maximization of $\hat{\rho}$ will not necessarily minimize M_X. Experiments with stopping rules on autoregressive equations (24) of successively higher order showed that the addition of longer lags does reduce the over-all extrapolation error in some cases where it does not increase $\hat{\rho}$. Such reductions, however, are, on the whole, small. The experiments indicate that the smallest extrapolation errors are obtained by using five-term lags for GNP and industrial production, and two-term lags for consumption and plant and equipment expenditures.[37]

Table 1-7 (columns 3 and 4, lines 1–8) shows the proportions of systematic error in the extrapolative forecasts (U_X/M_X) and the coefficients of correlation between the extrapolated and observed changes (r_{AX}). As would be expected, the autoregressive predictions are largely free of significant biases: the systematic components are small, not only for the models selected here but typically also for those with fewer or more lagged terms in the range covered in these tests.[38] The correlations r_{AX} are high for the autoregressive predictions of levels, but (except in the case of investment) rather low for changes. Here the results often differ considerably, depending on the number of the lagged terms included in the models. But the models selected, which are those with the lowest M_X values, also turn out, with only one exception, to be the models with the highest r_{AX} values (compare columns 5 and 6, lines 1–8).

We conclude that the autoregressive extrapolations, while not necessarily optimal, show a substantial margin of superiority over the usual naive models. This is partly because the former are less likely to be biased than the latter, and partly because they are more efficient. A relatively small number of lags is sufficient to produce satisfactory benchmarks in terms of minimizing M_X.

[37] It should be noted that these particular conclusions are based on the entire forecast period 1953–63. The choice of numbers of lagged terms is thus *ex post,* utilizing more information than was available to the forecaster. But, as Table 1-7 shows, the effects of varying lag periods on the mean square extrapolation errors are rather small, at least in the selected data.

[38] Only for the changes in industrial production did some of the X models yield significant bias proportions.

EXTRAPOLATION ERRORS IN MULTIPERIOD FORECASTING

Consider a series that has an autoregressive representation (22). Suppose that, in addition to extrapolating one period ahead, we also want to extrapolate any number (k) of periods ahead: It can be shown [39] that an optimal (in the sense of minimum extrapolation error) extrapolation at $t - k$ for k spans ahead is achieved by substitution of the as yet unknown magnitudes in the autoregression (22) by their extrapolated values:

(25) $_t\hat{A}_{t-k} = \beta_1(_{t-1}\hat{A}_{t-k}) + \beta_2(_{t-2}\hat{A}_{t-k}) + \cdots + \beta_{k-1}(_{t-k+1}\hat{A}_{t-k})$

$$+ \beta_k A_{t-k} + \beta_{k+1} A_{t-k-1} + \cdots.$$

For example, let $k = 2$: We substitute

$$\hat{A}_{t-1} = \alpha + \beta_1 A_{t-2} + \beta_2 A_{t-3} + \cdots$$

into

(22a) $A_t = \alpha + \beta_1(\hat{A}_{t-1} + \epsilon_{t-1}) + \beta_2 A_{t-2} + \cdots + \epsilon_t$

obtaining

(26) $A_t = \alpha (1 + \beta_1) + (\beta_1^2 + \beta_2)A_{t-2} + (\beta_1\beta_2 + \beta_3)A_{t-3} + \cdots$

$$+ (\beta_1\epsilon_{t-1} + \epsilon_t).$$

According to (26), the mean square error of extrapolation in predicting A_t at time $t - 2$ is the variance of $(\beta_1\epsilon_{t-1} + \epsilon_t)$. Given the stationarity assumptions underlying the autoregressive model (22), which state that ϵ_t is not serially correlated and that the variance of ϵ_{t-k} is the same for all k, we have:

(27) $$_2M_X = (1 + \beta_1^2)\sigma^2(\epsilon).$$

It can be seen, by similar substitutions, that the mean square extrapolation error for any span (k) is equal to:

(28) $$_kM_X = (1 + \gamma_1^2 + \gamma_2^2 + \cdots + \gamma_{k-1}^2) \cdot \sigma^2(\epsilon),$$

where [40]

$$\gamma_i = \sum_{j=1}^{i} \beta_j \gamma_{i-j}, \quad (\text{with } \gamma_0 = 1).$$

[39] For a sophisticated mathematical treatment of this topic, see [11].

[40] For the derivation and a more intensive study of these patterns and their implications in forecasting see Mincer's "Models of Adaptive Forecasting" in this volume.

We see that in stationary linear autoregressive series, the extrapolation error $_kM_X$ increases with lengthening of the span k. The rate at which the predictive power of extrapolations deteriorates as the target is moved further into the future depends on the patterns of coefficients in the autoregression (22) (see reference in footnote 40).

To the extent that forecasts P rely on extrapolations, and the latter are based on, or can be represented by, linear autoregressions, we would expect their accuracy to deteriorate with lengthening of the span. There is, indeed, ample evidence that forecasts deteriorate with lengthening span.

This can be seen in Table 1-8, where mean square errors of forecasts $_kM_P$ and of extrapolation $_kM_X$ increase with span k (columns 1 through 4). As in the previously observed case $k = 1$, we now also find that forecast errors are generally smaller than extrapolation errors in multispan forecasting.

Accordingly, the relative mean square errors are, without exception, less than one (column 5). On the whole, the RM indexes are larger for changes than for levels, indicating that forecasts have a comparative advantage in predicting levels, regardless of span.

The mean square errors of forecasts and of extrapolations increase with span, as we expected. An interesting question is: Do forecasts or extrapolations deteriorate more rapidly? The answer is given by the RM indexes in Table 1-8 (column 5), which show a tendency to increase with span. With the exception of quarterly GNP forecasts (lines 1–8), this regularity is more closely observed in the corrected relative mean square errors RM^c (column 6).

Looking further into the components of $RM^c = \dfrac{1 - r_{AP.X}^2}{1 - r_{AX.P}^2}$, we see that the partials $r_{AP.X}$ decline with the extension of span (column 7), while $r_{AX.P}$ increases (column 8). Evidently, the contribution of the autonomous component of P to predictive efficiency tends to decline in longer-span forecasts. At the same time, the degree to which forecasts fail to utilize the predictive power of extrapolations tends to increase with lengthening of the span.

Our finding that the autonomous components of forecasts deteriorate with span faster than the extrapolations can be explained by the following: Consider the ingredients of general economic forecasts. In addition to extrapolations of some kind, forecasters use relations between the series to be predicted and known or estimated values of other variables; various anticipatory data, such as investment intention surveys and government budget estimates; and, finally, their own presumably informed judgments. Each of these potential sources of forecast is subject to deterioration with lengthening span. The forecasting relations between time series involve lags of various lengths. Typically, the relations weaken as the lags are increased. Most indicators and anticipatory data have relatively short effective forecasting leads beyond which their usefulness declines. Informed judgments and estimates will probably also serve best over short time ranges. Hence, a hypothesis that P would tend to improve relative to X for the longer spans may well be contradicted by the data, and apparently often is, according to Table 1-8.

Evidence presented elsewhere indicates that similar results are also obtained in comparing forecasts with certain simple trend extrapolations: The errors of forecasts tend to increase more than the errors of these extrapolations. Relative to the naive models N1 and N2, however, the performance of most forecasts improves with extensions of the span.[41] Clearly, these models fail to provide trend projections.

Such projections become more useful with lengthening of span. Forecasts do in part incorporate trend projections. Still greater reliance on them might improve forecasting performance in the longer spans.

SUMMARY

This study is an exposition of certain criteria and methods of evaluating economic forecasts, and provides examples of their empirical application. The forecasts are sets of numerical point predictions, classified by source (individuals or groups), subject (time series for aggregative economic variables), and span (time from issue to target date).

Analysis of absolute forecast errors proceeds from a simple scatter diagram and a regression of realizations on predictions. A forecast is *unbiased* if the mean values of the predictions and the realizations are equal, that is, if the average error is zero. It is *efficient* if the pre-

---

[41] Zarnowitz [13].

TABLE 1-8. Comparisons of Forecasts and Extrapolations for Varying Spans, 1953–63

Line	Code and Type of Forecast [a]	Span of Fore-cast [b] k	Mean Square Error [c]				Relative Mean Square Error		Partial Correlation Coefficients	
			$_kM_P$ (1)	$_kM_P^c$ (2)	$_kM_X$ (3)	$_kM_X^c$ (4)	RM (col. 1 ÷ col. 3) (5)	RM^c (col. 2 ÷ col. 4) (6)	$r_{AP.X}$ (7)	$r_{AX.P}$ (8)
	A. Gross National Product									
	Quarterly forecasts, 1953–63									
	Forecast G (20)									
1	Level	1	83.6	68.5	205.2	160.6	.407	.427	.771	−.228
2	Level	2	99.5	62.3	340.3	247.2	.292	.252	.873	−.234
3	Level	3	243.0	223.1	512.3	498.6	.474	.447	.751	−.162
4	Level	4	306.4	91.5	446.6	311.4	.686	.294	.840	.048
5	Change	1	36.9	29.3	52.7	44.0	.700	.666	.589	.138
6	Change	2	89.0	71.1	119.5	100.0	.744	.712	.614	.352
7	Change	3	306.8	252.0	377.0	377.0	.814	.668	.599	.079
8	Change	4	211.4	136.7	221.0	191.4	.957	.714	.614	.357
	Semiannual forecasts, 1955–63									
	Forecast D (16)									
9	Level	1	160.0	87.6	265.0	186.6	.604	.470	.728	.048
10	Level	2	327.1	211.3	429.8	288.7	.761	.732	.562	.254
11	Change	1	67.1	61.9	143.9	107.0	.466	.579	.649	.020
12	Change	2	223.0	181.2	273.2	203.6	.816	.890	.390	.217
	Forecast G (16)									
13	Level	1	79.5	45.5	265.0	186.6	.300	.244	.888	−.360
14	Level	2	169.0	87.2	429.8	288.7	.393	.302	.836	−.016
15	Change	1	53.2	38.0	143.9	107.0	.370	.355	.804	.075
16	Change	2	179.1	99.2	273.2	203.6	.656	.487	.719	.097

(continued)

TABLE 1-8 (concluded)

Line	Code and Type of Forecast [a]	Span of Fore-cast [b] k	Mean Square Error [c] $_kM_P$ (1)	$_kM_P^c$ (2)	$_kM_X$ (3)	$_kM_X^c$ (4)	Relative Mean Square Error RM (col. 1 ÷ col. 3) (5)	RM^c (col. 2 ÷ col. 4) (6)	Partial Correlation Coefficients $r_{AP.X}$ (7)	$r_{AX.P}$ (8)
				B. Index of Industrial Production						
	Quarterly forecasts, 1953–63									
	Forecast G (19)									
17	Level	1	14.4	10.3	68.6	60.4	.210	.171	.922	−.352
18	Level	2	25.4	20.0	100.3	80.9	.253	.247	.868	.002
19	Level	3	88.4	36.4	113.9	94.1	.776	.387	.786	.121
20	Level	4	73.7	52.3	163.0	108.8	.452	.480	.730	.165
21	Change	1	9.9	9.0	18.9	18.4	.524	.488	.743	.287
22	Change	2	23.8	23.6	51.1	40.1	.467	.588	.698	.356
23	Change	3	49.9	45.9	83.2	59.3	.600	.773	.593	.402
24	Change	4	76.5	66.8	126.6	79.1	.604	.845	.528	.383
	Semiannual forecasts, 1955–63									
	Forecast D (16)									
25	Level	1	29.1	29.1	85.9	78.9	.339	.369	.764	.104
26	Level	2	69.7	69.7	165.8	123.3	.420	.570	.667	.382
27	Change	1	32.3	32.3	56.4	49.0	.573	.659	.537	.262
28	Change	2	75.7	75.7	136.4	94.4	.555	.802	.455	.369
	Forecast G (16)									
29	Level	1	18.0	14.9	85.9	78.9	.210	.189	.901	−.069
30	Level	2	70.3	55.9	165.8	122.3	.424	.457	.751	.210
31	Change	1	40.0	17.2	56.4	49.0	.708	.352	.808	.114
32	Change	2	75.6	64.4	136.4	94.4	.554	.682	.615	.300

[a] Number of predictions for each forecast set *per span* is given in parentheses.

[b] Quarterly forecasts refer to levels and changes in the given series one, two, three, and four quarters following the quarter (base period) in which the forecast was made. Semiannual forecasts refer to levels and changes in the series one and two halves following the half (base period) in which the forecast was made. Changes are computed from the base period to the relevant quarter (or half).

[c] Lines 1–16, billions of dollars squared; lines 17–32, index points squared (1947–49 = 100).

dictions are uncorrelated with errors, so that the slope of the regression equals unity. A convenient summary measure is the mean square error, which includes the variance of the residuals from that regression as well as two other components reflecting the bias and inefficiency of the forecast, respectively. The mean component is zero for an unbiased forecast, and the "slope component" is zero for an efficient forecast; hence, if the predictions are both unbiased and efficient, the mean square error reduces to the residual variance.

In dealing with limited samples of predictions and realizations, statistical tests are necessary to ascertain whether the forecasts are *significantly* biased or inefficient, or both. Measures of accuracy and decomposition of mean square errors are presented for several sets of business forecasts, along with test statistics for lack of bias and for efficiency. Bias is found most often in predictions of GNP and consumption. The residual variance accounts for most of the total mean square error, while the slope component is the smallest.

Another fact revealed by the accuracy analysis of forecasts of changes is the tendency to underestimate the absolute size of changes, a tendency reported in other studies. This tendency may be due to underestimation of levels in upward-trending series, or to an apparent underestimation of the variance of actual changes. The latter is theoretically implicit in efficient forecasting and is, therefore, not in itself a forecasting defect. In the forecasts examined here, however, it is the underestimation of levels that mainly accounts for the observed underestimation of changes. There is also evidence that increases in series with strong upward trends are likely to be underpredicted, but this is not so for decreases in series with little or no such trends. In short, the one established phenomenon is a tendency toward a conservative estimation of growth prospects.

Extrapolations of past values are relatively simple and inexpensive forecasting procedures which can be defined and reproduced. A forecast may be judged satisfactory according to íts absolute errors; but if a less costly extrapolation is about as accurate, the comparative advantage is on the side of the extrapolation. We compared forecast errors to extrapolation errors in the form of a ratio of the two mean square errors. This ratio, the relative mean square error, can thus be viewed as an index of the *marginal* rather than *total* productivity of business forecasting. Moreover, it provides a degree of commensurability for diverse forecasts whose absolute errors cannot be meaningfully compared.

Optimal, that is predictively most accurate, extrapolations are difficult to construct. As convenient substitutes, we use autoregressive extrapolations of a relatively simple sort, based on information available to the forecaster. Unlike the naive models, which have been widely used as standard criteria of forecast evaluation, the autoregressive benchmarks take partial account of the statistical structure of the time series to be predicted. They are largely free of bias and definitely superior to the naive models.

It is possible for a forecast to be less accurate than the benchmark extrapolations, yet to be superior after correction for bias and inefficiency. Even without such corrections, our collection of forecasts shows a consistently greater accuracy than autoregressive predictions.[42] The margin of superiority is increased when corrected forecasts are compared to corrected extrapolations.

Extrapolation is an alternative, but not an exclusive, method of forecasting. It is, to some degree, incorporated in the business forecasts, and, to that degree, implicit extrapolation errors are a part of observed forecast errors. Our analysis permits us to decompose observed forecasts into extrapolative and other (autonomous) components, and to estimate the relative contributions of each to the predictive accuracy of the forecast.

It is, of course, the autonomous component that is responsible for the superior efficiency of forecasts over the benchmark extrapolations. At the same time, we find that available extrapolative information is largely utilized by forecasters. The extrapolative component of forecasting is clearly more pronounced in strongly trending and relatively smooth series than in others.

In the final section we extend our accuracy analyses to multispan forecasting. We compare errors of forecasting one quarter to four quarters ahead. On the average, forecast errors increase with length of predictive span. One reason for this is that forecasts consist, in part, of extrapolations whose accuracy declines for more distant target dates. However, longer-term forecasts are generally *worse* than

---

[42] Some other forecasts, however, particularly those for GNP components and longer spans, were found to be inferior to extrapolative benchmark predictions; see Zarnowitz [13, pp. 86–104].

the short ones, when compared with such extrapolations. Evidently, the predictive power of the autonomous components of forecasts deteriorates more rapidly with lengthening span. In addition, the potential of extrapolative prediction is utilized to a lesser degree by the longer-span forecasts. Such forecasts, therefore, can gain from increased reliance on trend projection.

REFERENCES

[1] Alexander, S. S., and Stekler, H. O., "Forecasting Industrial Production – Leading Series vs. Autoregression," *Journal of Political Economy,* August 1959.

[2] Christ, Carl, "A Test of an Econometric Model for the U.S. 1921–1947," in *Conference on Business Cycles,* NBER, New York, 1951.

[3] Cunnyngham, Jon, "The Short-Term Forecasting Ability of Econometric Models," NBER, unpublished.

[4] Hickman, W. Braddock, "The Term Structure of Interest Rates: An Exploratory Analysis," NBER, 1942, mimeographed.

[5] Muth, J. F., "Rational Expectation and the Theory of Price Movements," *Econometrica,* July 1961.

[6] Okun, A. M., "A Review of Some Economic Forecasts for 1955–57," *Journal of Business,* July 1959.

[7] Theil, H., *Applied Economic Forecasting,* Chicago, 1966.

[8] ———, *Economic Forecasts and Policy,* Amsterdam, 1961.

[9] ———, *Optimal Decision Rules for Government and Industry,* Amsterdam, 1964.

[10] Wald, A., and Mann, H. B., "On the Statistical Treatment of Linear Stochastic Difference Equations," *Econometrica,* July 1943.

[11] Whittle, P., *Prediction and Regulation,* London, 1963.

[12] Yaglom, A. M., *Stationary Random Functions,* Englewood Cliffs, N.J., 1962.

[13] Zarnowitz, Victor, *An Appraisal of Short-Term Economic Forecasts,* Occasional Paper 104, New York, NBER, 1967.

TWO

Data Errors
and Forecasting Accuracy

ROSANNE COLE

INTRODUCTION

A basic requirement for successful economic forecasting is accurate
data. Though it is widely recognized that most economic statistics contain measurement errors, relatively little effort has been made to determine how much of the error in forecasts might be attributed to errors in
the underlying data. An analysis of the importance of this source of
forecast error, however, is indispensable for a proper evaluation of
forecasting accuracy. For example, conclusions about the quality of a
set of forecasts (and hence the model used to generate them) would
vary according to whether data errors were found to be a major or a
negligible component of forecast error. Moreover, an analysis of data
errors can provide an indication of the potential for improving forecasts by improving the accuracy of the underlying data.

The major difficulty confronting an empirical analysis of the effects
of data errors on forecasting accuracy is that very little is known about
the errors in many economic series. One type of information is avail-

NOTE: The reader who has traveled the preceding chapter will recognize throughout
this report my indebtedness to Jacob Mincer and Victor Zarnowitz. This is my opportunity to do so. I should also like to thank Phillip Cagan, John Kendrick, and Julius
Shiskin for their helpful comments on an earlier version of the paper.

able, however, and it approximates the data problems of a forecasting situation rather well. The data underlying many forecasts are preliminary estimates. Revised estimates based on more complete information are published at a later date. Since the revised estimates are presumably more accurate, the consequences of using preliminary rather than revised data can be viewed as an illustration of the effects of data errors.[1]

Another difficulty arises from the fact that the majority of published forecasts are not scientific: neither the forecasting models nor the data they use are explicitly specified. Such forecasts are nevertheless of considerable and practical interest to a broad class of business and economic analysts. Since they cannot be replicated, the effect of data errors on their accuracy cannot be assessed directly. However, by relating their errors to errors in data available at the time the forecasts were made, it is possible to infer indirectly the element of forecast error attributable to data errors. More specifically, forecasts may be assumed to rely partly on extrapolations of recent levels of the series to be predicted. Any shortcomings in these data would thus be transferred to the forecasts and become a source of error.

This chapter shows the effect of using preliminary rather than revised data on the accuracy of three types of short-term forecasts of GNP and its major components: (1) forecasts which consist only of extrapolations (naive models); (2) business forecasts which may rely partly on extrapolations and partly on other information; and (3) an analytical model of consumption in which the as yet unknown value of an exogenous variable is obtained by extrapolation. The main emphasis is thus on errors in the data underlying the extrapolative component of a forecast. The effects of errors in other data on which business forecasts may rely are not explicitly considered.

The first section of this study contains an analysis of the ways in which data errors would impair forecast accuracy and a brief review of the characteristics of the errors (as indicated by subsequent revisions) in preliminary GNP data. These errors are shown to be a potential source of forecast bias as well as inefficiency. Though the

---

[1] A recent study of this nature was made by Denton and Kuiper [2]. They constructed a small econometric forecasting model based on the Canadian national accounts, generated forecasts, and observed directly the effects of using preliminary rather than revised data on the parameters of the model and on the accuracy of the simulated forecasts.

analysis is formulated in terms of errors in the data underlying the extrapolative component of forecasts, it is general enough to apply to errors in any data on which forecasts may draw.

In the empirical analysis that follows, estimates are made of the extent to which the use of preliminary rather than revised GNP data reduced the over-all accuracy of naive projections and business forecasts. The importance of data errors as a source of bias and inefficiency in business forecasts is then assessed. Finally, the effect of such errors on the parameter estimates and predictive accuracy of a quarterly consumption function is shown. The findings are summarized in the last section.

I. THE DATA ERROR COMPONENT OF FORECASTS, REALIZATIONS, AND FORECAST ERRORS

An observed forecast error may contain data errors of two kinds: (1) measurement errors in the data used to construct the forecast and (2) measurement error in the realized value. Data errors of the first kind will be a component of the true forecast error. Data errors of the second kind will cause the observed forecast error to differ from the true error. In order to illustrate their different effects, we shall first assume that realizations are measured without error and consider only the consequences of errors in the data underlying forecasts. This assumption will then be relaxed and the effect of errors in realizations shown.

ERRORS IN THE UNDERLYING DATA

Let A be the series forecast. A forecast P_t, made in period $t-1$, of the value of A in period t can be considered as consisting partly of a projection of past values of the series as in

(1) $$P_t = \gamma_1 A^\circ_{t-1} + \gamma_2 A^\circ_{t-2} + \gamma_3 A^\circ_{t-3} + \cdots + h_t,$$

where A° denotes the series of estimates available to the forecaster at the time the forecast is made; γ_i is the weight assigned to A°_{t-i}, the value of the series in period $t-i$; and h_t is an autonomous component summarizing all other information on which the forecast may draw. The linear formulation is assumed for the sake of simplicity.

Most forecasters use the series of best available estimates. This series $(A°)$ consists of mixed data: The values for the most recent periods are provisional estimates while those for periods further into the past have been revised at least once. An estimate from this series of the value of A in period $t - i$ differs from the final series by the error ϵ. In symbols,

$$(2) \qquad\qquad A^{\circ}_{t-i} = A_{t-i} + \epsilon_{t-i}.$$

As a consequence of using preliminary $(A°)$ rather than final data (A), errors in $A°$ are incorporated into the forecast. Using equation (2), the forecast can be rewritten as the sum of P'_t, the forecast that could have been made if final data were available to the forecaster, and an element of data error,

$$(1') \qquad\qquad P_t = \Sigma\gamma_i A_{t-i} + h_t + \Sigma\gamma_i\epsilon_{t-i} = P'_t + \Sigma\gamma_i\epsilon_{t-i},$$

where $P'_t = \Sigma\gamma_i A_{t-i} + h_t$.

The forecast error (u) is defined

$$(3) \qquad u_t = P_t - A_t = (P'_t - A_t) + \Sigma\gamma_i\epsilon_{t-i} = u'_t + \Sigma\gamma_i\epsilon_{t-i},$$

where u' is the error of the forecast (P') based on final data. Errors in the preliminary data $(A°)$ are thus a component of both the forecast and its error.

Let us first consider the case in which the preliminary data are unbiased [i.e., $E(A°) = E(A)$, such that $E(\epsilon) = 0$, where E denotes expected value]. How would such data errors affect forecasting accuracy? The expected value of the forecast error,

$$(4) \qquad\qquad E(u) = E(P) - E(A) = E(u') + \Sigma\gamma_i E(\epsilon),$$

is a measure of the bias. Forecasts are unbiased if $E(P) = E(A)$ and in that case $E(u) = 0$. It is clear from (4) that if the preliminary data were unbiased $[E(\epsilon) = 0]$, their error would not be a source of bias in P.

Whether the preliminary data are biased or not, their errors are likely to reduce forecasting efficiency. Provided the two components of the forecast error in (3) are uncorrelated, the variance of the forecast error is

$$(5) \qquad\qquad \sigma^2(u) = \sigma^2(u') + \sigma^2(\Sigma\gamma_i\epsilon_{t-i}),$$

and $\sigma^2(u)$ must exceed $\sigma^2(u')$. The observed forecast (P) is therefore less efficient than the forecast (P') that could have been made with final data.

A particular aspect of inefficiency is the presence of a "slope error." This obtains if a linear correction of the forecast would reduce the variance of its error.[2] Such a correction is given by a least squares regression of A on P:

$$(6) \qquad A_t = \alpha + \beta P_t + v_t.$$

The corrected forecast is $\alpha + \beta P_t$ and the variance of its error is the residual variance, $\sigma^2(v) = (1 - \rho_{AP}^2)\sigma^2(A)$, where ρ_{AP}^2 denotes the coefficient of determination. The variance of the forecast error can then be expressed as the sum of a potentially reducible, or systematic, component and the residual variance,

$$(7) \qquad \sigma^2(u) = (1 - \beta)^2\sigma^2(P) + (1 - \rho_{AP}^2)\sigma^2(A).$$

It is clear that unless $\beta = 1$, P would be inefficient because $\sigma^2(u)$ would exceed $(1 - \rho_{AP}^2)\sigma^2(A)$.

It can be readily shown that the forecast would be efficient (i.e., $\beta = 1$) only if it is uncorrelated with its error. The correction factor β is, by definition,

$$(8) \qquad \beta = \frac{\text{Cov }(A,P)}{\sigma^2(P)}.$$

It follows from the identity $A \equiv P - u$ that

$$(9) \qquad 1 - \beta = \frac{\text{Cov }(u,P)}{\sigma^2(P)},$$

and Cov $(u,P) = 0$ implies $\rho_{uP} = 0$.

We have seen, however, that P and u share a common error $(\Sigma\gamma_i\epsilon_{t-i})$, which creates a positive correlation between them. As a result, $1 - \beta$ would not equal zero even if P' and u' were uncorrelated, since, using $(1')$ and (3),

$$(9') \qquad 1 - \beta = \frac{\text{Cov }(u', P') + \sigma^2(\Sigma\gamma_i\epsilon_{t-i})}{\sigma^2(P)}.$$

[2] Jacob Mincer and Victor Zarnowitz in Chapter 1 of this volume propose this component of forecast (in)efficiency in their decomposition of mean square errors.

Random data errors could therefore augment the slope component of $\sigma^2(u)$. They would also increase the residual variance component. If ϵ_{t-i} were uncorrelated with A and P', and if β' denotes the regression coefficient, and $\rho^2_{AP'}$, the coefficient of determination, in the regression of A on P', the slope component would be [3]

$$(10) \qquad (1 - \beta)^2\sigma^2(P) = (1 - \beta')^2\sigma^2(P') + (1 - \beta'\beta)\sigma^2(\Sigma\gamma_i\epsilon_{t-i}),$$

and the residual variance would be [4]

$$(11) \qquad (1 - \rho^2_{AP})\sigma^2(A) = (1 - \rho^2_{AP'})\sigma^2(A) + \beta'\beta\sigma^2(\Sigma\gamma_i\epsilon_{t-i}).$$

The extent to which data errors increase the mean square error and each of its three components can now be seen. The mean square error of P' is defined as $E(P' - A)^2$ and equals

$$(12) \qquad M' = [E(P' - A)]^2 + (1 - \beta')^2\sigma^2(P') + (1 - \rho^2_{AP'})\sigma^2(A).$$

Because of data errors, the mean square error of the observed forecast P would be

$$(13) \quad M = [E(P' - A + \Sigma\gamma_i\epsilon_{t-i})]^2 + [(1-\beta')^2\sigma^2(P') + (1-\beta'\beta)\sigma^2(\Sigma\gamma_i\epsilon_{t-i})]$$
$$+ [(1 - \rho^2_{AP'})\sigma^2(A) + \beta'\beta\sigma^2(\Sigma\gamma_i\epsilon_{t-i})].$$

Let P' be unbiased and efficient. Then $E(P' - A) = 0$ and $\beta' = 1$. The first two components of M', the mean and slope components, would then vanish and $M' = (1 - \rho^2_{AP'})\sigma^2(A)$. However, the mean component of M would be

$$[E(\Sigma\gamma_i\epsilon_{t-i})]^2;$$

the slope component would be

$$(1 - \beta)\sigma^2(\Sigma\gamma_i\epsilon_{t-i});$$

and the residual component would be

$$(1 - \rho^2_{AP'})\sigma^2(A) + \beta\sigma^2(\Sigma\gamma_i\epsilon_{t-i}).$$

---

[3] Since $\beta = \beta' \dfrac{\sigma^2(P')}{\sigma^2(P)}$ and $\sigma^2(P) = \sigma^2(P') + \sigma^2(\Sigma\gamma_i\epsilon_{t-i})$, $(1 - \beta)^2\sigma^2(P) = \sigma^2(P') +$

$\sigma^2(\Sigma\gamma_i\epsilon_{t-i}) - 2\beta'\sigma^2(P') + \beta'^2\sigma^2(P') \dfrac{\sigma^2(P')}{\sigma^2(P)}$. Add and subtract $\beta'^2\sigma^2(P')$ and rearrange terms to obtain equation (10).

[4] The proof is similar to that given in footnote 3.

Thus, errors in the underlying data could convert an unbiased, efficient forecast into a biased, inefficient one. The size of the bias would be $E(\Sigma\gamma_i\epsilon_{t-i})$.[5] The variance of the forecast error would be augmented by $\sigma^2(\Sigma\gamma_i\epsilon_{t-i})$ in such a way that a slope error of $(1-\beta)\sigma^2(\Sigma\gamma_i\epsilon_{t-i})$ would be created and the residual variance would be augmented by $\beta\sigma^2(\Sigma\gamma_i\epsilon_{t-i})$.

On the assumption that P' is unbiased and efficient, M would reduce to

$$(13') \qquad M = (1 - \rho_{AP'}^2)\sigma^2(A) + E(\Sigma\gamma_i\epsilon_{t-i})^2.$$

Let the relative magnitude of errors in the preliminary data be $k^2 = \dfrac{E(\epsilon)^2}{\sigma^2(A)}$. The data error component of M can then be expressed

$$(14) \qquad E(\Sigma\gamma_i\epsilon_{t-i})^2 = \Sigma\gamma_i^2 k^2 \sigma^2(A),$$

provided that $E(\epsilon_{t-i})^2 = E(\epsilon)^2$ for all i.

The relative mean square error, $RM' = M/M'$, shows the extent to which data errors increase the pure forecast error. Substituting (14) into (13'),

$$(15) \qquad RM' = \frac{(1 - \rho_{AP'}^2)\sigma^2(A) + \Sigma\gamma_i^2 k^2 \sigma^2(A)}{(1 - \rho_{AP'}^2)\sigma^2(A)} = 1 + \frac{\Sigma\gamma_i^2 k^2}{1 - \rho_{AP'}^2}.$$

Thus, given the relative size of errors in the preliminary data (k^2), the increase in forecast error will be greater, the greater the weights assigned to these data ($\Sigma\gamma_i^2$) and the better the forecast (i.e., the greater $\rho_{AP'}^2$).

ERRORS IN REALIZATIONS

Thus far it has been assumed that realizations are measured without error, and we have seen only the effect of errors in the data underlying forecasts. In practice, however, realizations are also likely to contain measurement errors which obscure true forecast errors. In keeping with the preceding example of measurement errors, let us now assume that realizations consist of preliminary ($A°$) rather than revised (A) data. The observed forecast error ($u°$) is then defined as $P - A°$ and equals

---

[5] If the preliminary data are unbiased [i.e., $E(\epsilon_{t-i}) = 0$ for all i], the size of the bias would of course be zero.

(16)
$$u_t^\circ = P_t - A_t^\circ = (P_t' + \Sigma\gamma_i\epsilon_{t-i}) - (A_t + \epsilon_t) = u_t - \epsilon_t = u_t' + \Sigma\gamma_i\epsilon_{t-i} - \epsilon_t.$$

With the aid of (16), three types of forecast error can be distinguished and their relation to each other shown: the observed forecast error (u°); the true forecast error (u); and the pure forecast error (u'). If there were no data errors, the three forecast errors would be identical. Errors in the data used to construct forecasts $(\Sigma\gamma_i\epsilon_{t-i})$ augment the pure forecast error (u') and become a component of the true forecase error (u). Errors in realizations data (ϵ_t) cause the observed error (u°) to differ from the true error (u).

The observed error thus consists of a pure forecast error and two components of data error. The expected value of u° is

(17)
$$E(u^\circ) = E(u - \epsilon) = E(u') + (\Sigma\gamma_i - 1)E(\epsilon),$$

provided $E(\epsilon_{t-i}) = E(\epsilon)$ for all i; and the variance is

(18)
$$\sigma^2(u^\circ) = \sigma^2(u') + \sigma^2(\Sigma\gamma_i\epsilon_{t-i}) + \sigma^2(\epsilon_t) - 2 \text{ Cov } (\Sigma\gamma_i\epsilon_{t-i},\epsilon_t),$$

provided u' and ϵ are uncorrelated.

If the two sets of data errors are independent of each other; that is, if ϵ is serially independent, the covariance term in (18) would vanish. The variance of the forecast error would then be augmented by the errors in the realizations data, $\sigma^2(\epsilon_t)$, as well as by errors in the data underlying the forecast, $\sigma^2(\Sigma\gamma_i\epsilon_{t-i})$.

However, $\sigma^2(\epsilon_t)$ would not be distributed among the slope and residual components in the same way as $\sigma^2(\Sigma\gamma_i\epsilon_{t-i})$. If β° and $\rho^2_{A^\circ P}$ denote the coefficients of regression and determination, respectively, the observed mean square error (M°) equals

(19)
$$M^\circ = [E(P - A^\circ)]^2 + (1 - \beta^\circ)\sigma^2(P) + (1 - \rho^2_{A^\circ P})\sigma^2(A^\circ).$$

The mean component of M° would equal

$$[E(P - A^\circ)]^2 = [E(u - \epsilon)]^2 = [E(u') + (\Sigma\gamma_i - 1)E(\epsilon)]^2;$$

the slope component would be

$$(1 - \beta^\circ)^2\sigma^2(P) = (1 - \beta)^2\sigma^2(P);$$

and the residual component would be

$$(1 - \rho^2_{A^\circ P})\sigma^2(A^\circ) = (1 - \rho^2_{AP})\sigma^2(A) + \sigma^2(\epsilon),$$

provided Cov $(\epsilon_t, \epsilon_{t-i})$ and Cov (A, ϵ) are zero. If P' is unbiased and efficient, $M°$ would become, using (10) and (11),

$$(19') \quad M° = [(\Sigma\gamma_i - 1)E(\epsilon)]^2 + [(1 - \beta)\sigma^2(\Sigma\gamma_i\epsilon_{t-i})] + [(1 - \rho_{AP'}^2)\sigma^2(A)$$
$$+ \beta\sigma^2(\Sigma\gamma_i\epsilon_{t-i}) + \sigma^2(\epsilon)].$$

Data errors would thus affect observed forecasting accuracy in the following ways: Given that errors in the data used to construct the forecast are independent of errors in the realized values (i.e., ϵ is serially independent), then, if the preliminary data are biased, the bias in realizations data would tend to offset the bias induced by errors in the data underlying the forecast. Indeed, in the special case in which $\Sigma\gamma_i = 1$, the biases would be exactly offsetting. Both sets of data errors would reduce forecasting efficiency. Errors in the underlying data would increase the variance of the forecast error by $\sigma^2(\Sigma\gamma_i\epsilon_{t-i})$. They would create a slope error of $(1 - \beta)\sigma^2(\Sigma\gamma_i\epsilon_{t-i})$ and increase the residual variance by $\beta\sigma^2(\Sigma\gamma_i\epsilon_{t-i})$. Errors in realizations would have no effect on slope error; they would reduce the forecast's efficiency by augmenting the residual variance by $\sigma^2(\epsilon_t)$.

There would be a smaller reduction in forecasting efficiency if the two data errors were related. If ϵ were serially correlated, the reduction in efficiency arising from errors in the underlying data would be attenuated by errors in the realizations data. The extent to which the two data errors are offsetting depends, as (18) shows, on the weights assigned to the underlying data $(\Sigma\gamma_i)$ and the strength of the serial correlation in ϵ (ρ_ϵ). At the one extreme, in the special case in which $\Sigma\gamma_i = 1$ and $\rho_{\epsilon_t\epsilon_{t-i}} = 1$ for all i, errors in realizations would exactly offset the reduction in efficiency caused by errors in the underlying data. Then $\sigma^2(u°) = \sigma^2(u') < \sigma^2(u)$, and the observed forecast error would be an unbiased, efficient estimate of the pure forecast error. At the other extreme, $\rho_{\epsilon_t\epsilon_{t-i}} = 0$ for all i, and, as we have seen, errors in realizations would augment the reduction in efficiency and $\sigma^2(u°) > \sigma^2(u) > \sigma^2(u')$. In practice, the effect of errors in the realizations data is likely to fall somewhere in between.

ERRORS IN PRELIMINARY GNP DATA

Table 2-1 shows summary statistics of the errors (as measured by revisions) in preliminary estimates of GNP and its components. We would expect the preliminary data to be unbiased and their errors to be serially independent if they were generated by a probability sampling process. This is not the case, however, for the national accounts estimates. As Table 2-1 shows, and, as is well documented elsewhere,[6] the preliminary product (or expenditures) data have a negative bias: the preliminary estimates underestimate revised levels of GNP and most of its components. These data could thus be a source of negative bias in forecasts which rely on them. Since the biases in the detailed variables do not offset one another, we could expect the bias induced by data errors to be larger in forecasts of aggregates than in forecasts of detailed variables.

Errors in aggregate variables, however, would be likely to increase the mean square error (from M' to M) in forecasts of these variables less than that of the detailed variables. This is suggested by the k-ratios in column 4 of Table 2-1. The relative size of the data errors (k) tends to be larger in details than in aggregates. Thus, other things being constant (i.e., $\Sigma\gamma_i^2$ and $\rho_{AP'}^2$), data errors would be expected to cause the greatest increase in the over-all error of forecasts of net exports, expenditures on consumer and producer durables, new construction, and change in business inventories; they should have the smallest effect on the accuracy of forecasts of GNP, personal consumption, and government expenditures on goods and services.

Errors in the preliminary data for some GNP components show strong, positive serial correlation (column 5). Therefore, the errors would tend to be offsetting when these data are used as realizations as well as inputs to forecasts. Indeed, the possibility for offsetting the errors in the data underlying forecasts by the errors in realizations data has led several investigators to choose preliminary rather than revised GNP data as the set of realized values.[7] In effect, they are using the observed forecast error (u°) to approximate the pure forecast error (u'). The accuracy of this approximation depends, as shown elsewhere,

[6] See, for example, [7], [1], and Rosanne Cole, "Errors in Provisional Estimates of Gross National Product," NBER, forthcoming.

[7] See, for example, [5], [6], and Chapter 1 of this volume.

TABLE 2-1. Errors in Preliminary Estimates of Annual Levels of Gross National Product and Its Components, 1953–63 [a] (*dollars in billions*)

Variable	Mean Error $\bar{\epsilon}$ (1)	Standard Deviation of Error S_ϵ (2)	Root Mean Square Error $\sqrt{M_\epsilon}$ (3)	k-Ratio $\sqrt{\dfrac{M_\epsilon}{\sigma^2(A)}}$ (4)	Serial Correlation Coefficient $r_{\epsilon_t \epsilon_{t-1}}$ (5)
Gross national product	−11.0	4.5	12.8	.166	.570
Personal consumption expenditures	−6.0	1.6	6.2	.125	.841
Durables	−2.9	1.6	3.2	.508	.976
Nondurables	1.8	1.9	2.5	.141	.948
Services	−4.9	1.4	5.1	.198	.457
Gross private domestic investment	−4.2	2.7	4.9	.441	.429
Producers durable equipment	−0.5	2.9	2.8	.642	.464
New construction	−2.7	2.6	3.6	.764	.976
Change in business inventories	−1.0	1.6	1.8	.625	.176
Gov't expend. on goods and services	1.0	1.7	1.9	.114	.574
Federal	0.6	1.6	1.6	.239	.679
State and local	0.3	0.8	0.8	.072	.568
Net exports	−1.8	0.7	1.9	.905	.958

[a] Errors are computed as $\epsilon = A° - A$, where $A°$ denotes provisional estimates and A, the 1965 statistically revised estimates. Provisional estimates of the value of GNP and its components during a given year are from the next year's February issue of the *Survey of Current Business* (*SCB*). The 1965 statistically revised estimates are from the August 1965 *SCB*. The figures published are the result of both statistical and definitional revisions. The major definitional change was to exclude interest paid by consumers from the estimates (see the report article, "National Income and Product Accounts," *SCB*, August 1965, Tables 2 and 3). This item was added to the published figures (expenditures on consumer services, and hence to the aggregates, personal consumption expenditures and gross national product), to obtain estimates of only the statistically revised data. This procedure does not entirely eliminate the definitional changes, and the resulting series (A), therefore, includes some minor definitional changes in federal government expenditures and net exports.

on the strength of the serial correlation in ϵ and on the importance of the extrapolative component in the forecast.

In the following sections, estimates are made of the extent to which errors in the preliminary data augmented the pure forecast error of three types of forecasts of GNP and its components. Though u' (and hence the effect of data errors) can be directly observed for two of the three, it must be estimated indirectly for the third, business forecasts. Two estimates of u' are made for business forecasts. Regression analysis is used to decompose u into its two components: u' and $\Sigma \gamma_i \epsilon_{t-i}$. The results are then compared with those obtained when $u°$ is used as an estimate of u'.

II. EFFECT OF DATA ERRORS ON THE ACCURACY
OF NAIVE PROJECTIONS

Naive models are a class of forecasts constructed from past values of the target series. They are widely used not so often as forecasts per se but as yardsticks for appraising the performance of more sophisticated forecasts.

Table 2-2 shows the root mean square errors of naive projections of annual levels in GNP and its components for the period 1953–63. Errors of projections constructed with preliminary and with revised (1965) data are compared for three types of naive projections, denoted N1, N2, and N3. The projections based on preliminary data, P_t, are specified

$$\text{N1:} \quad P_t = A_{t-1}^{\circ}$$

$$\text{N2:} \quad P_t = A_{t-1}^{\circ} + (A_{t-1}^{\circ} - A_{t-2}^{\circ})$$

$$\text{N3:} \quad P_t = A_{t-1}^{\circ} + (A_{t-1}^{\circ} - A_{t-n}^{\circ})/n,$$

where n is the number of observations in the series. The projections based on revised data, P_t', are the same except that A_{t-i} replaces A_{t-i}° in each case.

These models are thus special cases of the forecast described in equation (1) above, in which the autonomous component of the forecast (h_t) is zero, and the weights (γ_i) assigned to past values of the series are set arbitrarily. In the case of N1, γ_1 equals unity and all other γ coefficients are zero. The model N2 projects the last known level plus the last known change in the series ($\gamma_1 = 2$, $\gamma_2 = -1$, and $\gamma_i = 0$ for $i > 2$); N3 projects the last known level plus the average change [$\gamma_1 = (n + 1)/n$, $\gamma_n = -1/n$, and $\gamma_i = 0$ for $1 < i < n$].

Table 2-2 shows that preliminary data errors increase the root mean square error in naive projections of GNP by 12 to nearly 40 per cent (line 1, columns 7–9). Of the four major sectors, errors in the early estimates of government expenditures affect forecast accuracy the least. The greatest reductions in accuracy are produced by errors in the detailed components of personal consumption expenditures and of gross private domestic investment data.

TABLE 2-2. Effect of Data Errors on the Accuracy of Three Naive Model Projections of Annual Levels of Gross National Product and Its Components, 1953–63

| Line | Variable | Root Mean Square Error of: [a] | | | | | | Relative Root Mean Square Error [b] | | |
| | | Naive Model N1 | | Naive Model N2 | | Naive Model N3 | | | | |
		$\sqrt{M}$ (1)	$\sqrt{M'}$ (2)	$\sqrt{M}$ (3)	$\sqrt{M'}$ (4)	$\sqrt{M}$ (5)	$\sqrt{M'}$ (6)	$\sqrt{RM'_1}$ (7)	$\sqrt{RM'_2}$ (8)	$\sqrt{RM'_3}$ (9)
1	Gross national product	28.4	22.9	20.6	18.4	16.4	11.9	1.240	1.120	1.378
2	Personal consumption expenditures	13.0	12.3	11.6	10.1	7.9	6.2	1.057	1.148	1.274
3	Durables	6.3	4.0	8.8	6.0	5.2	3.8	1.575	1.467	1.368
4	Nondurables	3.4	4.6	6.5	8.9	3.9	1.7	.739	.730	2.294
5	Services	5.9	6.4	4.5	2.4	2.9	1.0	.922	1.875	2.900
6	Gross private domestic investment	11.2	7.6	17.2	15.4	9.9	7.4	1.474	1.117	1.338
7	Producers durable equipment	4.4	2.7	5.4	6.9	4.7	2.6	1.630	.783	1.808
8	New construction	5.4	2.6	5.5	2.9	3.9	2.3	2.077	1.896	1.696
9	Change in business inventories	5.4	3.8	21.3	17.9	5.7	4.0	1.421	1.190	1.425
10	Gov't. expend. on goods and services	5.6	5.7	4.8	5.3	6.0	5.5	.982	.906	1.091
11	Federal	4.0	4.0	3.9	5.5	5.6	5.7	1.000	.709	.982
12	State and local	2.1	3.0	1.7	1.8	1.0	0.7	.700	.944	1.428
13	Net exports	2.5	1.9	2.8	2.9	2.7	2.4	1.316	.966	1.125

[a] In billion dollars. See text for a description of the naive models N1, N2, and N3; see Table 2-1, note a, for sources of data.

[b] Relative root mean square error is defined $\sqrt{RM'_i} = \sqrt{\frac{M_i}{M'_i}}$, where i denotes the naive model.

The data errors do not always increase forecast error. For some variables (line 4 or line 10, for example), the bias arising from the data offsets the bias in projections.[8] On the whole, however, Table 2-2 shows that data errors reduce the accuracy of the naive models, particularly that of the simple trend projection, N3. The root mean square errors of this projection were increased by an average of 55 per cent.

III. EFFECT OF DATA ERRORS ON THE ACCURACY OF BUSINESS FORECASTS

FORECASTS OF ANNUAL LEVELS

Naive projections can be considered scientific forecasts in the sense that the models generating the predictions are specified and the projections can be replicated. The exact weights (γ_i) that naive models assign to past values of the series are known. It was, therefore, possible to compute directly the element of forecast error that can be traced to data errors.

The effect of data errors on the accuracy of business forecasts, however, must be determined indirectly. The models underlying the forecasts in the Zarnowitz sample are not explicitly specified and it is necessary to infer their dependence on preliminary GNP statistics. Some of the forecasts may rely primarily on extrapolations; others may use them hardly at all. Mincer and Zarnowitz found that the patterns of observed forecast errors are consistent with a hypothesis that forecasters tend to be selective and use extrapolations when they provide the greatest advantage: Forecasts of fairly smooth and strongly serially correlated series rely more on extrapolations than do forecasts of somewhat volatile series. For example, forecasts of consumption expenditures tend to rely more on extrapolations than do investment forecasts.

It might be tempting, therefore, to predict that errors in the preliminary statistics would reduce the accuracy of consumption more than that of investment forecasts. Other things being equal, this prediction would be correct. But the "other things" are, according to (15),

---

[8] Note from equations (12) and (13) above that $M' > M$ if $[E(u') + \Sigma\gamma_i E(\epsilon)]^2 < [E(u')]^2$, or, in other words, if $E(u')$ and $\Sigma\gamma_i E(\epsilon)$ are of opposite sign.

the relative magnitudes of the data errors (k^2) and the efficiency of the pure forecast ($\rho^2_{AP'}$). Even though consumption forecasts may rely more on preliminary statistics than do forecasts of more volatile GNP components, the errors in the aggregate consumption data tend to be smaller (as shown by the k-ratios in Table 2-1). The effect on the forecast error depends not only on the importance of extrapolations to the forecast but on the size of the data errors as well.

In order to determine the effect of data errors on the accuracy of business forecasts, let us assume that these forecasts contain an extrapolative component and that it is a linear combination of past values of the target series as expressed in equation (1) above. The forecast error (u) would then consist of the pure forecast error (u') and the error ($\Sigma \gamma_i \epsilon_{t-i}$) induced by errors in the preliminary data, as shown in equation (3) above.

Provided u' and ϵ_{t-i} are uncorrelated, a least squares regression of u_t on past data errors decomposes u into its two components:

$$(20) \qquad u_t = \gamma_1 \epsilon_{t-1} + \gamma_2 \epsilon_{t-2} + \gamma_3 \epsilon_{t-3} + \cdots + u'_t, \quad \text{or}$$

$$u_t = \gamma_0 + \gamma_1 \epsilon_{t-1} + \gamma_2 \epsilon_{t-2} + \gamma_3 \epsilon_{t-3} + \cdots + w_t,$$

where $u'_t = \gamma_0 + w_t$. If the forecast contains an extrapolative component (i.e., if the weights γ_i are not zero), then data errors would be a source of error in the forecast and they would account for part of its variability. The regression intercept (γ_0) provides an estimate of the mean error, $\overline{u'}$, and the residual variance [$\sigma^2(w)$], an estimate of $\sigma^2(u')$. Regression (20) can thus be used to determine whether or not data errors are a component of business forecast errors. If they are, they can be a source of bias and will reduce the forecast's efficiency.

Regressions of forecast errors on past data errors were computed for sixteen forecasts from the Zarnowitz sample.[9] Table 2-3 shows error statistics for these forecasts and the corresponding regression

[9] The forecasts are from the eight different sets of business forecasts, denoted by eight capital letters, A–H. They are a subset of the records of several hundred forecasts which were assembled for the NBER study of short-term economic forecasting. The particular variables predicted differ from one forecast set to another; however, all eight sets include forecasts of GNP and two of them (B and F) include forecasts of the major GNP components. For purposes of illustration, only the eight GNP forecasts and eight GNP component forecasts are used here. Though a somewhat different subset of forecasts is used by Mincer and Zarnowitz in Chapter 1 of this volume, we both include the GNP forecasts of sets E, F, and G and the personal consumption forecasts of set F.

TABLE 2-3. Estimates of the Effect of Data Errors on the Accuracy of Forecasts of Annual Levels of Gross National Product and Its Major Components, 1953–63

Code of Forecast[a] and Period Covered	Line	Forecast Error (billion dollars)			Regression Estimates of Pure Forecast Error[b] (billion dollars)				Tests of Bias and Efficiency[c]				
									t-test for				
		$\bar{u}$ (1)	S_u (2)	$\sqrt{M}$ (3)	$\bar{u}'$ (4)	$S_{u'}$ (5)	$\sqrt{M'}$ (6)	$\sqrt{RM'}$ (7)	$E(u)=0$ (8)	$E(u')=0$ (9)	r_{pu} (10)	$r_{pu'}$ (11)	Adjusted $R^2_{u\cdot\epsilon_{t-1},\cdots,\epsilon_{t-k}}$ (12)
Gross National Product													
Set A, 1954–63	1	−19.1	11.6	22.1	−23.0	8.8	24.5	.902	5.20 *	2.80 *	.473	.417	.432
Set B, 1953–63	2	−13.8	11.2	17.5	−7.3	6.5	9.7	1.804	4.09 *	1.42	.061	−.091	.659 *
Set C, 1958–63	3	−14.5	11.0	17.7	14.5	9.5	16.9	1.047	3.23 *	0.52	.179	−.073	.260
Set D, 1956–63	4	−18.5	9.9	20.7	3.5	6.5	7.0	2.957	5.27 *	0.19	−.012	−.305	.569 *
Set E, 1953–63	5	−21.8	13.5	25.3	−13.8	7.7	15.6	1.622	5.35 *	2.28 *	−.240	.210	.677 *
Set F, 1953–63	6	−15.8	8.8	18.0	−6.6	7.6	9.8	1.837	5.95 *	1.00	.315	.257	.264
Set G, 1953–63	7	−9.2	7.9	11.0	−8.2	7.4	10.8	1.018	3.88 *	1.30	.684 *	.778 *	.122
Set H, 1954–63	8	−19.7	10.5	22.1	−24.6	6.1	25.3	.873	5.95 *	4.59 *	.432	.408	.668 *
Personal Consumption Expenditures													
Set B, 1953–63	9	−7.3	6.4	9.5	2.1	4.7	4.9	1.939	3.82 *	0.62	.338	−.045	.460 *
Set F, 1953–63	10	−9.1	5.0	10.2	4.1	4.5	5.9	1.729	6.09 *	0.50	.550 *	.582 *	.181
Gross Private Domestic Investment													
Set B, 1953–63	11	−6.9	6.7	9.4	−8.2	3.6	8.9	1.056	3.40 *	3.65 *	.264	−.288	.718 *
Set F, 1953–63	12	−5.5	5.0	7.3	−10.8	3.6	11.3	.646	3.61 *	2.70 *	.372	.473	.494 *
Gov't. Expend. on Goods and Services													
Set B, 1953–63	13	2.2	3.2	3.8	1.4	3.2	3.3	1.152	2.35 *	1.13	.015	.203	−.007
Set F, 1953–63	14	1.2	2.5	2.7	1.3	2.6	2.8	.964	1.56	1.27	−.156	.171	−.105
Net Exports													
Set B, 1953–63	15	−1.9	2.2	2.9	−0.7	2.2	2.3	1.261	2.82 *	0.54	.497	.386	−.001
Set F, 1953–63	16	−2.5	1.6	2.9	−1.4	1.7	2.1	1.381	5.01 *	0.70	−.015	.116	−.070

Note: * denotes significance at the 10 per cent level.

[a] For a description of the forecasts, see Zarnowitz [6] and footnote 9 above.

[b] Error statistics are from regression (20) in text:

$$u_t = \gamma_0 + \gamma_1 \epsilon_{t-1} + \gamma_2 \epsilon_{t-2} + \gamma_3 \epsilon_{t-3} + \gamma_4 \epsilon_{t-4} + w_t.$$

$\bar{u}'$ is estimated as the regression intercept γ_0; $S_{u'}$ as the adjusted standard error of estimate, $\sqrt{\gamma_0^2 + (n-1)/n \, S_{w}^2}$, where n is the number of observations.

S_{u} and $\sqrt{M'}$ is computed as $\sqrt{\gamma_0^2 + (n-1)/n \, S_{w}^2}$, where n is the number of observations.

A step-wise regression was used and the number of lags (up to 4) that produced the maximum adjusted R^2 was used. The statistics for: lines 1, 5, 7, 8, 10, and 12 are based on 4 lags; lines 2–4 are based on 3 lags; line 11 is based on 2 lags; and lines 6, 9, 13–16 are based on 1 lag.

[c] The correlation coefficient $r_{pu'}$ is estimated as $r_{pu\mid\epsilon_{t-1},\cdots,\epsilon_{t-k}}$ where k is the number of lags used in the regressions above.

estimates of $\overline{u'}$, $\sigma^2(u')$, and M'. In addition, the table gives the results of tests for forecast bias and efficiency. The samples are small and sampling variation alone could produce a relation between forecast errors and data errors, as well as nonzero mean errors or nonzero correlations between forecasts and their errors. Tests of significance are therefore indicated.

There is some relation between forecast errors and data errors for each of the twelve sets of GNP, consumption, and investment forecasts, but judging by the coefficients of determination ($R^2_{u \cdot \epsilon_{t-1}, \ldots, \epsilon_{t-k}}$ in column 12), it is significant (at the 10 per cent level) in only seven cases. In these seven sets, however, data errors account for about 65 per cent of $\sigma^2(u)$. No relation is indicated between the errors in forecasts and errors in the preliminary data for government expenditures and net exports (column 12, lines 13–16).[10]

We have seen that though data errors would reduce the efficiency of P by augmenting the random component of $\sigma^2(u)$, they could also affect the systematic component. This is because data errors would create a positive correlation between P and u. Thus, in general, we would expect the correlation coefficient r_{Pu} to be greater than $r_{P'u'}$. If data errors were the only source of inefficiency, $r_{P'u'}$ would be zero. The partial correlation coefficient, $r_{P_tu_t \cdot \epsilon_{t-1}, \ldots, \epsilon_{t-k}}$, which holds the effect of data errors constant, provides an estimate of $r_{P'u'}$.

The two correlation coefficients, r_{Pu} and $r_{P'u'}$, are given in columns 10 and 11 of Table 2-3. A comparison shows that r_{Pu} exceeds $r_{P'u'}$ for six of the seven forecasts in which data errors comprise a significant element of forecast error. However, the correlations that data errors create between P and u are not strong, and we could conclude that data errors reduced the efficiency of P primarily by increasing the random component of $\sigma^2(u)$ rather than by increasing its slope component.

The hypothesis that each of the seven forecasts affected by data errors is unbiased would be rejected at the 10 per cent level in every case (column 8). This hypothesis for the forecasts net of data errors (P') would be rejected for four sets (column 9). Data errors, therefore, could be considered the only source of bias in three of the seven sets.

[10] Data errors are measured by revisions. Definitional revisions, however, have not been excluded from the revisions of government expenditures and net exports (see Table 2-1, note a). It is possible, therefore, that the definitional revisions obscure any relation that may exist between forecast errors and statistical data errors for these variables.

To sum up, the results in Table 2-3 suggest that at least seven of the sixteen forecast sets relied on extrapolations.[11] Errors in the data used to construct the extrapolations reduced the efficiency of these seven forecasts. The reduction was considerable: It is estimated that data errors account for 50 to 70 per cent of $\sigma^2(u)$. All seven forecasts are biased, and data errors could be considered the *primary* source of the bias in three.

FORECASTS OF ANNUAL CHANGES

Errors in forecasts of changes would be exactly the same as errors in forecasts of levels, except for the presence of data errors. The error of a forecast of the change in series A from year $t-1$ to year t is defined

$$(21) \quad u_{\Delta t} = (P_t - A_{t-1}^\circ) - (A_t - A_{t-1}) = (P_t - A_t) - (A_{t-1}^\circ - A_{t-1})$$

$$= u_t - \epsilon_{t-1} = u_t' + \Sigma \gamma_i \epsilon_{t-i} - \epsilon_{t-1},$$

where A_{t-1}° is the forecast base.[12] If there were no data errors, the error of both the change and level forecast would be u_t'.

Provided as before that u' and ϵ_{t-i} are uncorrelated, a least squares regression of the observed forecast error (u_Δ) on past data errors (ϵ_{t-i}) decomposes u_Δ into its two components:

$$(22) \quad u_{\Delta t} = u_t - \epsilon_{t-1} = \gamma_0 + (\gamma_1 - 1)\epsilon_{t-1} + \gamma_2 \epsilon_{t-2} + \gamma_3 \epsilon_{t-3} + \cdots + w_t,$$

where $u_t' = \gamma_0 + w_t$.

Since (22) is simply a linear transformation of (20), the regression equation for levels, all of the coefficients (except the coefficient of

---

[11] These results suggest less widespread use of extrapolations than that found by Mincer and Zarnowitz. This is because the method that they used to decompose forecasts into extrapolative and "autonomous" components, a regression of P_t on past values of A°, estimates the autonomous component as a residual. Thus, as they point out, the autonomous component would include only that element of the forecast that is statistically independent of past values of A°. If the forecast in fact relied on variable B, which is correlated with A_{t-i}°, its importance to the forecast would be attributed to A_{t-i}°. It is unlikely, however, that measurement errors in B would also be correlated with the measurement errors in A_{t-i}°. Therefore, a regression of the forecast *error* on the *errors* in past values of A° would be unlikely to associate B with the extrapolative component of the forecast.

[12] For the sake of simplicity, it is assumed that the forecaster's estimate of the current level of the series, the forecast base, equals the first official estimate, A_{t-1}°. This is a reasonable assumption: the forecaster's estimate of the base year is an average of the official estimates of the first three quarters and the forecaster's estimate of the fourth quarter.

ϵ_{t-1}), their standard errors, and the residual variance will be the same as in (20). The only difference would occur in the coefficient of determination. Generally one might expect this coefficient to be larger for levels than for changes because its denominator, the variance of the forecast error, would be expected to be smaller for levels than for changes. In other words, base errors (ϵ_{t-1}) and level errors (u_t) might be expected to be uncorrelated and, if so, $\sigma^2(u_\Delta) = \sigma^2(u) + \sigma^2(\epsilon)$.

However, it is clear from (21) that the presence of data errors in the forecast would create a positive correlation between u_t and ϵ_{t-1}, and as a result,

$$(23) \qquad \sigma^2(u_\Delta) \gtreqless \sigma^2(u) \quad \text{as} \quad r_{u_t\epsilon_{t-1}} \lesseqgtr \frac{1}{2}\frac{\sigma(\epsilon)}{\sigma(u)}.$$

This can be expressed differently: Since

$$(24) \qquad \sigma^2(u_\Delta) = \sigma^2(u) + \sigma^2(\epsilon_{t-1}) - 2\mathrm{Cov}(u_t,\epsilon_{t-1})$$

$$= \sigma^2(u) + (1 - 2\gamma_1 - 2\sum_{i=2} \gamma_i\rho_{\epsilon_{t-i},\,\epsilon_{t-1}})\sigma^2(\epsilon),$$

provided Cov $(u_t',\epsilon_{t-i}) = 0$ and $\sigma^2(\epsilon_{t-i}) = \sigma^2(\epsilon)$ for all i, then even if there were no serial correlation in ϵ (i.e., $\rho_{\epsilon_{t-i},\epsilon_{t-1}} = 0$), as long as γ_1, the weight that the forecast assigns to the forecast base (A_{t-1}°, the last known value of the series), exceeds $\frac{1}{2}$, data errors would be a smaller component of predicted change than of predicted level errors and $\sigma^2(u_\Delta)$ would be smaller than $\sigma^2(u)$.

Table 2-4 shows error statistics for forecasts of annual change in GNP and its major components similar to those given in Table 2-3 for level forecasts. A comparison shows that data errors were indeed a smaller component of predicted change errors than of level errors (column 7 and 12 in Table 2-4 compared with columns 7 and 12 in Table 2-3).

Comparison of columns 8 through 11 in Table 2-4 with the corresponding columns in Table 2-3 shows a striking difference between the characteristics of change and level forecast errors. Though both show systematic, or potentially reducible, error, it takes a different form: Change forecasts show much less bias than level forecasts, but they tend to be inefficient (in the sense that the predicted changes are correlated with their errors) whereas level forecasts do not. It might be

TABLE 2-4. Estimates of the Effect of Data Errors on the Accuracy of Forecasts of Annual Changes in Gross National Product and Its Major Components, 1953–63

| Line | Code of Forecast [a] and Period Covered | Forecast Error (billion dollars) | | | Regression Estimates of Pure Forecast Error [b] (billion dollars) | | | | Tests of Bias and Efficiency [c] | | | | |
| | | | | | | | | | t-test for | | | | Adjusted |
		$\bar{u}$ (1)	S_u (2)	$\sqrt{M}$ (3)	$\bar{u}'$ (4)	$S_{u'}$ (5)	$\sqrt{M'}$ (6)	$\sqrt{RM'}$ (7)	$E(u)=0$ (8)	$E(u')=0$ (9)	r_{pu} (10)	$r_{pu'}$ (11)	$R^2_{u \cdot e_{t-1}, \ldots, e_{t-k}}$ (12)
						Gross National Product							
1	Set A, 1954–63	−7.8	11.7	13.6	−23.0	8.8	24.5	.555	2.11 *	2.80 *	.730 *	.736 *	.441
2	Set B, 1953–63	−4.2	8.8	9.8	−7.3	6.5	9.7	1.010	1.76	1.42	.436	.246	.452 *
3	Set C, 1958–63	−2.7	10.1	9.6	14.5	9.5	16.9	.568	0.66	0.52	.722 *	.628 *	.115
4	Set D, 1956–63	−6.2	8.1	9.7	3.5	6.5	7.0	1.386	2.16 *	0.19	.487	.446	.357
5	Set E, 1953–63	−11.4	10.2	15.0	−13.8	7.7	15.6	.962	3.71 *	2.28 *	.483	.262	.435
6	Set F, 1953–63	−5.2	8.4	9.5	−6.6	7.6	9.8	.969	2.05 *	1.00	.726 *	.782 *	.185
7	Set G, 1953–63	0.1	8.9	9.0	−8.2	7.4	10.8	.833	0.04	1.30	.684 *	.602 *	.237
8	Set H, 1954–63	−8.9	10.1	13.1	−24.6	6.1	25.3	.518	2.79 *	4.59 *	.672 *	.607 *	.642 *
						Personal Consumption Expenditures							
9	Set B, 1953–63	−2.4	4.9	5.3	2.1	4.7	4.9	1.082	1.62	0.62	.548 *	.585 *	.102
10	Set F, 1953–63	−3.6	4.7	5.8	4.1	4.5	5.9	.983	2.54 *	0.50	.850 *	.858 *	.101
						Gross Private Domestic Investment							
11	Set B, 1953–63	−2.2	6.6	6.6	−8.2	3.6	8.9	.742	1.11	3.65 *	.405	.371	.707 *
12	Set F, 1953–63	−1.4	5.1	5.1	−10.8	3.6	11.3	.451	0.91	2.70 *	.358	.556	.513 *
						Gov't. Expend. on Goods and Services							
13	Set B, 1953–63	0.7	3.1	3.1	1.4	3.2	3.3	.939	0.75	1.13	.274	−.377	−.036
14	Set F, 1953–63	0.3	2.2	2.1	1.3	2.6	2.8	.750	0.45	1.27	−.322	−.356	−.062
						Net Exports							
15	Set B, 1953–63	−0.2	1.7	1.6	−0.7	2.2	2.3	.696	0.39	0.54	−.532 *	−.624 *	.013
16	Set F, 1953–63	−0.4	1.6	1.6	−1.4	1.7	2.1	.762	0.83	0.70	−.236	−.268	.081

Note: * denotes significance at the 10 per cent level. See notes to Table 2-3.

supposed that data errors are the primary source of the correlations between P and u, but the correlations remain when data errors are held constant (columns 10 and 11 of Table 2-4).

As Mincer and Zarnowitz showed in the preceding chapter, however, the criteria for efficient change forecasts are more stringent than those for levels. Consider the regression

$$(25) \qquad A_t - A_{t-1} = \alpha_\Delta + \beta_\Delta(P_t - A_{t-1}^\circ) + v_t'.$$

A change forecast is efficient if $\beta_\Delta = 1$. The coefficient is, by definition,

$$(26) \qquad \beta_\Delta = \frac{\text{Cov } (A_t - A_{t-1}, P_t - A_{t-1}^\circ)}{\sigma^2(P_t - A_{t-1}^\circ)}.$$

Using the identity $(A_t - A_{t-1}) \equiv (P_t - A_{t-1}^\circ) - u_{\Delta t}$, $\beta_\Delta = 1$ only if Cov $(P_t - A_{t-1}^\circ, u_{\Delta t}) = 0$. Since

$$(27) \quad 1 - \beta_\Delta = \frac{\text{Cov } (P_t - A_{t-1}^\circ, u_{\Delta t})}{\sigma^2(P_t - A_{t-1}^\circ)} =$$

$$\frac{(1 - \Sigma\gamma_i\rho_{\epsilon_{t-i}, \epsilon_{t-1}})\sigma^2(\epsilon) + \text{Cov } (u_t', P_t') - \text{Cov } (u_t', A_{t-1})}{\sigma^2(P_t - A_{t-1}^\circ)},$$

a change forecast would be efficient if there were no data errors and if both $r_{u_t'P_t'}$ and $r_{u_t'A_{t-1}}$ are zero. The last requirement means that the forecast should utilize the extrapolative potential of the series. Otherwise, the forecast error could be reduced by taking account of the last known value of the series. The estimate of this value that would be available for the forecast is the preliminary estimate A_{t-1}°. Thus, in some respects the forecaster is in a box: Full use of A_{t-1}° would transfer its error to the forecast, but failure to do so would also result in an inefficient forecast.

The data in Table 2-4 suggest that forecasting efficiency was impaired much less by data errors than by failure to use the forecasting potential of the series. Eight of the forecasts of change are inefficient before as well as after the effect of data errors is taken into account (column 10 compared with column 11). Since six of these forecasts were not considered inefficient level forecasts (i.e., $r_{P'u'}$ did not differ significantly from zero in Table 2-3, column 10), we could conclude that the change forecasts were inefficient because they did not make effective use of A_{t-1}° (i.e., $r_{u_t'A_{t-1}} \neq 0$).

Failure of forecasts to use A_{t-1}° effectively could cause the variance of predicted changes to exceed that of actual changes. Efficient use of A_{t-1}° requires the forecast to take account of the serial correlation in A, such that $r_{P_t'A_{t-1}} = r_{A_tA_{t-1}}$. The variance of the predicted change is $\sigma^2(P_t - A_{t-1}^{\circ}) = \sigma^2(P_t' - A_{t-1}) + (\Sigma\gamma_i^2 + 1 - 2\Sigma\gamma_i\rho_{\epsilon_{t-i}, \epsilon_{t-1}})\sigma^2(\epsilon)$. Since $\sigma^2(P_t' - A_{t-1}) = \sigma^2(P_t') + \sigma^2(A_{t-1}) - 2r_{P_t'A_{t-1}}\sigma(P_t')\sigma(A_{t-1})$,

$$(28) \quad \sigma^2(P_t - A_{t-1}^{\circ}) = \sigma^2(P_t') + \sigma^2(A_{t-1}) - 2r_{P_t'A_{t-1}}\sigma(P_t')\sigma(A_{t-1})$$
$$+ (\Sigma\gamma_i^2 + 1 - 2\Sigma\gamma_i\rho_{\epsilon_{t-i}, \epsilon_{t-1}})\sigma^2(\epsilon).$$

The variance of the actual change is

$$(29) \quad \sigma^2(A_t - A_{t-1}) = \sigma^2(A_t) + \sigma^2(A_{t-1}) - 2r_{A_tA_{t-1}}\sigma(A_t)\sigma(A_{t-1}).$$

Thus $\sigma^2(P_t - A_{t-1}^{\circ})$ could exceed $\sigma^2(A_t - A_{t-1})$ because of data errors, because $\sigma^2(P')$ exceeds $\sigma^2(A)$, or because the forecast did not make sufficient use of the serial correlation in A (i.e., $r_{P_t'A_{t-1}} < r_{A_tA_{t-1}}$).

Table 2-5 compares the variance of level and change forecasts, both adjusted and unadjusted for data errors, with the variance of actual levels and changes. Regressions of forecast errors on past data errors were used to obtain estimates of the variance of forecasts net of data errors. That is, $\sigma^2(P')$ was estimated as

$$S_{P'}^2 = S_P^2 - R_{u \cdot \epsilon_{t-1}, \dots, \epsilon_{t-k}}^2 S_u^2,$$

where S_P^2 is the variance of the forecast (level or change); S_u^2, the variance of its error (level or change, respectively); and $R_{u \cdot \epsilon_{t-1}, \dots, \epsilon_{t-k}}^2$, the coefficient of determination in the regression of u on ϵ_{t-i}.

The variance of GNP, consumption, and investment forecasts exceeds that of the actual values, especially for the changes. Data errors were only in part responsible. Although they increased the variance of predicted levels by about 1 per cent and that of predicted changes by 5 to 25 per cent, the variance of the adjusted predictions in most cases exceeds that of actuals. Comparison of the two correlation coefficients [13] shows that $r_{P_t'A_{t-1}}$ is generally less than $r_{A_tA_{t-1}}$. Thus failure to exploit the extrapolative potential of the series is the main reason why the change forecasts are inefficient and why the variance of forecasts exceeds the variance of realizations.

[13] The partial correlation coefficient, $r_{P_t'A_{t-1}^{\circ} \cdot \epsilon_{t-1}, \dots, \epsilon_{t-k}}$, which holds the effect of data errors constant, was used to estimate $r_{P_t'A_{t-1}}$.

TABLE 2-5. Estimates of the Effect of Data Errors on the Variability of Forecasts of Annual Levels and Changes in Gross National Product and Its Major Components, 1953–63 (*dollars in billions*)

Line	Code of Forecast and Period Covered	Level Forecasts			Change Forecasts			$r_{P'_t A_{t-1}}$	$r_{A_t A_{t-1}}$
		S_P	$S_{P'}$	S_A	S_P	$S_{P'}$	S_A		
		(1)	(2)	(3)	(4)	(5)	(6)	(7)	(8)
	Gross National Product								
1	Set A, 1954–63	78.1	77.4	73.3	18.7	17.0	12.9	.976	.986
2	Set B, 1953–63	77.0	76.4	77.1	13.2	11.9	12.3	.986	.988
3	Set C, 1958–63	53.4	53.2	52.6	18.3	17.9	13.0	.926	.973
4	Set D, 1956–63	62.4	62.0	60.9	13.7	12.8	11.1	.980	.985
5	Set E, 1953–63	79.3	78.5	77.1	13.4	11.0	12.3	.989	.989
6	Set F, 1953–63	79.5	79.3	77.1	17.0	16.6	12.3	.979	.989
7	Set G, 1953–63	82.3	82.2	77.1	16.6	15.8	12.3	.989	.989
8	Set H, 1954–63	77.2	76.8	73.3	17.4	15.4	12.9	.979	.986
	Personal Consumption Expenditures								
9	Set B, 1953–63	48.9	48.7	49.5	5.4	5.1	4.9	.997	.996
10	Set F, 1953–63	52.1	42.0	49.5	8.3	8.1	4.9	.990	.996
	Gross Private Domestic Investment								
11	Set B, 1953–63	12.5	11.2	11.1	7.1	4.4	7.4	.804	.764
12	Set F, 1953–63	12.0	11.4	11.1	7.6	6.6	7.4	.748	.764
	Gov't. Expend. on Goods and Services								
13	Set B, 1953–63	16.4	16.4	16.7	4.0	4.0	4.8	.983	.963
14	Set F, 1953–63	16.1	16.1	16.7	3.6	3.6	4.8	.981	.963
	Net Exports								
15	Set B, 1953–63	2.0	2.0	2.1	0.7	0.7	2.2	.932	.465
16	Set F, 1953–63	1.4	1.4	2.1	1.1	1.1	2.2	.816	.465

Note: See notes to Table 2-3.

Data errors then were not the only source of systematic error in the business forecasts examined here: Though they could be considered the primary source of bias in three of the sixteen forecast sets, in no case were they the only source of the "slope component" of forecast errors. Data errors mainly impaired forecasting accuracy by augmenting the random component of the variance of the forecast error.

ALTERNATIVE ESTIMATES

Since the method of least squares necessarily yields an estimate of the maximum amount of the variation in u that is statistically related to data errors, and hence a minimum estimate of $\sigma^2(u')$, the regression estimates may overstate the effect of data errors on forecasting efficiency. This would be the case if u' were correlated with ϵ_{t-i}. A comparison of the regression estimates with alternative estimates of u' is therefore worthwhile.

An obvious alternative and one that is commonly used is the observed forecast error $u°$. It was argued earlier (Section I) that if ϵ is serially correlated, the error in realizations data (ϵ_t) would tend to offset the data errors $(\Sigma \gamma_i \epsilon_{t-i})$ transmitted to the forecast through its extrapolative component. Indeed, if $\Sigma \gamma_i = 1$, $E(u°) = E(u')$. The extent to which ϵ_t would offset the loss in forecast efficiency depends on the strength of the serial correlation in ϵ. If the correlation were perfect (and positive), $\sigma^2(u°) = \sigma^2(u')$, since

$$(30) \quad \sigma^2(u°) = \sigma^2(u'_t + \Sigma \gamma_i \epsilon_{t-i} - \epsilon_t)$$

$$= \sigma^2(u'_t) + \sigma^2(\Sigma \gamma_i \epsilon_{t-i}) + \sigma^2(\epsilon_t) - 2 \text{ Cov } (\Sigma \gamma_i \epsilon_{t-i}, \epsilon_t)$$

$$+ 2 \text{ Cov } (u'_t, \Sigma \gamma_i \epsilon_{t-i}) - 2 \text{ Cov } (u'_t, \epsilon_t).$$

In general, $\Sigma \gamma_i \neq 1$ and $u°$ is not a very satisfactory estimate of u'. For example, if the bias in $A°$ were in the same (opposite) direction as the bias in P', $E(u°)$ would understate (overstate) $E(u')$ for those forecasts in which $\Sigma \gamma_i < 1$. Moreover, ϵ is not perfectly serially correlated and $\sigma^2(u°)$ would generally exceed $\sigma^2(u')$. Indeed, $\sigma^2(u°)$ would exceed $\sigma^2(u)$ for those forecasts which do not rely on extrapolations at all $(\gamma_i = 0)$. Since $\sigma^2(u°)$ could overestimate, and the regression estimates could underestimate, the two would bracket $\sigma^2(u')$. The alternative estimates based on $u°$ are given in Table 2-6.

As expected, $S_{u°}$ exceeds the regression estimate of $S_{u'}$ for all of

TABLE 2-6. Alternative Estimates of the Effect of Data Errors on the Accuracy of Forecasts of Annual Levels of Gross National Product and Its Major Components, 1953–63 (*dollars in billions*)

Line	Code of Forecast and Period Covered	Alternative Estimates of Pure Forecast Error				
		$\bar{u}^{\circ}$ (1)	$S_{u^{\circ}}$ (2)	$\sqrt{M^{\circ}}$ (3)	$\sqrt{RM^{\circ}}$ (4)	t-test for $E(u^{\circ}) = 0$ (5)
	Gross National Product					
1	Set A, 1954–63	−7.1	13.5	12.5	1.768	1.68
2	Set B, 1953–63	−2.8	10.8	10.7	1.636	0.87
3	Set C, 1958–63	−3.2	11.6	11.0	1.609	0.67
4	Set D, 1956–63	−6.9	9.7	11.4	1.816	2.01 *
5	Set E, 1953–63	−10.8	13.4	16.7	1.515	2.68 *
6	Set F, 1953–63	−4.8	7.8	8.8	2.045	2.07 *
7	Set G, 1953–63	1.8	8.1	7.9	1.392	0.73
8	Set H, 1954–63	−7.8	9.7	12.0	1.842	2.52 *
	Personal Consumption Expenditures					
9	Set B, 1953–63	−1.3	5.6	5.7	1.667	0.76
10	Set F, 1953–63	−3.0	4.8	5.5	1.855	2.06 *
	Gross Private Domestic Investment					
11	Set B, 1953–63	−2.7	6.9	7.1	1.323	1.32
12	Set F, 1953–63	−1.3	4.4	4.4	1.659	1.00
	Gov't. Expend. on Goods and Services					
13	Set B, 1953–63	1.3	2.1	2.3	1.652	2.01 *
14	Set F, 1953–63	0.2	1.6	1.6	1.688	0.43
	Net Exports					
15	Set B, 1953–63	−0.1	1.8	1.7	1.706	0.22
16	Set F, 1953–63	−0.7	1.5	1.6	1.812	1.53

Note: * denotes significance at the 10 per cent level. See Table 2-3, note a, for source.

the forecasts of GNP, consumption, and investment expenditures (compare column 2, Table 2-6, with column 5, Table 2-3). The opposite relation, however, holds for forecasts of government expenditures and net exports and it is probably due to the fact that the errors in both the preliminary data and the forecasts primarily reflect definitional revisions (see footnote 10 above).[14] In most cases in which the regressions indicated no significant relation between past data errors and forecast errors, S_{u° exceeds S_u.

The estimates based on u° suggest that P' is biased downward. However, u° may underestimate the size of the bias in P' and therefore overestimate the importance of data errors as a source of bias in P. The hypothesis that P is unbiased would be rejected at the 10 per cent level for fifteen of the sixteen forecasts shown in Table 2-3 (column 8). This hypothesis for P' would be rejected for only six of the forecasts in Table 2-6 (column 5). Thus, when u° is used to estimate u', data errors would be considered the only source of bias in nine of the forecasts examined. The regression estimates, however, indicated that data errors were solely responsible for the bias in only three sets.

When there is a significant relation between forecast errors and past data errors, the regression estimates attribute a somewhat larger fraction of forecast error to data errors than that suggested by the alternatives based on u° (column 7, Table 2-3 compared with column 4, Table 2-6). These differences, however, are relatively small. The greatest differences occur for the nine forecasts that the regression estimates indicate were unaffected by data error. The alternative estimates suggest that data errors reduced the accuracy of these forecasts by an average of 70 per cent! This huge overestimation occurs because bias is a very large component of the over-all forecast error (M) and u° overstates the bias arising from data errors.[15] Thus, even though

---

[14] More explicitly, the definitional revisions would create a positive correlation between u_t and ϵ_t and therefore reduce the variance of u°. Since the regressions for these variables indicated γ_i not different from zero, $u_t = u'_t$ and

$$\sigma^2(u^\circ) = \sigma^2(u) + \sigma^2(\epsilon) - 2 \text{ Cov } (u, \epsilon).$$

[15] This is readily shown. The regressions for these nine forecasts did not show a relation between forecast errors (u_t) and past data errors (ϵ_{t-i}) strong enough to reject the null hypothesis $\gamma_i = 0$. Thus equation (16) would become

(16') $u_t^\circ = P_t - A_t^\circ = u_t - \epsilon_t = u'_t - \epsilon_t,$

and it follows that $E(u) = E(u')$, but $E(u^\circ) = E(u') - E(\epsilon)$.

the regression estimates may overstate the effect of data errors, they are preferable to the alternatives. The regression estimates permit a test for the presence of data errors; the alternative estimates indiscriminately adjust for data errors, whether they were incorporated into the forecast or not.

IV. EFFECT OF DATA ERRORS ON THE ACCURACY OF AN ANALYTICAL MODEL OF CONSUMPTION

The use of preliminary rather than final data affects not only the values of the variables underlying a forecast, it affects the estimates of the parameters of relationships among these variables as well. Thus far the indirect effects on forecasting accuracy of errors in the data used to estimate the parameters of the forecast model have not been considered. There are no indirect effects on naive models — their parameters are not estimated but set arbitrarily — and they could not be determined for business forecasts because the forecasting models are not explicitly specified. The backbone of many GNP models, however, is a consumption function of one kind or another, and one is therefore used in this section to illustrate the total effect (indirect as well as direct) on predictive accuracy of errors in the underlying data.

EFFECT ON PARAMETER ESTIMATES

The consumption function chosen is one of the quarterly models first estimated by Zellner [8] and reestimated with revised data by Griliches *et al.* [3]. This function is

$$(31) \qquad C_t = \alpha + \beta Y_t + \gamma C_{t-1} + v_t,$$

where C denotes personal consumption expenditures; Y, personal disposable income; and v, the residual.

The preliminary consumption (C°) and income (Y°) estimates are written

$$(32) \qquad C^\circ = C + \epsilon(C) \quad \text{and} \quad Y^\circ = Y + \epsilon(Y),$$

where $\epsilon(C)$ and $\epsilon(Y)$ are errors in measuring C and Y, respectively. If preliminary data are used, equation (31) becomes

(31') $$C_t^\circ = \alpha + \beta Y_t^\circ + \gamma C_{t-1}^\circ + v_t^\circ,$$

where $$v_t^\circ = v_t + \epsilon(C)_t - \beta\epsilon(Y)_t - \gamma\epsilon(C)_{t-1}.$$

It is well known that the method of least squares applied to (31') would yield biased estimates of the coefficients. The magnitude and direction of the bias would depend on the correlation between the explanatory variables $(r_{Y_t C_{t-1}})$ and on the relative magnitude of the data errors $(\lambda_C = \sigma^2[\epsilon(C)]/\sigma^2(C)$ and $\lambda_Y = \sigma^2[\epsilon(Y)]/\sigma^2(Y))$ as well as their intercorrelations.[16]

The following tabulation, where C and Y denote 1965 data, shows the relevant statistics for the sample periods used by Zellner and by Griliches et al.:

		Error Statistics				
Data Used	Period Covered [a]	λ_C	λ_Y	$r_{\epsilon(C)t,\,t-1}$	$r_{\epsilon(C)t\epsilon(Y)t}$	$r_{\epsilon(Y)t\epsilon(C)t-1}$
Zellner						
Available in July 1955	1947-I–55-I	.024	.006	.960	.365	.342
Griliches et al.						
Available in Aug. 1961	1947-I–55-I	.013	.004	.890	.013	−.048
	1947-I–60-IV	.003	.002	.832	−.129	−.202

		Correlations Among Dependent and Independent Variables		
		$r_{C_t Y_t}$	$r_{C_t C_{t-1}}$	$r_{Y_t C_{t-1}}$
1965 Revised Data				
Available in Aug. 1965	1947-I–55-I	.984	.994 [b]	.983 [b]
			.989 [c]	.981 [c]
	1947-I–60-IV	.996	.998 [b]	.995 [b]
			.997 [c]	.995 [c]

[a] Excluding 1950–III and 1951–I. [b] Based on Zellner method of excluding observations (see text below).
[c] Based on Griliches et al. method of excluding observations.

Though there is strong, positive serial correlation in the consumption data errors, the relative magnitude of these errors, as well as that of the income errors, is small. Thus, in the absence of intercorrelation (i.e., $r_{Y_t C_{t-1}} = 0$), the data errors would have only negligible effects on the estimated coefficients. However, $r_{Y_t C_{t-1}}$ is close to unity, indicating

[16] For a detailed treatment of the effects of errors in the variables, see Johnston [4, Chapter 6].

strong multicollinearity. As a consequence, the effects of the errors would be substantially magnified. The strong, positive serial correlation in $\epsilon(C)$ would tend to bias c, the estimated coefficient of lagged consumption, upward. Because of the multicollinearity, serial correlation in $\epsilon(C)$ would also affect b, the estimated coefficient of current income, and tend to bias it downward.

On the whole these expectations are borne out in Table 2-7, which compares the coefficients obtained by Zellner with those obtained from revised data. The coefficients based on preliminary data tend to underestimate β and overestimate γ.

Zellner found that b was not significantly different from zero (line 1, column 2). Griliches *et al.* reestimated the coefficients from revised data. Their estimates differed substantially from Zellner's and reversed the conclusion for b (line 5, column 2). But as they point out [3, p. 494, note 6]:

There is one minor difference between Zellner's and our way of computing the same equation. When Zellner leaves out an observation, e.g., 1951-I, in the next period the value of lagged consumption is taken to be that of two periods ago, whereas when we delete an "observation," we do not change the independent variables, and in 1951-II, C_{t-1} equals the actual C of 1951-I, even though this value itself does not appear in the series for the dependent variable. Whichever procedure is right depends on one's interpretation of why 1951-I is "out of line" and should be excluded in the first place.

As Table 2-7 shows, this small difference has a large effect on the coefficients. The Zellner method results in much lower estimates of the coefficient of Y_t and much higher estimates of the coefficient of C_{t-1} than those obtained using the method of [3]. Hence a simple comparison of the original Zellner coefficients (line 1) with the Griliches *et al.* coefficients (line 5) grossly overstates the effect of data errors. Indeed, if Griliches *et al.* had used the same method as Zellner, they too would have found the coefficient of current income lacking statistical significance (line 2, column 2), and if Zellner had used the Griliches *et al.* method, he would have found a statistically significant b (line 4, column 2). Estimates based on the 1965 data yield similar results (lines 3 and 6, column 2).

None of the coefficients estimated from data covering the longer period lacks statistical significance (lines 7–10). Moreover, it is worth noting that sets of considerably different coefficients are associated

TABLE 2-7 Coefficients of Zellner's Quarterly Consumption Function: Original Compared With Those Computed From Revised Data

			Coefficients of			
Line	Method of Excluding Observations [a]	Constant Term (1)	Y_t (2)	C_{t-1} (3)	R^2 (4)	LR MPC [b] (5)
	Period Covered: 1947-I–1955-I, Excluding 1950-III and 1951-I					
	Zellner Method					
1	Zellner (July 1955 data)	0.1	.128 (.093)	.870 (.127)	.978	.98
2	Griliches *et al.* (August 1961 data)	0.6	.071 (.099)	.928 (.129)	.984	.99
3	1965 revised data	0.3	.168 (.093)	.827 (.106)	.989	.97
	Griliches *et al.* Method					
4	Zellner data	13.1	.296 (.115)	.618 (.158)	.959	.77
5	Griliches *et al.* data	15.4	.335 (.130)	.574 (.169)	.971	.79
6	1965 revised data	3.1	.318 (.111)	.650 (.126)	.982	.91
	Period Covered: 1947-I–1960-IV, Excluding 1950-III and 1951-I					
	Zellner Method					
7	Griliches *et al.* data	2.7	.185 (.068)	.796 (.078)	.996	.91
8	1965 revised data	0.4	.258 (.069)	.728 (.073)	.997	.95
	Griliches *et al.* Method					
9	Griliches *et al.* data	3.1	.300 (.085)	.670 (.097)	.994	.91
10	1965 revised data	−0.4	.330 (.081)	.652 (.086)	.996	.95

[a] The Zellner data are in 1947–49 dollars, the Griliches *et al.* data are in 1954 dollars, and the 1965 revised data are in 1958 dollars.

[b] *LR MPC* is the long-run marginal propensity to consume, computed by dividing the coefficient of current income by 1 minus the coefficient of lagged consumption.

with the same long-run marginal propensity to consume (line 7 compared with line 9 and line 8 compared with line 10).

To sum up, errors in the underlying data bias estimates of the coefficients of the consumption function in (31): The coefficient of current income was biased downward by about 25 per cent and the coefficient of lagged consumption was biased upward by about 7 per cent when the Zellner method of excluding observations is used. The biases are much smaller when the Griliches *et al.* method is used. The effect of data errors on the coefficients, however, was much weaker than the effect of a small difference in the method of excluding observations.

EFFECT ON PREDICTIVE ACCURACY

Strictly considered, the consumption function in (31) is not a forecasting model because it requires knowledge of the value of personal disposable income during the prediction period $t + 1$. It could be used as one if a prediction of income $\hat{Y}_{t+1}$ were somehow obtained. Since we are interested in the effect of errors in the preliminary data, an obvious choice is a simple extrapolation of these data,

(33)
$$\hat{Y}^\circ_{t+1} = d_0 + d_1 Y^\circ_t + d_2 Y^\circ_{t-1} + \cdots = d_0 + \Sigma d_i Y_{t-i+1} + \Sigma d_i \epsilon(Y)_{t-i+1}.$$

The forecast, made in period t, of consumption in period $t + 1$ $(\hat{C}^\circ_{t+1})$ would then be

(34)
$$\hat{C}^\circ_{t+1} = a + b\hat{Y}^\circ_{t+1} + cC^\circ_t,$$

where a, b, and c are the coefficients estimated from preliminary data.

If (31) were correctly specified, and if the true values of the variables are denoted C and Y, the value of consumption in period $t + 1$ is

(35)
$$C_{t+1} = \alpha + \beta Y_{t+1} + \gamma C_t + v_{t+1}.$$

The error of the forecast is then defined

(36)
$$\hat{C}^\circ_{t+1} - C_{t+1} = (a - \alpha) + (b - \beta)Y_{t+1} + (c - \gamma)C_t + b(\hat{Y}^\circ_{t+1} - Y_{t+1})$$
$$+ c(C^\circ_t - C_t) - v_{t+1}.$$

In addition to the error (v) arising because the forecast model (31) is a stochastic rather than an exact relation, (36) shows that error in $\hat{C}^\circ_{t+1}$

could also arise from: (1) biased parameter estimates, (2) error in extrapolating income, and (3) error in the preliminary consumption data.

If Y were a linear autoregressive series, Y_{t+1} would be

$$(37) \qquad\qquad Y_{t+1} = \delta_0 + \Sigma \delta_i Y_{t-i+1} + w_t,$$

and the error of the income extrapolation would be

$$(38)$$
$$\hat{Y}^\circ_{t+1} - Y_{t+1} = (d_0 - \delta_0) + \Sigma(d_i - \delta_i)Y_{t-i+1} + \Sigma d_i \epsilon(Y)_{t-i+1} - w_{t+1}.$$

Thus the error in extrapolating income would be partly induced by errors in the preliminary income data. These errors would affect the forecast directly as well as indirectly through their effects on the estimated parameters of the extrapolation model.

Now if C and Y and their respective errors, $\epsilon(Y)$ and $\epsilon(C)$, were stationary series, their means would be independent of t. Then

$$(39) \quad a - \alpha = \overline{\epsilon(C)} - (b - \beta)\bar{Y} - (c - \gamma)\bar{C} - b\overline{\epsilon(Y)} - c\overline{\epsilon(C)},$$

and

$$(40) \qquad\qquad d_0 - \delta_0 = \overline{\epsilon(Y)} - \Sigma(d_i - \delta_i)\bar{Y} - \Sigma d_i \overline{\epsilon(Y)},$$

where the bar denotes mean value. Using (38), (39), and (40) to rewrite (36), the forecast error would become

$$(41)$$
$$\hat{C}^\circ_{t+1} - C_{t+1} = \overline{\epsilon(C)} + b\overline{\epsilon(Y)} + (b - \beta)(Y_{t+1} - \bar{Y}) + (c - \gamma)(C_t - \bar{C})$$
$$+ b\Sigma(d_i - \delta_i)(Y_{t-i+1} - \bar{Y}) + c[\epsilon(C)_t - \overline{\epsilon(C)}]$$
$$+ b\Sigma d_i[\epsilon(Y)_{t-i+1} - \overline{\epsilon(Y)}] - v_{t+1} - bw_{t+1}.$$

Though errors in the independent variables would bias the parameter estimates [i.e.. $E(b - \beta)$, $E(c - \gamma)$, and $E(d_i - \delta_i)$ would not equal zero], it is well known that biased parameter estimates would not bias the forecast if C, Y, and their errors were stationary series. Under stationarity assumptions,

$$E(Y_{t-i+1} - \bar{Y}), \ E(C_t - \bar{C}), \ E[\epsilon(C)_t - \overline{\epsilon(C)}], \ \text{and} \ E[\epsilon(Y)_{t-i+1} - \overline{\epsilon(Y)}]$$

would all be zero, and hence the bias in b, c, and d_i would create no bias in $\hat{C}^\circ_{t+1}$. This is not to say that $\hat{C}^\circ_{t+1}$ would be unbiased, however. The expected value of the forecast error would be

(42) $$E(\hat{C}^{\circ}_{t+1} - C_{t+1}) = \overline{\epsilon(C)} + b\overline{\epsilon(Y)},$$

assuming $E(v)$ and $E(w)$ are zero. Thus the forecast would be unbiased only if the preliminary data were unbiased. Since these data have a negative bias, we would expect that consumption forecasts would also have a negative bias, and Table 2-8 shows that they do.

Table 2-8 illustrates the direct as well as indirect effects of using preliminary rather than revised data on the accuracy of consumption forecasts. The table shows error statistics for forecasts constructed in three ways: (1) by inserting variables based on preliminary data ($\hat{Y}^{\circ}_{t+1}$ and C°_t) into the equation estimated from preliminary data; (2) by inserting variables based on 1965 revised data ($\hat{Y}^{65}_{t+1}$ and C^{65}_t) into the preliminary equation; and (3) by inserting the revised data variables into the equation estimated from revised data. The effect of errors in the variables used to construct the forecast (the direct effect) is shown by comparing the errors in forecasts of type (1) with those in forecasts of type (2). The effect of data errors on the parameter estimates (the indirect effect) is shown by comparing the errors in type (2) forecasts with those in type (3) forecasts. The total effect of data errors is seen by comparing the errors in type (1) with those in type (3) forecasts.

The use of preliminary rather than revised data resulted in a *doubling* of the forecast error (line 1 compared with line 3, 4 with 6, and 7 and 9 with 11). Though the direct effect is clearly more important and accounts for most of the increase in error, the indirect effect is by no means negligible.[17]

V. SUMMARY

According to our analysis, the use of preliminary rather than revised GNP data impaired forecasting accuracy and by a substantial amount: The accuracy of naive model projections of GNP and its components

---

[17] Denton and Kuiper [2] found somewhat similar results for the Canadian data: The direct effects were much larger than the indirect effects of errors in the preliminary data. This is not to say that the parameter estimates were unaffected. Indeed, they found that the choice of data had a stronger effect on the estimates of the parameters of their small econometric model than that resulting from the choice of estimating procedures (direct least squares or two-stage least squares).

TABLE 2-8. Effect of Data Errors on the Predictive Accuracy of Zellner's Quarterly Consumption Function, 1961-I–1964-IV [a]

| | Prediction Equation: $\hat{C}_{t+1} = a + b\hat{Y}_{t+1} + cC_t$ | | Prediction Errors (billion 1958 dollars) | | |
| | | Variables Based on Preliminary or | $\bar{E}$ | S_E | $\bar{M}$ |
Line	Coefficients	Revised Data	(1)	(2)	(3)
	1947-I–1960-IV				
	Zellner Method				
	Preliminary Data Coefficients				
1	$a = 2.7, b = .185, c = .796$	Preliminary	−7.2	3.8	8.1
2		Revised	−4.0	2.4	4.6
	1965 Revised Data Coefficients				
3	$a = 0.4, b = .258, c = .728$	Revised	−3.0	2.3	3.7
	Griliches et al. Method				
	Preliminary Data Coefficients				
4	$a = 3.1, b = .300, c = .670$	Preliminary	−7.3	3.8	8.2
5		Revised	−5.0	2.4	5.5
	1965 Revised Data Coefficients				
6	$a = -0.4, b = .330, c = .652$	Revised	−3.6	2.3	4.2
	1947-I–1955-I				
	Zellner Method				
	Zellner Coefficients				
7	$a = 0.1, b = .128, c = .870$	Preliminary	−5.5	3.7	6.6
8		Revised	−4.0	2.4	3.0
	Griliches *et al.* Coefficients				
9	$a = 0.6, b = .071, c = .928$	Preliminary	−6.3	3.8	7.3
10		Revised	−2.3	2.4	3.3
	1965 Revised Data Coefficients				
11	$a = 0.3, b = .168, c = .827$	Revised	−1.7	2.4	2.9

[a] The sample period excludes 1950-III and 1951-I. The coefficients are from Table 2-7. The predictions in lines 1, 4, 7, and 9 are based on C_t^o, $\hat{Y}_{t+1}^o$; the remainder are based on C_t^{65}, $\hat{Y}_t^{65}$, and the actual value is C_{t+1}^{65}; where C_{t+1}^{65} and C_t^{65} denote 1965 statistically revised estimates, C_t^o denotes preliminary estimates, and $\hat{Y}_{t+1}^o$ and $\hat{Y}_{t+1}^{65}$ denote extrapolations based on preliminary and on 1965 statistically revised estimates, respectively.

The coefficients used to obtain $\hat{Y}_{t+1}^o$ were estimated from the data used by Griliches. Those used to obtain $\hat{Y}_{t+1}^{65}$, were estimated from the 1965 revised data. In both cases the regression was of the form

$$Y_t = d_0 + d_1 Y_{t-1} + \cdots + d_6 Y_{t-6} + v_t$$

and the sample period was 1948-II–1960-IV. Extrapolations, $\hat{Y}_t = d_0 + d_1 Y_t + \cdots + d_6 Y_{t-5}$, were then generated for the 1961-I–1964-IV period, $\hat{Y}_{t+1}^o$ used preliminary data in the equation estimated from the Griliches data and $\hat{Y}_{t-1}^{65}$ used 1965 data in the equation estimated from revised data.

was reduced by about 30 per cent, while that of business forecasts was reduced by nearly 40 per cent.

Data errors were not the major source of systematic error in the business forecasts examined here. Though they could be considered the primary source of the bias in three of the sixteen forecast sets, in no instance did they materially contribute to the slope component of inefficiency. This does not mean that forecast efficiency was unaffected. Indeed, the reduction in efficiency was considerable. It is estimated that data errors accounted for 50 to 70 per cent of the variance of the error in seven of the sixteen forecasts.

Data errors affect not only the variables underlying a forecast (the direct effect); they affect the estimates of the parameters of the relationships among these variables as well (the indirect effect). A well-known quarterly consumption function was used to illustrate the indirect as well as direct effects of data errors. Consumption forecasts were generated from preliminary and from 1965 revised data. The use of preliminary rather than revised data led to a *doubling* of the forecast errors. The direct effect accounted for 70 per cent of the increase; the remaining 30 per cent was due to the indirect effect of data errors on the parameter estimates.

These results suggest that there is considerable scope for improving forecasting accuracy by improving the accuracy of preliminary data.

REFERENCES

[1] De Janosi, Peter E., "A Note on Provisional Estimates of the Gross National Product and Its Major Components," *Journal of Business,* October 1962.

[2] Denton, Frank T. and Kuiper, John, "The Effect of Measurement Errors on Parameter Estimates and Forecasts: A Case Study Based on the Canadian Preliminary National Accounts," *Review of Economics and Statistics,* May 1965.

[3] Griliches, Zvi, Maddala, G. S., Lucas, R., and Wallace, N., "Notes on Estimated Aggregate Quarterly Consumption Functions," *Econometrica,* July 1962.

[4] Johnston, J., *Econometric Methods,* New York, 1963.

[5] Suits, Daniel, "Forecasting and Analysis with an Econometric Model," *American Economic Review,* March 1962.

[6] Zarnowitz, Victor, *An Appraisal of Short-Term Economic Forecasts,* Occasional Paper 104, NBER, New York, 1967.
[7] Zellner, Arnold, "A Statistical Analysis of Provisional Estimates of Gross National Product and Its Components, of Selected National Income Components, and of Personal Savings," *American Statistical Association Journal,* March 1958.
[8] ———, "The Short-Run Consumption Function," *Econometrica,* October 1957.

THREE

Models of
Adaptive Forecasting

JACOB MINCER

I. INTRODUCTION

Economic behavior is frequently a response to an anticipated future rather than to the past or present. Consequently, anticipated rather than actual values must be assigned to some of the variables in empirical economic models. Unfortunately, data on anticipatory magnitudes are scarce. Even when such data are obtainable, as in some surveys, they pose questions of reliability going beyond matters of sampling or measurement error. Reliable anticipatory values are those on which economic agents are, indeed, acting. *Ex ante* reports of such values are necessarily imperfect.

In the absence of reliable data or, more commonly, of any anticipations data, the economic analyst is forced to ascribe certain methods of formation of expectations to the subjects of his analysis. The issue cannot be ignored: The use of current rather than anticipated values is equivalent to a hypothesis that expectations are largely based on current magnitudes and do not differ from them in any systematic way.

A more sophisticated approach is to employ realized future values as proxies for anticipations of them. Such proxies are most appropriate when it is believed that economic agents forecast successfully, so that differences between anticipations and realizations are small.[1]

The usefulness of the implicit approach is obviously limited. Hence, the search for explicit models of expectations is a growing preoccupation of econometricians. In principle, the best model is one that most closely approximates the effective anticipatory values in economic behavior. However, to be useful the model must be relatively simple conceptually and statistically tractable.

In practice, most of the expectational models used in econometric analyses are extrapolations of current and past values of the time series, the future value of which is anticipated. In most cases the extrapolation function is linear: The forecast value of the variable Y is obtained by a weighted sum of past values of the series. Denoting forecast value by an asterisk, the date at which the forecast is formed (date of forecast base) by the right-hand subscript, and the date to which the forecast applies (date of forecast target) by the left-hand subscript, the extrapolated value for the next future period is:[2]

$$(1) \qquad\qquad {}_{t+1}Y_t^* = \sum_{j=0}^{\infty} \beta_j Y_{t-j}$$

The purpose of this paper is to inquire into the applicability and properties of several classes of forecasting models within the general class of linear extrapolations (1). The analysis suggests considerations

---

[1] This approach, known as the "implicit expectations" model was suggested by Mills [1]. If implicit forecast errors are not very small, the approach leads to unbiased estimation of parameters only when forecast errors are uncorrelated with realizations. It is worth noting, however, that the zero correlation assumption suggests *inefficient* forecasting:

If P = forecast, A = realization, and u = forecast error, zero correlation between u and A implies a nonzero correlation between u and P. Assuming $P = A + u$ is unbiased, a regression of A on P yields $A = \alpha + \beta P + v$, with $\beta < 1$. A corrected forecast $P' = \alpha + \beta P$ is clearly more efficient than P, as $\sigma^2(v) < \sigma^2(u)$. Proof: The coefficient of determination between A and P equals $1 - \dfrac{\sigma^2(u)}{\sigma^2(P)} = 1 - \dfrac{\sigma^2(v)}{\sigma^2(A)}$, and $\sigma^2(A) < \sigma^2(P)$.

[2] Functions of form (1) arise also in nonforecasting contexts. Thus, an observed value Z_t may constitute a response to the current and past values of the variable Y_{t-j}. While such distributed lag functions are clearly distinguishable in concept from extrapolation functions dealt with here, econometric practice has seldom differentiated among them. For a comprehensive survey of conceptual and practical issues in the application of both functions in econometric analyses, see Griliches [2].

which, to some extent, may guide the specification of such models. These considerations may help in determining when and where simplicity should be traded for greater realism. On the positive side, the analysis permits discrimination among several models of expectational behavior, when actual, albeit imperfect, forecasting data are available. Empirical illustrations are shown in the conclusion of the paper.

II. EXPONENTIAL COEFFICIENTS AND LINEAR EXTRAPOLATION

The specification of expectational models (1) is a specification of the coefficients β_j. The usual though not necessary restrictions are for the β_j to be nonnegative, less than unitary, and — particularly in the forecasting context — declining into the past. If Y is a trendless series, and (1) contains no intercept, the coefficients must sum to unity [3] to produce an unbiased forecast Y^*.

A widely used extrapolation function of form (1), which obeys the restrictions listed above, is the "geometrically declining weights," or exponential forecasting function:

$$(1a) \qquad {}_{t+1}Y_t^* = \beta \sum_{j=0}^{\infty} (1 - \beta)^j Y_{t-j}.$$

Several reasons account for the popularity of forecasting formula (1a):

1. Only one coefficient β need be supplied or estimated.

2. The formula is theoretically appealing because it can be derived from a simple and rather plausible model of expectations adapting to unforeseen developments:

$$(2) \qquad {}_{t+1}Y_t^* - {}_tY_{t-1}^* = \beta(Y_t - {}_tY_{t-1}^*).$$

According to (2) expectations are formed by error learning; they are revised in consequence of (and in proportion to) currently experienced surprises. By successive substitution for the lagged term in (2), and

---

[3] If the series is trending with a rate of growth g, the coefficients must sum to $(1 + g)$.

by a reduction procedure on (1), due to Koyck [3], the two formulations can be shown to be equivalent.

3. More recently, strong support for exponential forecasting (1a) has been adduced from the statistical theory of optimal prediction.[4] It has been shown that such forecasts are optimal linear predictions, in the sense of minimizing the mean square error of forecast, for certain types of nonstationary time series.[5]

The knowledge that exponential extrapolation (1a) expresses a type of adaptive, error-learning behavior, and that it is an optimal forecasting scheme under certain conditions, lends a degree of confidence to this specification, which is often sound. It is not, of course, a claim on generality. As yet, the limitations on the appropriateness of exponential forecasting have not been fully explored.

One way to proceed is to consider the appropriateness of alternative formulations. A start can be made by inquiring into the applicability and interpretation of forecasting behavior (1) when the β_j coefficients *do not decline exponentially*. Can it still serve as an optimal predictor? Under what conditions?

The simplest class of time series for which the answer is readily available has been discussed by Muth [4].

Let the time series Y_t, which is being forecast, originate as a linear function of independent random shocks:

$$(3) \qquad Y_t = \epsilon_t + \sum_{i=1}^{\infty} w_i \epsilon_{t-i},$$

with zero mean and common variance for all ϵ. Exponential forecasting (1a) is optimal for such time series, if and only if all w_i are the same and equal β. And, whether the w_i are equal or not, (3) is a sufficient condition[6] for the optimal forecasting function to be linear in the past values of the series Y_t, as is (1). Here:

$$(4) \qquad {}_tY_{t-1}^* = \sum_{j=1}^{\infty} \beta_j Y_{t-j}.$$

[4] In particular, see the works of Muth [4], Nerlove and Wage [5], and Whittle [6].

[5] A series is stationary if its auto-covariance matrix is independent of calendar time.

[6] The linear extrapolation (1) is optimal for a wider class of processes than (3), as was indicated in note 4 for the exponential case.

The condition of optimality is that the β_j of (4) and the w_i of (3) are related by [7]:

$$(5) \qquad w_i = \sum_{j=1}^{i} \beta_j w_{i-j}, \quad \text{with} \quad w_0 = 1.$$

III. THE GENERAL LINEAR ADAPTATION HYPOTHESIS

As assumption (3) illustrates, linear extrapolation (1) can be an optimal predictor without having exponentially declining weights. But does it, in that case, cease to represent adaptive, error-learning behavior? The answer is no. Indeed, all linear forecasts (1) which are optimal under (3) imply adaptive behavior as optimal forecasting for any number of spans. However, the revision function (2) describes adaptive behavior only in the exponential case. In the general case it is replaced by a set of revision functions, closely resembling (2), but not identical with it.

Consider optimal predictions for (3) for more than one period ahead. Start with forecasts made at $(t - 2)$ for target date (t): The smallest error such a forecast can have is $(\epsilon_t + w_1\epsilon_{t-1})$, as is apparent from assumption (3), because ϵ_t and ϵ_{t-1} are not known yet at time $(t - 2)$. Generally, the minimal forecast error for a k-span forecast is:

$$(6) \qquad Y_t - {}_tY^*_{t-k} = \epsilon_t + \sum_{i=1}^{k} w_i\epsilon_{t-i}.$$

Now, we can show that a forecast at $(t - k)$ for k spans ahead will achieve this minimal error by substitution for the as yet unknown values in the extrapolation function (4) by their optimal forecast values:

---

[7] Substitute (3) into (4) to obtain:

$$(4a) \qquad {}_tY^*_{t-1} = \sum_{i=1}^{\infty} M_i\epsilon_{t-i}, \quad \text{where} \quad M_i = \sum_{j=1}^{i} \beta_j w_{i-j}, \ (w_o = 1).$$

Since ϵ_t is not known at $(t - 1)$ when the forecast is made, the optimal forecast ${}_tY^*_{t-1} = Y_t - \epsilon_t = \sum_{i=1}^{\infty} w_i\epsilon_{t-i}$. Hence $M_i \equiv w_i$.

(7)
$$_tY^*_{t-k} = \beta_1(_{t-1}Y^*_{t-k}) + \beta_2(_{t-2}Y^*_{t-k}) + \cdots + \beta_{k-1}(_{t-k+1}Y^*_{t-k}) + \beta_k Y_{t-k}$$
$$+ \beta_{k+1}Y_{t-k-1} + \cdots .$$

A succession of substitutions, such as

$$_{t-k+1}Y^*_{t-k} = Y_{t-k+1} - \epsilon_{t-k+1}; \quad _{t-k+2}Y^*_{t-k} = Y_{t-k+2} - (\epsilon_{t-k+2} + \beta_1\epsilon_{t-k+1});$$

and so on, leads to the conclusion that optimality condition (6) is fulfilled.[8]

Compare now optimal forecasts made at different dates in the past for the same future target:

(7a) $$_{t+1}Y^*_t = \beta_1 Y_t + \beta_2 Y_{t-1} + \cdots ,$$

and

(7b) $$_{t+1}Y^*_{t-1} = \beta_1(_tY^*_{t-1}) + \beta_2 Y_{t-1} + \cdots .$$

Subtracting (7b) from (7a) we obtain:

(8) $$_{t+1}Y^*_t - _{t+1}Y^*_{t-1} = \beta_1(Y_t - _tY^*_{t-1}).$$

Equation (8), which we shall call a one-span revision function, can be viewed as a description of adaptive expectational behavior. It is, indeed, very similar to adaptive equation (2). But note the generality of (8): *It is implied by any optimal linear extrapolation* (4) under model (3), while (2) is implied only by the exponential extrapolation. Note also the difference: The forecast target in (2) shifts forward just as the forecast base does. In (8) the forecast target is fixed, and the forecast is revised only because the forecast base has moved forward.

In the exponential case, both (2) and (8) must hold, with $\beta_1 = \beta$. It follows that $_{t+1}Y^*_{t-1} = _tY^*_{t-1}$. More generally, exponential forecasting implies that the same expectations are held for any span in the future.[9]

Since, in the general case, adaptive hypotheses (2) and (8) are distinct, they can be applied to distinguish empirically between exponential and nonexponential expectational behavior.[10]

---

[8] In the two-span case: $_tY^*_{t-2} = \beta_1(_{t-1}Y^*_{t-2}) + \beta_2 Y_{t-2} + \beta_3 Y_{t-3} + \cdots .$ Since $_{t-1}Y^*_{t-2} = Y_{t-1} - \epsilon_{t-1}$, and $_tY^*_{t-1} = Y_t - \epsilon_t$, it follows that $_tY^*_{t-2} = _tY^*_{t-1} - \beta_1\epsilon_{t-1} = Y_t - (\epsilon_t + \beta_1\epsilon_{t-1})$. Condition (6) is fulfilled, as $\beta_1 = w_1$ by (5). Generalization to k spans is straightforward.

[9] This result is well known. For example, see Muth [4].

[10] See Section V, below.

Revision functions for k-span forecasts can be derived by the same procedure as that which produced (8). Subtracting

$$_{t+k}Y_{t-1}^* = \beta_1(_{t+k-1}Y_{t-1}^*) + \beta_2(_{t+k-2}Y_{t-1}^*) + \cdots + \beta_k(Y_{t-1}^*) + \cdots$$

from

$$_{t+k}Y_t^* = \beta_1(_{t+k-1}Y_t^*) + \beta_2(_{t+k-2}Y_t^*) + \cdots + \beta_k Y_t + \cdots$$

yields

$$(9) \quad _{t+k}Y_t^* - _{t+k}Y_{t-1}^* = \beta_1(_{t+k-1}Y_t^* - _{t+k-1}Y_{t-1}^*) + \beta_2(_{t+k-2}Y_t^* - _{t+k-2}Y_{t-1}^*)$$
$$+ \cdots + \beta_k(Y_t - _tY_{t-1}^*).$$

Since (9) is recursive, repeated substitutions produce:

$$(10) \qquad\qquad _{t+k}Y_t^* - _{t+k}Y_{t-1}^* = \gamma_k(Y_t - _tY_{t-1}^*).$$

The revision coefficient γ_k is a function of the weights $\beta_1, \beta_2, \ldots, \beta_k$ in the linear autoregressive forecasting function (4). In particular, we have seen in (8) that for $k = 1$, $\gamma_1 = \beta_1$. In general, the expression for the kth span revision coefficient is: [11]

$$(11) \qquad\qquad \gamma_k = \sum_{j=1}^{k} \beta_j \gamma_{k-j}, \quad (\gamma_0 = 1).$$

Now compare (11) with (5). Since $\gamma_1 = \beta_1 = w_1$, it follows that:

$$(12) \qquad\qquad \gamma_i \equiv w_i, \quad \text{for all } i = k.$$

We have reached the following conclusions:

1. The general autoregressive extrapolation (4) is consistent with an error-learning model of type (10) which uses different revision coefficients for different spans in the future.

2. Given observed revision coefficients γ_i, we can reconstruct the autoregressive extrapolation which generates the adaptive behavior by means of identities (5).

3. In the exponential case there is only one adaptation function, since all revision coefficients are the same. Forecasts and revisions for all future spans are the same. Adaptation function (2) is equivalent to (8).

4. If the time series can be described by the linear process (3) and the extrapolation is optimal for it, the revision coefficients γ_i in equa-

---

[11] This result is obtained by straightforward, though laborious, substitutions in (9).

tions (10) must be equal to the coefficients w_i in (3). Thus, there are as many distinct adaptive equations (10) as there are distinct parameters w_i in the linear process (3).

If extrapolations are available for more than one span, it is possible to test whether the extrapolations are optimal by comparing the mean square errors of the forecasts for each of the available spans with the revision functions corresponding to these spans.

The mean square error of an optimal forecast of Y_t in (3) for k periods ahead is:

(13)
$$M_k = \sigma^2(\epsilon_t + w_1\epsilon_{t-1} + \cdots + w_{k-1}\epsilon_{t-k+1})$$
$$= (1 + w_1^2 + w_2^2 + \cdots + w_{k-i}^2) \cdot \sigma^2(\epsilon),$$

where

$$\sigma^2(\epsilon) = M_1,$$

from which

(14)
$$w_i^2 = \frac{M_{i+1} - M_i}{M_1} = \gamma_i^2.$$

If M_i and γ_i are observable, a test of the right-hand equality in (14) is a test of optimality of the observed forecasts.[12]

IV. NONEXPONENTIAL FORECASTING AND STABILITY OF EXPECTATIONS

The pattern of coefficients γ_i in the adaptive equations (10) describes the pattern of revisions of future forecasts in response to current surprises. Implicit in these patterns are notions about stability of expectations. Thus, γ_i coefficients declining with span imply greater stability of long-term than of short-term expectations. That is, longer-term expectations remain relatively unaffected by unforeseen current developments. Conversely, γ_i coefficients increasing with span imply a greater sensitivity to such developments on the part of long-run

---

[12] Provided the forecasts are extrapolations, and the structure of Y is given by (3). Actual forecasts are seldom mere extrapolations (see the discussion in Section IX of this paper).

rather than short-run expectations. It would seem, perhaps, that in the trendless case, or in the case where expectations concerning trends do not change, the pattern of relatively greater stability of long-term expectations is more plausible.[13] However, the issue need not be decided a priori. Observed revision equations (10) can, in principle, provide insights into actual behavior.

The variation of γ_i with span i need not be monotonic. The implications about comparative stability of short- versus long-term expectations does, however, suggest a special interest in the monotonic cases over the relevant time span. Let us call *convex* forecasting behavior that which manifests itself in declining with span revision coefficients γ_i, and *concave* (or "explosive") that which shows the opposite pattern of coefficients in the revision equations (10).

Suppose we require an expectational model in which long-term expectations are comparatively more stable. This requirement rules out concave and exponential forecasting, that is, all linear extrapolation functions (4) which yield revision equations with fixed or increasing revision coefficients. What pattern must be imposed on the coefficients β_j of the extrapolation (4) to yield convex forecasts? Since the β_j coefficients must decline geometrically in order to yield fixed revision coefficients γ_i, must they, in some sense, decline more than exponentially, in order to generate declining γ_i? The answer is yes, if we adhere to the restrictions on β_j: that they must be positive, less than unitary, and strictly declining.

Convexity can be produced without these restrictions. That is to say, declining revision coefficients γ_i can be achieved with linear extrapolation functions (4) in which some of the β_j can be negative, exceed unity, and oscillate with j. Since the restrictions are often encountered in empirical work, and the pattern of β_j is easier to identify under such restrictions, we shall employ them for illustrative purposes.

It will be useful first to compare the coefficients β_j of single-span forecasting functions (4) with the corresponding coefficients of k-span forecasting functions (7), when the latter is reduced (by successive substitutions) to a function of past observed values only. Call the coefficients $\beta_j^{(k)}$ (in particular $\beta_j^{(1)} = \beta_j$), and consider $k = 2$. Then, by (7):

---

[13] The opposite pattern is certainly plausible when current developments lead to changed beliefs about future trends.

$$_{t+2}Y_t^* = \beta_1(_{t+1}Y_t^*) + \beta_2 Y_t + \beta_3 Y_{t-1} + \cdots$$

which reduces to:

(15) $\quad _{t+2}Y_t^* = (\beta_1^2 + \beta_2)Y_t + (\beta_1\beta_2 + \beta_3)Y_{t-1} + (\beta_1\beta_3 + \beta_4)Y_{t-2} + \cdots.$

Here, then:

(15a) $\qquad \beta_1^{(2)} = \beta_1^2 + \beta_2, \quad$ and $\quad \beta_j^{(2)} = \beta_1\beta_j + \beta_{j+1}.$

Similarly, for $k = 3$:

$$\beta_1^{(3)} = \beta_1\beta_1^{(2)} + \beta_2^{(2)} = \beta_1^3 + 2\beta_1\beta_2 + \beta_3,$$

and

$$\beta_j^{(3)} = \beta_1\beta_j^{(2)} + \beta_2\beta_j + \beta_{j+2}.$$

And, more generally, for $k = i$:

(16) $\qquad \beta_j^{(i)} = \beta_1\beta_j^{(i-1)} + \beta_2\beta_j^{(i-2)} + \cdots + \beta_{i-1}\beta_j + \beta_{i+j-1}.$

Inspection reveals that, for $j = 1$, expression (16) is exactly the same as (5) and (11).

Hence:

(17) $\qquad\qquad\qquad\qquad \beta_1^{(i)} \equiv \gamma_i \equiv w_i.$

In words: *The coefficient attached to the forecast base value in the ith span forecasting function is equal to the ith span revision coefficient.* Note that this result follows without any restriction on β_j. Note also: [14]

(18) $\qquad \sum\limits_{j=1}^{\infty} \beta_j = 1 \quad$ implies $\quad \sum\limits_{j=1}^{\infty} \beta_j^{(i)} = 1, \quad$ for all $k = i$.

Expressing the i-span forecast by:

(19) $\qquad _{t+i}Y_t^* = \beta_1^{(i)}Y_t + \beta_2^{(i)}Y_{t-1} + \beta_3^{(i)}Y_{t-2} + \cdots,$

we conclude that, since $\beta_1^{(i)} = \gamma_i = w_i$ and $\sum\limits_{j} \beta_j^{(i)} = 1$, declining revision coefficients γ_i imply that the further we forecast into the future the lesser the absolute and the relative weight attached to the most re-

---

[14] For $i = 2$: $\sum\limits_{j} \beta_j^{(2)} = \beta_1 \sum\limits_{j} \beta_j + \sum\limits_{j} \beta_{j+1} = \beta_1 + (1 - \beta_1) = 1.$ The proof for any i follows by mathematical induction.

cent observations $\beta_1^{(i)}$ and the greater the weights attached to the more distant observations.

The opposite is true when γ_i (and w_i) increase with i. It is easily seen that in the exponential case the weights $\beta_j^{(i)}$ are the same for all spans.

This is another way of explaining why, in this case, forecast values for all future spans are identical.

To repeat: When the γ_i (and w_i) decline, the $\beta_j^{(i+1)}$ coefficients for the $(i + 1)$-span forecasting function are at first smaller but eventually larger than the corresponding $\beta_j^{(i)}$ coefficients for the i-span forecasting function. If we assume strictly declining β_j with j this property formally means that:

$$(20) \qquad \frac{\beta_j^{(i+1)}}{\beta_j^{(i)}} < \frac{\beta_{j+1}^{(i+1)}}{\beta_{j+1}^{(i)}} \quad \text{for all } j.$$

Using (15a) to substitute in the numerator we get, for $i = 1$:

$$\frac{\beta_1\beta_j + \beta_{j+1}}{\beta_j^{(i)}} < \frac{\beta_1\beta_{j+1} + \beta_{j+2}}{\beta_{j+1}^{(i)}}.$$

Hence:

$$(21) \qquad \frac{\beta_{j+1}}{\beta_j} < \frac{\beta_{j+2}}{\beta_{j+1}}.$$

The meaning of (21) is that the forecasting functions, $_{t+1}Y_t^*$, have coefficients β_j whose rate of decline diminishes as j increases. When the inequality sign in (21) is reversed, the $\gamma_i^{(i)}$ increase; when (21) is an equality, the γ_i coefficients are constant.

The latter case is, of course, *exponential:* The rate of decline of β_j with j is fixed. The extrapolation function is *convex* when the rate of decline of β_j diminishes with j, and *concave* in the opposite case.

Note that inequality (21) is a sufficient condition of convexity. It is not required by the latter, except under the restriction of strictly declining β_j in the extrapolation function.[15]

Finally, inequality (21) suggests another way of describing the implications for stability of expectations in each of the three classes:

---

[15] The terms convexity and concavity are derived from the time shape of log β_j, as illustrated in Figure 3-1. But they apply to all forecasts which generate declining (or increasing) revision coefficients.

When the forecast is formed at relatively high values of the time series Y_t, convex forecasting implies that $_{t+i+1}Y_t^* < {_{t+i}Y_t^*}$. The opposite is true when the forecast base value Y_t is relatively low. More generally, convex forecasting implies that forecast values for successive spans trace out a monotonic path (upward or downward) from the base toward positions of "normalcy." No such "return to normalcy" is implied by exponential or concave forecasts. Movements away from normalcy are implied in the latter, and a horizontal path in the former. This relation between the patterns of β_j and of multispan predictions is shown in Figure 3-1.

The relation shown in this figure is illustrated for extrapolation functions with strictly declining coefficients β_j. But it is more general: Return to normalcy is a tendency in all convex forecasts. And the movement away from normalcy is a phenomenon in all concave forecasting.

Return to normalcy is best defined, in terms of our discussion, as a tendency to observe a negative correlation between current levels of Y_t and the direction of the predicted future flow, e.g., $(_{t+k}Y_t^* - {_{t+1}Y_t^*})$:

$$(22) \qquad _{t+k}Y_t^* - {_{t+1}Y_t^*} = b(Y_t - \tilde{Y}) + v_t = c + bY_t + v_t,$$

where v_t is a residual and $\tilde{Y}$ is a "normal" level of Y, which changes slowly. It is here impounded in the constant c.

Since $_{t+k}Y_t^* = \sum_{j=1}^{\infty} \beta_j^{(k)} Y_{t-j}$, (22) becomes

$$(23) \qquad _{t+k}Y_t^* - {_{t+1}Y_t^*} = (\beta_1^{(k)} - \beta_1)Y_t + v_t.$$

Recall that $\beta_1^{(k)} = \gamma_k$, by (17). Hence

$$(24) \qquad _{t+k}Y_t^* - {_{t+1}Y_t^*} = (\gamma_k - \gamma_1)Y_t + v_t,$$

where

$$v_t = \sum_{j=2}^{\infty} (\beta_j^{(k)} - \beta_j)Y_{t-j}.$$

Clearly, $b = (\gamma_k - \gamma_1)$ is negative in convex forecasts, positive in concave forecasts, and zero in exponential forecasts.[16]

---

[16] The sign of the correlation in (24) depends also on the sign, size, and correlation of the remainder term v_t with the independent variable Y_t. If the autocorrelation in Y is weak, the remainder term will have little effect. If the autocorrelation is substantial and positive, as it is more commonly, the relation can be expected to hold more dependably for low than for high values of k.

FIGURE 3-1. Exponential, Convex, and Concave Expectations Hypothetical
Weight Patterns and Forecasts

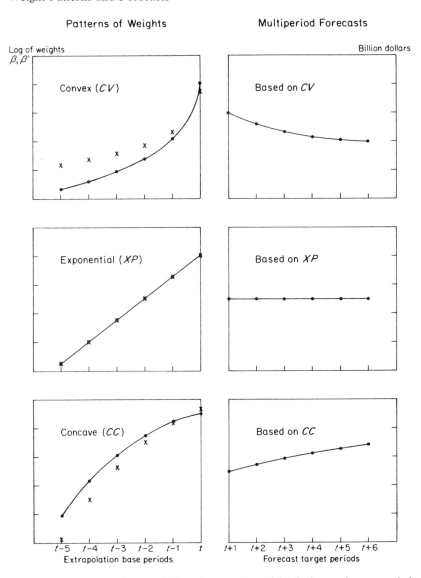

Patterns of Weights   Multiperiod Forecasts

Log of weights   Billion dollars
β, β^1

Convex (*CV*)   Based on *CV*

Exponential (*XP*)   Based on *XP*

Concave (*CC*)   Based on *CC*

$t-5$ $t-4$ $t-3$ $t-2$ $t-1$ t $t+1$ $t+2$ $t+3$ $t+4$ $t+5$ $t+6$
Extrapolation base periods   Forecast target periods

Note: In the left panel, the solid line shows β, the weights in forecasting one period
ahead; the crosses show β^1, the weights in forecasting two spans ahead.

The return to normalcy as an aspect of stability of expectations should be distinguished from the usual characterization of expectational stability by a less than unitary "elasticity coefficient of expectations" [β in adaptation function (2)]. Actually, so long as all β_j in (4) are less than 1 (a generalization of less than unitary elasticity), the forecast value for any span will be intermediate between high or low values of Y_t and normal levels. In this sense, all moving average extrapolations imply a return to normalcy. Convexity, however, adds a dynamic aspect to these stability characteristics: The path of expected movement persists in the direction of normal levels.[17]

A phenomenon closely related to the return to normalcy is known in the literature as regressivity in forecasting. This has been defined as a negative correlation between predicted change and past change in the time series.[18] If regressivity is basically a notion that future values of a series are expected to move in the direction of its mean, then a negative correlation in (22) is a better statement of this tendency.[19] If so, we may conclude that regressivity is an implication of convex forecasting.

V. STATIONARITY, OPTIMALITY,
AND AGGREGATION

The time series Y_t arising from the linear process (3) is stationary, if $\sigma^2(Y) = \sigma^2(\epsilon) \sum_{i=1}^{\infty} w_i^2$ is finite. In that case, the w_i must converge to zero. Hence, the revision coefficients derived from an optimal ex-

---

[17] The need to introduce a return to normalcy feature into a basically exponential expectational model led Allais [7] to the addition of a separate term to the exponential extrapolation. Such a "splicing" is unnecessary in convex extrapolations.

[18] For references, see Bossons and Modigliani [8]. Bossons and Modigliani define regressivity specifically as a negative correlation between $(_tY_{t-1}^* - Y_{t-1})$ and $(Y_{t-1} - Y_{t-k})$.

[19] Equation (22) avoids the overlapping term Y_{t-1} in the Bossons-Modigliani definition. This can produce the appearance of regressivity even when forecasting $(_tY_{t-1}^*)$ is random. Equation (22) also generalizes predicted change to more than one span, and substitutes "deviation from normal" for "past change."

In proposing optimal predictions of future interest rates, Harberger [9] does, indeed, formulate regressivity by (22). His optimal forecasts are clearly convex: Compare his figure 1 [9, p. 137] with our Figure 3-1.

trapolation must eventually decline, even if they rise or fluctuate at first. Thus, optimal forecasts of stationary time series are, at least eventually, convex. However, convex forecasts may be optimal for structure (3) even when the latter is not stationary. This happens when the w_i coefficients decline, but do not converge.

It can be shown that convex forecasts are optimal for certain stationary time series whose stochastic process is somewhat more complex than (3):

Consider the following time series:

$$(25) \qquad Y_t = X_t + U_t,$$

$$X_t = \sum_{i=1}^{n} \alpha_i X_{t-i} + \epsilon_t,$$

$$U_t = \sum_{h=1}^{m} \delta_h U_{t-h} + \eta_t.$$

ϵ_t and η_t are neither autocorrelated nor intercorrelated; Y_t and X_t are stationary.

For this latent structure of time series, a class of forecasts which attains a minimal mean square error is a weighted sum of several exponentially weighted averages of past values of Y_t:[20]

$$(26) \qquad {}_{t+1}Y_t^* = \sum_{j=0}^{\infty} \sum_{i=1}^{n} C_i \lambda_i (1 - \lambda_i)^j Y_{t-j}.$$

In terms of the general linear autoregression (4), the coefficients attached to past values Y_{t-j} are:

$$(27) \qquad \beta_j = \sum_{i=1}^{n} C_i \lambda_i (1 - \lambda_i)^j.$$

The interesting thing about function (26) is that, provided the λ_i are distinct, positive, and less than unity, *it is necessarily convex.*

Recall the condition of convexity, when $0 < \beta_j < 1$:

$$(21) \qquad \beta_j^2 < \beta_{j-1} \cdot \beta_{j+1}.$$

Applied to (27), the following inequality must hold as a condition of convexity:

[20] See Bailey [10] for derivation.

$$(28) \quad \left[\sum_i C_i \lambda_i (1 - \lambda_i)^j \right]^2 < \left[\sum_i C_i \lambda_i (1 - \lambda_i)^{j-1} \right] \left[\sum_i C_i \lambda_i (1 - \lambda_i)^{j+1} \right].$$

Define

$$a_i = [C_i \lambda_i (1 - \lambda_i)^{j-1}]^{1/2},$$

$$b_i = [C_i \lambda_i (1 - \lambda_i)^{j+1}]^{1/2}.$$

By the Schwartz inequality:

$$\left(\sum_i a_i b_i \right)^2 < \sum_i a_i^2 \sum_i b_i^2.$$

Since, in our case, $b_i = (1 - \lambda_i)a_i$, it is easily seen that the equality sign holds only when $(1 - \lambda_i)$ is the same for all i (or when $n = 1$). Otherwise the convexity of the forecasting function (26) must hold.[21]

Function (26) may arise as an aggregation phenomenon rather than as an optimal extrapolation for an assumed type of time series. If individuals $(i = 1, \ldots n)$ forecast exponentially, the aggregated (market?) forecast will appear to be convex, in terms of the β_j coefficients, if not all λ_i are identical;[22] similarly if a forecast of an aggregate, say GNP, was obtained by aggregating sectoral forecasts, each of which was exponential with different parameter λ_j.

Note, however, that even if the aggregated function (26) appears to have convex coefficients β_j, it does not imply declining revision coefficients γ_i: If each individual, or sector forecast is exponential, individual multispan forecasts are identical for each span. Therefore, the aggregated (weighted averages) multispan forecasts also remain fixed regardless of span, and the (aggregated) revision coefficients remain fixed. Thus, when reported on aggregates, the revision equations (10) provide better insight into the true nature of forecasting behavior than the extrapolation function itself.[23]

---

[21] Intuitively, the conclusion that a linear combination of exponentials is necessarily convex is perhaps best visualized as follows: Since exponentials are linear in logs, only geometric averages of exponentials are exponential. Arithmetic averages exceed geometric averages, hence (21) is nonlinear in logs. It is convex, because the arithmetic average is biased toward the higher and more steeply declining $\log \lambda_i (1 - \lambda_i)^j$ for small values of j, and again toward the higher and flatter $\log \lambda_i (l - \lambda_i)^j$ for larger values of j.

[22] See Bierwag and Grove [11].

[23] If individual forecasting is exponential, the revision coefficient is a weighted average of the λ_i. The degree of convexity in the aggregated extrapolation function clearly depends on the variance of λ_i across individuals. Taken together, the extrapolation and revision functions provide information on the distribution of λ_i among individuals.

VI. FORECASTING STOCK OR FLOW VARIABLES

The discussion in the preceding sections suggests that, despite the widespread use and asserted success of the exponential forecasting formula, convexity may often be a better description of extrapolative expectations.

Successful exponential forecasting need not be inconsistent with this conclusion. First, the degree of convexity may not be sufficiently strong to affect the forecasting errors very much. More important, the relevant variables which need to be forecast for purposes of management decisions are often discounted flows of predicted future values rather than single-span predictions. The redeeming feature of the exponential forecast is that even when it is unsatisfactory as a forecast of a single future value, its error as a forecast of a discounted multispan flow is likely to be much smaller:

Denote the single span prediction of the flow at i by $_{t+i}P_t^*$, and the prediction of the stock (converted into the same dimension as a flow in perpetuity) by P_t^*. Then, *exponential* forecasting of $_{t+i}P_t^*$ means that $P_t^* = {}_{t+1}P_t^*$. This is because $_{t+i}P_t^* = {}_{t+1}P_t^*$ for all i.

$$(29) \qquad P_t^* = r\left[\frac{1}{1+r}\,{}_{t+1}P_t^* + \frac{1}{(1+r)^2}\,{}_{t+2}P_t^* + \cdots\right]$$

$$= {}_{t+1}P_t^*\, r \sum_{i=1}^{\infty} \frac{1}{(1+r)^i} = {}_{t+1}P_t^*.$$

When nonexponential forecasting is appropriate but exponential is used, the exponential forecasts of flows $_{t+i}P_t^*$ will be too high for near spans and too low for higher spans, or conversely. Since P_t^* is a weighted average [24] of $_{t+i}P_t^*$, the error of using it as a forecast of P_t will be smaller than the average error of $_{t+i}P_t^*$ as a forecast of P_{t+i}.

In the case of the consumption function, for example, an incorrect exponential formulation of "permanent" income may yield errors in predicting consumption which are only slightly larger than the errors resulting from a correct convex formulation. At the same time, the

---

[24] Weighted by $\dfrac{r}{(1+r)^i}$. The attentuation of error will be greater the lower the discount rate r.

differences in the errors of forecasting the next period's income by the two forecasting functions could be sizeable. Similarly, even a relatively poor exponential forecast of the next period's sales may be a relatively good forecast of the discounted flow of future sales. If the latter decision variable is superior to the former, the incorrectly formulated forecast may be sufficiently useful.

Equation (29) suggests two important properties of exponential forecasts of perpetuities (discounted stocks): First, they are the same as forecasts of single-period flows, and second, the forecast value does not depend on the discount rate. For example, if permanent income (Y_P) is estimated by exponential extrapolation of past incomes, its forecast is the same as the forecast of the next period's income, $Y_P = {}_{t+1}Y_t^*$. More important, the exponential forecast does not depend on the discount rate, and cannot, therefore, be used to estimate the discount rate: The exponentially declining weights with parameter β do not provide any information on the size of the discount rate r.[25]

When the relevant variable to be forecast is a discounted future flow, it is natural to raise the question about possible relations between the discount rate r and the expectational coefficients β_j. A small r denotes "longsightedness" into the future. Similarly, a small β_1 means that a longer past was taken account of in forming expectations. It is tempting to postulate a positive correlation between the two parameters of behavior: Horizons are both longer or shorter symmetrically with respect to the future and to the past. And, as discount rates change, so do expectational coefficients.[26] It is clear, however, that no such connection needs to exist if the extrapolative weights β_j are dictated exclusively by the structure of the time series, while the size of the discount rate does not depend on the experienced variations in the time series.

---

[25] See Friedman's analysis of the consumption function [12] and [13]. In the latter article Friedman proposes a different expectational interpretation of his estimating procedure in [12], precisely for the reasons indicated above.

[26] A hypothesis which has some resemblance to this one was introduced by Allais [7].

VII. EXTRAPOLATION, AUTONOMOUS FORECASTING, AND EMPIRICAL INVESTIGATION OF FORECASTING BEHAVIOR

It is not reasonable to assume that forecasts F_t of a future value of Y_t are based exclusively on extrapolations of that series. We may represent the actual forecast as consisting of two parts:

$$(30) \qquad {}_{t+1}F_t = {}_{t+1}Y_t^* + {}_{t+k}u_t,$$

where ${}_{t+1}Y_t^*$ is the extrapolative component and ${}_{t+k}u_t$ an independent remainder, or autonomous component of the forecast. The autonomous component presumably utilizes information based on relations with other series and other objective or subjective data.[27]

The preceding discussion of forecasting functions refers to the extrapolative component in (30). Before empirical observations can be analyzed, we need to know in what way the presence of autonomous components affects our conclusions. We proceed to an analysis of revision equations in the presence of autonomous components.

Expression (30) refers to a one-span forecast. If forecasts for longer spans are obtained recursively, that is, by substitution of intervening-span forecasts for as yet unknown values of Y_{t+i}, so that:

$$(31) \qquad {}_{t+k}Y_t = \beta_1({}_{t+k-1}F_t) + \beta_2({}_{t+k-2}F_t) + \cdots + \beta_k Y_t$$
$$+ \beta_{k+1}Y_{t-1} + \cdots + {}_{t+k}u_t,$$

then the general term of (30) for k spans is:

$$(32)$$
$$ {}_{t+k}F_t = {}_{t+k}Y_t^* + \sum_{j=0}^{k-1} \gamma_j({}_{t+k-j}u_t) \quad (\gamma_0 = 1, \quad \text{and} \quad \gamma_k = \sum_{j=i}^{k} \beta_j \gamma_{k-j}).$$

Revision functions (10) now become:

$$(33) \qquad {}_{t+k}F_t - {}_{t+k}F_{t-1} = \gamma_k (Y_t - {}_t F_{t-1})$$
$$+ (\Delta_k u + \gamma_1 \Delta_{k-1} u + \cdots + \gamma_{k-1}\Delta_1 u),$$

where $\Delta_k u = {}_{t+k}u_t - {}_{t+k}u_{t-1}$.

[27] See Chapter 1 of this volume, pp. 23 ff.

It is possible to conceive of expectational behavior in which multi-span forecasting is recursive only in the extrapolative component. The autonomous component is then superimposed. In such a case expression (30) generalizes directly for any span k:

(30a) $$_{t+k}F_t = {}_{t+k}Y_t^* + {}_{t+k}v_t.$$

And the revision functions (33) become:

(33a) $$_{t+k}F_t - {}_{t+k}F_{t-1} = \gamma_k(Y_t - {}_tF_{t-1}) + \Delta_k v + \gamma_k\,{}_tv_{t-1},$$

since

$$_tF_{t-1} = {}_tY_{t-1}^* + {}_tv_{t-1}.$$

Even if expectational behavior is not described by (30a), empirical data which we take as representing F may contain some systematic nonforecasting components [28] or, more commonly, measurement errors. Revision equation (33a) would then be interpreted as reflecting extrapolation observed with some error.

If data on forecasts are available for several spans, empirical estimates of revision equations can be used to ascertain important features of expectational behavior:

1. Estimated coefficients γ_k indicate whether expectational behavior is exponential, convex, or concave.

2. The extrapolation function can be reconstructed from the γ_k coefficients.

3. The coefficient of determination in revision equations (33) is less than unity, because of the presence of nonextrapolative components in forecasts. Its size reflects the importance of revisions of autonomous components or of change in nonforecasting components in the observed revisions of F.

It is of interest to note that, under model (31), the residual variance in empirical regressions of the revision functions increases with span, as the right-hand term in (33) cumulates. This is not true in (33a), where the residual variance grows or declines together with the coefficients γ_k, thus *decreasing* in convex forecasting.

Denoting the forecast error $(Y_t - {}_tF_{t-1}) = \epsilon$, and assuming $\Delta_k u$ are uncorrelated over spans and of equal variance, we can derive coefficients of determination for the various spans of the revision functions (33):

---

[28] Such as the liquidity premium in forward interest rates. See Kessel [14].

(34) $\sigma^2(\Delta_k F) = \gamma_k^2 \sigma^2(\epsilon) + (1 + \gamma_1^2 + \gamma_2^2 + \cdots + \gamma_{k-1}^2)\sigma^2(\Delta u).$

Hence, coefficients of determination in empirical revision equations for span k are given by

(35) $$\frac{R_k^2}{1 - R_k^2} = \frac{\gamma_k^2}{1 + \gamma_1^2 + \gamma_2^2 + \cdots + \gamma_{k-1}^2} \cdot \frac{\sigma^2(\epsilon)}{\sigma^2(\Delta u)}.$$

Putting $k = 1$ into (34) makes it possible to replace the unobservable term $\dfrac{\sigma^2(\epsilon)}{\sigma^2(\Delta u)}$ in (35) by the observable $\dfrac{1}{\gamma_1^2 \dfrac{1 - R_1^2}{R_1^2}}$, since

$$\frac{R_1^2}{1 - R_1^2} = \frac{\sigma^2(\epsilon)}{\gamma_1^2 \sigma^2(\Delta u)},$$

which yields:

(36) $$\frac{R_i^2}{1 - R_i^2} = \frac{\gamma_i^2}{1 + \gamma_1^2 + \gamma_2^2 + \cdots + \gamma_{i-1}^2} \cdot \frac{1}{\gamma_1^2} \cdot \frac{R_1^2}{1 - R_1^2}.$$

Clearly, R_k^2 declines as k increases in convex and in exponential forecasts. It may increase, though it need not, in concave forecasts. If the revision functions are interpreted as (33a) rather than (33), the coefficients of determination follow:

(35a) $$\frac{R_k^2}{1 - R_k^2} = \frac{\gamma_k^2 \sigma^2(\epsilon)}{\gamma_k^2 \sigma^2(v) + \sigma^2(\Delta_k v)} = \frac{\sigma^2(\epsilon)}{\sigma^2(v) + \dfrac{1}{\sigma_k^2} \cdot \sigma^2(\Delta v)}.$$

Assuming that $\sigma_k^2(v)$ and $\sigma^2(\Delta_k v)$ do not vary systematically with k, it follows from (35a) that R^2 declines with increasing span in convex forecasts (even though the residual variance declines), increases in concave forecasts, and remains unchanged in exponential forecasting.

Taking models (33) and (33a) together — and they are not mutually exclusive if a nonforecasting component is present in the data on F — it appears that the coefficient of determination in the revision equations is most likely to decline in convex forecasts, remain constant in exponential forecasts, and increase in concave forecasting.

If empirical data on forecasts are available for two spans only, discrimination between exponential and nonexponential forecasting can still be achieved by a comparison of estimated revision functions (8) with (2):

(8) $_{t+1}F_t - _{t+1}F_{t-1} = \beta_1(Y_t - _tF_{t-1})$,

(2) $_{t+1}F_t - _tF_{t-1} = \beta(Y_t - _tF_{t-1})$.

If forecasting is exponential, the two equations should yield the same results. However, estimated β_1 should be greater than β if forecasting is convex, and smaller than β if concave.

To see this, perform a Koyck-type reduction in the general case:

$$_{t+1}F_t = \beta_1 Y_t + \beta_2 Y_{t-1} + \cdots$$

$$(1 - \beta_1)_tF_{t-1} = (1 - \beta_1)(\beta_1 Y_{t-1} + \cdots).$$

Subtracting, we obtain:

(2') $_{t+1}F_t - _tF_{t-1} = \beta_1(Y_t - _tF_{t-1}) + [\beta_2 - (1 - \beta_1)\beta_1]Y_{t-1}$

$$+ [\beta_3 - (1 - \beta_2) \cdot \beta_2]Y_{t-2}.$$

In the exponential case, all terms beyond the first on the right-hand side of (2') vanish, yielding adaptive equation (2). However, in the convex case, lagged terms of Y_t enter with negative coefficients [since $\beta_2 < \beta_1(1 - \beta_1)$], and in the concave case, with positive coefficients.

With positive serial correlation in Y usually present, leaving out the lagged terms [that is, using (2) instead of (2')] will make the estimated β smaller than β_1 in the convex case, larger in the concave case.

If data are available for one span only, equation (2') can, in principle, still serve the purpose: Convexity is suggested by significant lagged terms with negative coefficients, concavity by the same terms with positive coefficients. No lagged terms appear in the exponential case.

THE TERM STRUCTURE OF INTEREST RATES

Revision equations (10) were first introduced into the empirical literature by Meiselman [15] in his study of the term structure of interest rates. While previous research based on adaptive hypothesis (2) was invoked to justify the use of (10), the distinction between the two formulations of adaptive behavior received no attention in that study.[29]

Meiselman tested the hypothesis that the "forward" rate $_{t+k}F_t$ is

---

[29] The expectational aspects of the term structure are intensively explored within the present framework by Stanley Diller in Chapter 4 of this volume. In this section we draw on some of his findings.

a forecast of the future (spot) rate A_{t+k}, by means of empirically fitted revision functions (10), for $k = 1, 2, \ldots$, eight spans. The fact that good fits were obtained is consistent with a hypothesis that forward rates embody linear autoregressive forecasts of future spot rates. They also embody autonomous forecasting components, as well as nonforecasting components such as liquidity premia. The existence of the nonextrapolative component in the forward rate creates correlations that are less than one in Meiselman's revision function. This component is responsible for the weakening of the Meiselman correlations as the span increases. As Diller shows (Table 4-1), the pattern of decline in R^2 is closely predictable on the assumption of recursive multispan forecasting, as in our equation (36).

Meiselman's revision equations show continuously declining estimates of revision coefficients γ_i from .703 in the first span to .208 in the eighth span. This pattern is clearly consistent with convex forecasting.[30]

While the pattern of eight revision coefficients constitutes more comprehensive evidence of convex forecasting, it might be of interest to illustrate the discrimination between hypotheses of exponential and nonexponential forecasting, using only the first revision equation in a

---

[30] It is also interesting to note that the revision coefficients (γ_i) in Meiselman's Table 1 seem to decline almost geometrically. If the coefficients for the more remote spans are disregarded, the pattern can be approximated by a straight line in logs (as noted by Meiselman, p. 21).

(24a) $$\lg \gamma_i = \alpha + i \log \gamma$$

with α close to unity, so that:

(24b) $$\gamma_i = \gamma^i.$$

If such an approximation is imposed, it turns out that the linear autoregressive extrapolation which would give rise to such revision coefficients is of a very simple form:

(24c) $$_{t+1}A_t^* = \beta_1 \cdot A_t.$$

And, in terms of forward rates:

(24d) $$_{t+1}F_t = \beta_1 \cdot A_t + u_t.$$

Proof: Recall (11)

$$\gamma_i = \sum_{j=1}^{i} \beta_j \gamma_{i-j} \quad (\gamma_0 = 1).$$

Substituting (24b) into (11) yields $\beta_1 = \gamma_1$, all other $\beta_j = 0$. In a recent article, Pye [16] shows that Meiselman's revision coefficients could have been produced by a particular first order Markov chain. This is equivalent to result (24c) which is a first order autoregression. See also L. Telser [17].

comparison with adaptive equation (2). The results were:

$$(8) \qquad {}_{t+1}F_t - {}_{t+1}F_{t-1} = .703 \ (A_t - {}_tF_{t-1}), \quad R^2 = .906,$$

$$(2) \qquad {}_{t+1}F_t - {}_tF_{t-1} = .558 \ (A_t - {}_tF_{t-1}), \quad R^2 = .774.$$

As expected in convex forecasting, the regression coefficient in (8) exceeds the regression coefficient in (2). Equation (2) also shows a weaker fit and a larger residual variance, while the variance of the dependent variable is smaller than in (8).

Diller finds suggestions of convex forecasting also in other bodies of interest rate data. However, Conard [18, Table 10] reports a study of government securities in which neither revision coefficients nor (the very high) coefficients of determination change with span. If these data reflect forecasting behavior, then according to (35a) the findings suggest exponential extrapolation, without autonomous components.

BUSINESS FORECASTS

In a recent NBER study of short-term economic forecasting, Victor Zarnowitz [19] compiled and analyzed a variety of recent forecasts of aggregate economic activity in the United States. The forecasts come from a variety of sources.[31] Most of them are predictions of the next year's business, but some include forecasts of several semiannual or quarterly spans.

One of the conclusions of Zarnowitz's study is that these forecasts in part represent extrapolations of the past. In order to ascertain whether business forecasts are better characterized as exponential, concave, or convex, regressions were fit to the two alternative forms of revision functions (2) and (8).

Columns 1 to 4 in Table 3-1 show results of fitting the shifting-target function (2); columns 5 to 8 are results of fitting the fixed-target function (8).

Clear patterns of convexity are visible in GNP forecast G, for which five spans are available. Otherwise, the evidence is unclear. Since the business forecasts contain apparently sizeable autonomous components, the correlations are not strong.[32]

---

[31] For a detailed description, see [19, Chapter 1].

[32] Another reason is that the forecast base values contain errors of measurement. Forecasters use preliminary available data which are subject to revision. Data revisions are, in effect, a part of the forecasting error. For a discussion of this issue, see Rosanne Cole, Chapter 2 of this volume.

TABLE 3-1. Relations Between Forecast Revisions and Forecast Errors, Selected Forecasts of GNP and Plant and Equipment Outlays for Spans Varying From Three to Eighteen Months [a]

| | | Revision Function (2) Regressions of Constant-Span Revisions | | | Revision Function (8) Regressions of Reduced-Span Revisions | | | |
Line	Span of Forecast, in Months (before and after revision) (1)	Intercept a_1 (2)	Coefficient of Regression b_1 (3)	Correlation Coefficient r_1 (4)	Span of First and Span of Revised Forecast (in months) (5)	Intercept a_2 (6)	Coefficient of Regression b_2 (7)	Correlation Coefficient r_2 (8)
				GNP Forecasts: C				
1	3	5.07 (2.25)	2.034 (.684)	.668	3;0	−1.57	.892	.428
2	6	6.68 (2.65)	1.391 (.803)	.463	6;3	0.54 (2.07)	.814 (.627)	.365
3	9	8.44 (2.35)	.253 (.714)	.106	9;6	0.72 (1.94)	.657 (.588)	.319
				GNP Forecasts: D				
4	6	12.87 (4.54)	−.050 (.359)	−.037	12;6	9.07 (2.86)	−.112 (.227)	−.131
				GNP Forecasts: G				
5	6	12.23 (2.40)	.265 (.256)	.250	6;0	−3.77 (2.00)	.565 (.214)	.551
6	9	13.23 (2.33)	−.063 (.249)	−.063	9;3	−2.97 (1.59)	.422 (.170)	.528
7	12	14.15 (2.45)	−.226 (.262)	−.211	12;6	−1.07 (1.94)	.289 (.207)	.329
8	15	14.51 (3.04)	−.372 (.334)	−.306	15;9	−1.17 (2.49)	.070 (.274)	.074
9	18	14.81 (2.99)	−.452 (.330)	−.368	18;15	−.13 (2.56)	−.041 (.281)	−.042
				Anticipations of Plant and Equipment Outlays (OBE-SEC)				
10	3	.66 (.16)	1.033 (.228)	.548	6;3	.13 (.09)	.675 (.127)	.609

Period covered: 1952-II through 1964-III. The figures in parentheses are standard errors.

VIII. OPTIMALITY, ONCE AGAIN

In the early sections of this paper the formal generation of optimal forecasts was exclusively determined by assumptions about the stochastic structure of time series. This was a matter of mathematical and expositional simplicity. In general, an optimal formulation of forecasts depends not only on the stochastic structure of time series but also on the criterion of optimization, that is, on the "loss function" of the forecast error. Minimization of an economically motivated loss function need not yield the same results as, for example, the mean square error criterion.

In particular, minimizing the cost of error may lead to convex forecasting even when the mean square error criterion implies concavity, or conversely.[33] We have seen that convex forecasting means larger revisions of short-term than of long-term expectations, in response to current (unexpected) developments. If short-term plans are based on short-term expectations, and if economic considerations lead to greater flexibility in the short run than in the long run, such considerations may lead to convex forecasting. For example, if revisions of (short-run) production schedules are less costly than those of (longer-run) capital investment plans, economic optimization would influence the formation of convex forecasts of future demand.[34]

We noted previously (p. 90) that, if multispan forecasts are available, the revision coefficients of equation (10) not only provide a means for testing the form and reconstructing the extrapolation function (4), but also for ascertaining whether the extrapolation function is optimal, provided the time series can be described by the stochastic process (3). When the forecasts consist of extrapolations only, the answer is obtained by testing the equality (14) $\gamma_i^2 = \dfrac{M_{i+1} - M_i}{M_1}$, where M_i is the mean square error of the ith span forecast. If the equality holds, then $\gamma_i = w_i$ in (3), and forecasting behavior is indeed optimal in the mean square error sense. If the equality does not hold, forecasting behavior may still be optimizing, but either (3) is false or forecasters follow a different optimization criterion.

The test becomes less meaningful in the presence of nonextrapolative components in forecasting. To the extent that these components are either nonforecasting (e.g., measurement errors) or ineffective as forecasting components, they enter the mean square errors M_i.

The contribution of autonomous components to the size of forecasting error was observed to increase relative to that of extrapolation with increasing span in the NBER collection of business forecasts. We

---

[33] In this case, the revision coefficients γ_k in (10) are no longer equal to the coefficients w_i in the latent structure (3), even if such a structure could be assumed.

[34] As another example, Harberger [9] advocates convex forecasting of future interest rates in optimal planning schemes.

may infer from this pattern that, even if equality (14) held for pure extrapolations, the addition of autonomous components augments the numerator $(M_{i+1} - M_i)$ more than the denominator (M_i). Hence, estimates of $\dfrac{M_{i+1} - M_i}{M_i}$ would exceed estimates of σ_i^2, and by an increasing proportion with increasing span. If the ratios $\dfrac{M_{i+1} - M_i}{M_1}$, while differing from γ_i^2, nevertheless vary in the same direction, this is consistent with a weak hypothesis of optimization, in the sense that convex (concave) forecasting is used because the true series itself is convex (concave).

Table 3-2 compares $\dfrac{M_{i+1} - M_i}{M_1}$ of forward interest rates with corresponding γ_i^2 in Meiselman's revision equations.

TABLE 3-2. Observed and Predicted Revision Coefficients in Forward Rates

Span	i	1	2	3	4	5	6	7	8
Observed [a]	γ_i^2	.50	.28	.16	.10	.08	.06	.06	.04
Predicted [b]	$\dfrac{M_{i+1} - M_i}{M_1}$	.99	.90	.87	.60	.52	.42	.24	.34

[a] γ_i are regression coefficients in Meiselman revision equations.
[b] Calculated using residual variances in the regressions of Y_{t+k} on $_{t+k}F_t$, from Diller's Table 4-21, this volume. The residual variances are, in effect, mean square errors adjusted for bias.

The observed $\dfrac{M_{i+1} - M_1}{M_1}$ do, indeed, decline as the γ_i^2, though they are larger and decline more slowly. Here the joint hypothesis of optimizing forecasting in a linear time series process (3) cannot be rejected.

No comparable statements can be made about the business forecasts analyzed by Zarnowitz. The forecasts are prima facie not optimal, since they vary by forecaster for the same time series.

IX. CONCLUSION

Can we learn from available forecast data how these forecasts were generated? The analysis presented above arises from an attempt to answer this question. The answer is positive, to a degree believed to be useful, provided forecasts are available for several successive future periods at a given time.

When direct forecast data are not available, empirical insights on how expectations are formed should provide some guidance for specification of expectational forms in econometric models. The usual procedure in this usual case has been to assume a simple extrapolation value for the expectational magnitude on which the observed behavior is based. This extrapolation is often a naive projection of past values or past changes in them, or a more sophisticated geometrically weighted or exponential extrapolation. In addition to relative simplicity, the following claims have been put forth on behalf of the exponential extrapolation: That it represents a type of error-learning forecasting behavior, and that it is an optimal predictor, in the mean square error sense, in certain nonstationary time series.

In this paper we have shown that wide classes of nonexponential extrapolations can also be interpreted as error-learning behavior, and that they can be optimal in types of time series for which the exponential is not optimal. For example, the extrapolation which is optimal for certain stationary linear processes is not exponential but convex, at least in some range. Convex forecasts have properties of regressivity, a behavioral characteristic often desired in the specification of the model.

We also recognize that forecasts or anticipations do not consist exclusively, or even mainly, of extrapolations. We have shown that revision functions (10), which relate revisions of forecasts to the last observed error of forecast, permit not only an analysis of the type of extrapolation embedded in the forecast but also an analysis of the nature and importance of nonextrapolative components in the observed forecasts.

The diagnostic usefulness of the analysis developed in this paper is illustrated more concretely in Diller's investigation of the term structure of interest rates in the following chapter.

REFERENCES

[1] Mills, Edwin, *Price, Output, and Inventory Policy,* New York, 1962.
[2] Griliches, Zvi, "Distributed Lags: A Survey," *Econometrica,* January 1967.

[3] Koyck, L. M., *Distributed Lags and Investment Analysis*, Amsterdam, 1954.

[4] Muth, J. F., "Optimal Properties of Exponentially Weighted Forecasts," *Journal of the American Statistical Association*, June 1960.

[5] Nerlove, M. and Wage, S., "On the Optimality of Adaptive Forecasting," *Management Science*, 1964.

[6] Whittle, P., *Prediction and Regulation by Least Squares*, London, 1963.

[7] Allais, M., "A Restatement of the Quantity Theory of Money," *American Economic Review*, December 1966.

[8] Bossons, J. and Modigliani, F., "Statistical vs. Structural Explanations of Understatement and Regressivity in Rational Expectations," *Econometrica*, April 1966.

[9] Harberger, A., "Techniques of Project Appraisal," in *National Economic Planning*, Universities-National Bureau Conference 19, New York, 1967.

[10] Bailey, M. J., "Prediction of an Autoregressive Variable . . . ," *Journal of the American Statistical Association*, March 1965.

[11] Bierwag, G. O. and Grove, M. A., "Aggregate Koyck Functions," *Econometrica*, October 1966.

[12] Friedman, Milton, *A Theory of the Consumption Function*, Princeton University Press for NBER, 1957.

[13] ———, "Windfalls, the Horizon, and Related Concepts . . . ," in *Measurement in Economics: Studies in Memory of Y. Grunfeld*, C. Christ et al., Stanford, Calif., 1963.

[14] Kessel, R., *The Cyclical Behavior of the Term Structure*, NBER Occasional Paper 91, New York, 1965.

[15] Meiselman, D., *The Term Structure of Interest Rates*, Englewood Cliffs, N.J., 1962.

[16] Pye, G., "A Markov Model of the Term Structure," *Quarterly Journal of Economics*, February 1966.

[17] Telser, L. G., "A Critique of Some Recent Empirical Research . . ." *The Journal of Political Economy*, Part II, August 1967.

[18] Conard, J., *The Behavior of Interest Rates*, NBER, New York, 1966.

[19] Zarnowitz, V., *An Appraisal of Short-Term Economic Forecasts*, NBER Occasional Paper 104, New York, 1966.

FOUR

Expectations in the
Term Structure of
Interest Rates

STANLEY DILLER

I. INTRODUCTION

Since J. R. Hicks' *Value and Capital* [6] appeared, and even before, a controversy has persisted over what determines the yield differentials among securities identical except for the term left to maturity. Formerly a technical subject on the fringe of monetary affairs, the term structure of interest rates has recently become a policy issue, involving as it does the relationship between long- and short-term interest rates. "Operation Twist," for example, a widely publicized policy in the early 1960's, involved the government's attempt to keep the long-term rate low in order to encourage domestic investment and the short-term rate high to discourage capital outflow through adjusting the supply of different maturities.

The effectiveness of this policy depends, of course, on the determinants of the term structure. In this respect, there are essentially two points of view: One holds that the market for securities consists of a group of separate nonoverlapping markets defined for different maturities, with no tendency for the rates in the different markets to assume any particular relation to each other. This point of view, stated here in its extreme, says in effect: that there is no theory of the term structure. On the other side are those who regard the securities market as a collection of interrelated markets and the term structure of rates as subject to some unifying principle. Ordinarily, the principle involves some form of forecasting. The term structure, according to the second view, is determined, at least in part, by the market's forecasts of future rates. David Meiselman, who sparked the latest round of discussion, argues vigorously for the so-called pure expectations hypothesis [11]. More recently, Reuben Kessel [8] revitalized Hicks' idea that the term structure depends on some combination of market anticipations and liquidity preference.

For our own work we tentatively accept the expectations hypothesis that the yield differentials are explainable in terms of market forecasting (with or without the liquidity component) and consider how the forecasts are actually formed. We find that a substantial part of the variation of the forecasts inferred from the term structure is related to an extrapolation of past spot rates. In other words, a moving average of past spot rates can predict a substantial part of the implicit forecasts themselves. We find, however, that the forecasts are no more (and even a little less) effective in forecasting future spot rates than are *linear* extrapolations of past spot rates; that is, extrapolations based on moving averages whose weights are specifically selected to yield the best predictions of future spot rates.

Most of this chapter is devoted to an interpretation of these findings. In particular, one can interpret the linear extrapolative model as a summary of many explicit behavioral models in the same way that a resultant force can be said to summarize the effects of component forces. Since it is the resultant that we observe, the issue becomes: What can we infer about the behavioral models contributing to the final effect?

In Section III we investigate the relationship between the error-learning mechanism that Meiselman used to test the expectations hypothesis and the extrapolative model. From the statistical results of the error-learning model reported by Meiselman we are able to infer a particular method of extrapolation and show that this method fits the actual data better than some plausible alternative methods.

The significance of this experiment lies in our ability to generalize the work of Meiselman and others into a form from which one can draw additional implications about the way market forecasts are made.

One characteristic of the term structure that has received wide attention and evoked general agreement, from Keynes to Kessel, is the inverse relation that exists between the slope of the yield curve and the level of short rates. This observation is ordinarily explained by the so-called expected return to normalcy hypothesis: When current rates deviate from their normal level, future rates are expected to move in the direction of the normal level. Part of Section III demonstrates that this hypothesis is implied by the particular extrapolative model that fits Meiselman's data. As before, the significance of this experiment is the connection it provides between the apparently mechanical procedure of extrapolation and an actual behavioral model.

Finally, we consider the relationship between economic indicators and extrapolative forecasting. Most of the observed connection between the indicators and the forecasts is picked up in the extrapolative procedure. This result is due to the common variation between the indicators and spot rates over the course of the business cycle. The extrapolative procedure implicitly takes account of this common relation. There is a net relation between the indicators and the forecasts that is independent of their common cyclical variation. This relation, it appears, grows as the span of forecast increases.

When we compare the accuracy of the implied forecasts with an autoregressive model designed to exhaust the full extrapolative potential of the data, we find the implied forecasts are inferior. This result follows largely from our analysis of the apparent method of market forecasting. Since the forecasts are based primarily on extrapolations, they are no more effective than the autoregressive model, which is itself an extrapolation. The margin of inferiority of the forward rate forecasts may also be due to the presence of a liquidity premium or some other nonforecasting component of the forward rates that obscures the variation of the forecast component.

The accuracy analysis also uncovers a bias in the forecasts: They are shown to be consistently too high. Kessel, having obtained a similar result, attributed it to the presence of a liquidity premium.

In summary, a substantial part of the variation of the yield differentials can be explained by relating them to market forecasts; the variation of the forecasts, in turn, is in large measure determined by an extrapolative procedure; and the extrapolative procedure is consistent with and related to several behavioral models that have been separately proposed as determinants of the term structure.

II. THE TERM STRUCTURE OF INTEREST RATES

FUTURE PRICES

There are various sets of time series data on individual and group anticipations that would be amenable to the analysis on which this study is based; surveys of business and consumer expectations, forecasts of national income components, sales forecasts, and so forth. There are far less data available on forecasts attributable to a market consensus. Perhaps the best example of this type of forecast is to be found in price data of future transactions. After allowing for various business costs, such as storage and default risk, the current price at which a commodity to be delivered in the future is transacted should, in principle, be equal to the price that is currently expected to prevail at that point in the future. In the special case where expectations are unanimously held and the market responds only to expected values, ignoring the risk of capital loss that fluctuating prices entails (leaving aside transactions and other business costs), the market is at the margin indifferent as to whether it transacts a future commodity at the forward price or waits until the delivery date and transacts at the then spot price. Unanimity is assumed because otherwise we would have to explain why a market deviant does not continue to transact until his funds are exhausted, borrowing to transact further until the discrepancy between his and the market's views are obliterated. It would contribute, perhaps, to verisimilitude if we explained the absence of indefinite transactions by assuming that expectations are not held with certainty and that the uncertainty increased with the number of transactions; or alternatively, that the existing capital market precludes the availability of an unlimited amount of funds to the market deviant. In this and other respects we have abstracted from descriptive complexity. The assumption that dispersion of prices is not relevant will be discussed later.

A particular kind of future price that has recently evoked wide discussion is the price of forward loans. Unlike the prices of commodity futures, the prices of forward loans are not explicitly quoted but are rather implied in the term structure of interest rates. Since these prices are free of the business costs that are part of commodity futures, their expectations content is more immediate; although a possible market response to the gamble is still present. The price of forward loans, like other forward prices, may include a risk premium. In the following pages we review briefly the determinants of the term structure, how the forward rates of return are inferred from the rates of return of securities differing only in the term left to their maturity, and the evidence for equating the forward rates with the expected rates. The recent literature has discussed this part of the subject quite thoroughly; therefore, this study will give it minimum coverage.

A yield curve for a given year and a given type of security is a locus of points relating the rate of return of a security, on the vertical axis, to the term remaining until its maturity, or the number of years remaining before the security is paid off, on the horizontal axis. A typical point on a yield curve for high-grade bonds reveals, as of a given time, the year for which the curve is drawn, the yield to maturity of a bond with a given term to maturity. On the same curve, another point shows the yield on a bond with a different term, and so on, each point for a different term to maturity. For a security of a given term, the yield on the curve associated with that term is the discount factor that is used to equate a stream of fixed payments – that is, the annual coupon payments plus the par value when the bond matures – with the present value of the security. The well-known formula for this computation is:

$$PV = \frac{C_1}{1+R} + \frac{C_2}{(1+R)^2} + \cdots + \frac{C_n + P}{(1+R)^n},$$

where: PV = present value of current market price of security; C_i = coupon payments; P = principle; and R = market yield of bond. Since in any one year there may be several bonds on the market with the same term to maturity but with somewhat different characteristics, it is necessary to fit a line to the points to reduce the array to a unique yield for each term to maturity.[1]

[1] See Durand [4]. The complete set of Durand data is listed in the National Industrial Conference Board's *Economic Almanac, 1967–1968*, p. 416.

A long-term yield is essentially an average of shorter-term yields covering the same period, although the particular form of this average depends on the assumption made with respect to the method of payment.[2] From the yields of two securities, identical except for the terms left to their maturities, one may infer a forward rate of return r that would apply to loans beginning at the time the shorter of the two securities matured and ending when the longer one matured. The formula for this computation of an i period loan is as follows: [3]

$$r_n = \frac{(1 + R_n)^n}{(1 + R_{n-i})^{n-i}} - 1.$$

With this formula one can compute a table of forward rates from the term structure of long-term rates that would reveal the rates of interest on forward loans up to n periods in the future.

THE EXPECTATIONS HYPOTHESIS

The purchase of a security with, say, ten years to maturity is conceptually identical with and can be regarded as the purchase of ten one-year securities that materialize consecutively from the time they were all purchased until the end of the tenth year.[4] Leaving aside attitudes toward the risk of capital loss or of fluctuations of income, since each investor has the option of waiting until a particular security is available and purchasing it at the then spot price, any tendency for the forward yield to deviate from the spot yield expected to prevail should be countered by a change in the demand for the source. For example, if the forward yield of a one-period security available five periods hence exceeds the yield that the market currently expects will prevail on the spot market five years hence, there should be enough investors around who, instead of waiting to deal on the spot market five years later, will move to buy the apparently cheap security now. The increased demand for the security would raise its current price until its yield approaches the expected spot yield. This mechanism is, of course, symmetrical.

This simple idea underlies the hypothesis that the forward rates are equal to the spot rates expected in the future. Since this equation re-

[2] See Macaulay [9, p. 29].

[3] This idea is explained in Hicks [6, pp. 1 and 5] and, in greater generality, in Wallace [16, Chapter I].

[4] See Wallace [16].

quires the willingness of a sufficient number of investors to implicitly transact in the forward market by rearranging the maturity mixture of their portfolios, a priori evaluations of the hypothesis hinge on whether a sufficient number of investors are, in fact, willing to alter their portfolios in response to anticipations.[5] The hedging theory holds that the markets for short- and long-term securities are independent and, therefore, that the equilibrating mechanism between forward and expected rates is nonexistent.[6] The liquidity preference theory acknowledges a relationship among the markets for different maturities (or, what amounts to the same thing, the substitutability of the different securities) but stops short of recognizing a single market for all maturities. In this theory the variance of the prices of securities is a direct function of maturity (not because prices of longer-term securities change more often, but because they fluctuate over a wider range); and, other things the same, the greater the variance the less valuable the security. Given two securities, identical except for maturity, the longer-term security would have to yield more to make the average investor indifferent between them. Therefore, between the pure expectations and the pure hedging theories there is a continuum of degrees of substitutability assumed to exist among the different maturities. At the one extreme, the substitutability is infinite, and the term structure of rates depends solely on expectations; at the other, the substitutability is zero, and the term structure of rates is determined by the supply and demand for each maturity. In between these extremes, the assumed substitutability depends on the relative degrees of price fluctuations that investors are assumed to anticipate, as well as the assumed extent of investors' abhorrence of risk or, obversely, their preference for insurance. In this case, the yield differential necessary for investors' indifference is the insurance or liquidity premium.[7]

In this intermediate position, there are two separate factors affecting the degree of substitutability among the various maturities: (1) in-

---

[5] The hypothesis does not imply one market for all securities regardless of maturity; nor, in the case of several markets, does it imply that all investors be indifferent about the maturity structure of their portfolios. It is necessary only that the several markets overlap and contain in their overlapping sections a sufficient number of lenders and borrowers whose respective cross elasticity of demand for or supply of securities of different terms to maturity is infinite. See Meiselman [11, Chapter I].

[6] See Culbertson [3, pp. 485–517].

[7] In this context the word "liquidity" refers strictly to the expected variance of security prices; the smaller the variance the greater the liquidity.

vestors' expectations of the variance of prices of different maturities; and (2) given the expected variances, investors' attitude with respect to the degree of risk of capital loss. Phillip Cagan, in his discussion of the first point, proposes that the differences in the expected variances are inversely related to the deviation of the actual level of rates from the normal level.[8] As for the second point, Reuben Kessel [8] finds that the required premium is greater the higher the level of rates. In both cases, since the liquidity premia will vary over time, there is no simple way to correct the forward rates for this factor in order to isolate the expectations component. The attempt to ascertain the basis for the forecast or the accuracy of the forecast is therefore marred by the presence of the varying liquidity premia.

The evidence that is typically offered for the existence of liquidity premia is the well-known tendency for yields on long-term securities to exceed those on short-term securities.[9] Any attempts, therefore, to measure the accuracy of forecasts by computing the mean square of the differences between the forward rates and the target spot rates will reveal a large error because of this bias. If, instead, the target rates are regressed on the forward rates,[10] the bias in the forward rates will fall out in the constant term. But the varying liquidity premia will lower the correlation and bias the regression coefficient toward zero, except for the special case when they are linearly related to the level of rates. In any case, the presence of a nonforecasting component, whether liquidity premia or some other random variable, hinders the evaluation of forecasts of interest rates.

III. LINEAR AUTOREGRESSIVE FORECASTING MODELS

LONG-TERM DATA

Error-learning model. The question of whether forward rates make accurate forecasts is, of course, independent of the question of whether

---

[8] See his "A Study of Liquidity Premiums on Federal and Municipal Securities" in *A Study of Interest Rates* [1].

[9] This phenomenon is often reversed in periods of high interest rates—a fact that is considered later in the study. For reasons not entirely clear, the reverse is also true in the mortgage market, where longer-term mortgages tend to yield less than shorter-term mortgages. On this point see Jack Guttentag's study of mortgage yields [1].

[10] The justification for this procedure is discussed more fully in Section IV.

forward rates are forecasts. Forecasting economic time series is notoriously difficult, even series that are far more stable than interest rates. Therefore, evidence of poor accuracy in no way impugns the expectations hypothesis or its liquidity preference variant. In his important study on the term structure, David Meiselman [11, Chapter II] devised an ingenious test to determine whether forward rates are, in fact, forecasts. His idea was to find some characteristics of known forecasts whose presence in a set of numbers would constitute evidence that this set behaved as though it consisted of forecasts. He formulated the characteristic he chose to isolate in terms of the error-learning model. Other studies in other areas have indicated a feedback mechanism in forecasting, whereby the error observed currently of previous forecasts inspires revisions of forecasts referring to a later period. Since the expectations hypothesis asserts that forward rates are, or contain, estimates of expected spot rates, a demonstration that forward rates follow a pattern similar to that of many known sets of forecast data is prima facie evidence that forward rates are or contain forecasts. The model that Meiselman tested is as follows:

$$_{t+n}r_t - _{t+n}r_{t-1} = a + \gamma_n(R_t - _tr_{t-1}) + u,$$

where $_{t+n}r_t$ = the forecast made in period t of the rate expected in period $t + n$; $_{t+n}r_{t-1}$ = the forecast made in $t - 1$ of the rate expected in $t + n$; R_t = the spot rate in period t; and $_tr_{t-1}$ = the forecast made in $t - 1$ of the spot rate in t. All rates are one-year rates. The left side of the equation denotes the revision in period t of the forecast made originally in $t - 1$, the forecast referring in both cases to the spot rate in period $t + n$. The right-hand side denotes a constant term a and the proportion γ of the current error $R_t - _tr_{t-1}$ that is projected into the revision of subsequent forecasts, and a random term, u. Meiselman tested this model with the Durand data for eight sets of revisions representing eight spans of forecast (where the span n is the number of years between the time the forecast is made and the time to which it refers). He found that as the span increases, γ falls together with the ability of the model to explain the variation of the revisions.

Because the regression coefficient was significantly different from zero in all eight regressions, as well as because of other characteristics of the results, Meiselman concluded that the model adequately represented the data and therefore that the data behaved as though they were forecasts.

Now, if the data on forward rates can be said to contain forecasts, the questions we raise are: How are the forecasts generated, and what are their behavioral properties? In the following, Meiselman's and other data on the term structure are probed to extend our insights into expectational behavior in the capital market.

The extrapolative model. In Chapter 3 of this volume, Jacob Mincer establishes a relationship between the Meiselman-type error-learning models and linear extrapolative forecasting models. In this extrapolation, the forecast value for any period in the future, $t + n$, is computed from a weighted average of past values of the same series taken sequentially back from the target date $t + n$ through the current period t and back into the past. Since the values of the series between periods t and $t + n$ are not known, the values forecast for each of these periods are substituted for the actual values.[11] In other words, a forecast of the period $t + n$ implies forecasts of the preceding periods, $t + n - 1, t + n - 2, \ldots, t + 1$. In symbols: [12]

$$(1) \qquad _{t+n}F_t = C + B_1(_{t+n-1}F_t) + B_2(_{t+n-2}F_t) + \cdots + B_n A_t$$
$$+ B_{n+1}A_{t-1} + \cdots + {_{t+n}E_t},$$

where $_{t+n-i}F_t = $ forecast made in period t referring to i periods prior to $t + n$; $A_{t-i} = $ actual value of series i periods into the past; $B_i = $ weights in linear combination; $C = $ constant term, by hypothesis equal to zero; and $E = $ autonomous component of forecast, i.e., the part not based on past values of the series. If the forecast were made in period $t - 1$ instead of in t, the fourth term on the right side of (1) would be $B_n(_tF_{t-1})$ instead of $B_n A_t$, since A_t could not be known in period $t - 1$. Let us write out the equations for the forecasts referring to $t + 1$ made in both t and $t - 1$:

$$(2) \qquad _{t+1}F_t = C + B_1 A_t + B_2 A_{t-1} + \cdots + B_{n+1}A_{t-n} + {_{t+1}E_t},$$

$$(3) \qquad _{t+1}F_{t-1} = C + B_1\,{_tF_{t-1}} + B_2 A_{t-1} + \cdots + B_{n+1} A_{t-n} + {_{t+1}E_{t-1}}.$$

[11] This procedure is optimal, in the sense of minimizing mean square error of forecast, for a particular class of time series. See p. 87, above.

[12] The symbols F and A represent forecasts and target (or actual) values of any series. When the F refers to forward rates, the nonextrapolative component E includes not only the autonomous component but any nonforecasting component, such as errors of measurement and liquidity premia.

Subtracting (3) from (2):

(4) $_{t+1}F_t - _{t+1}F_{t-1} = B_1(A_t - _tF_{t-1}) + (_{t+1}E_t - _{t+1}E_{t-1})$.

Let us apply the above procedure to the forecasts made in periods t and $t - 1$ referring to period $t + 2$:

(5) $_{t+2}F_t = C + B_1(_{t+1}F_t) + B_2A_t + B_3A_{t-1} + \cdots + _{t+2}E_t$.

(6) $_{t+2}F_{t-1} = C + B_1(_{t+1}F_{t-1}) + B_2(_tF_{t-1}) + B_3A_{t-1} + \cdots + _{t+2}E_{t-1}$.

Subtracting (6) from (5):

(7) $(_{t+2}F_t - _{t+2}F_{t-1}) = B_1(_{t+1}F_t - _{t+1}F_{t-1}) + B_2(A_t - _tF_{t-1})$

$$+ (_{t+2}E_t - _{t+2}E_{t-1}),$$

and the difference equation for $t + 3$:

(8) $(_{t+3}F_t - _{t+3}F_{t-1}) = B_1(_{t+2}F_t - _{t+2}F_{t-1}) + B_2(_{t+1}F_t - _{t+1}F_{t-1})$

$$+ B_3(A_t - _tF_{t-1}) + (_{t+3}E_t - _{t+3}E_{t-1}).$$

By recursive substitution of the lower span revisions, each revision becomes a linear function of the current forecasting error alone, generating Meiselman's equations for each span. Thus, we find that linear extrapolations of type (1) and (2) are consistent with Meiselman's error-learning model.

We note that Meiselman's revision coefficients γ_i and the R_i^2 decline steadily with increasing span i. Mincer has derived an expression that relates the decline in the coefficients of determination to the decline in the coefficients of regression, when multispan forecasting is assumed to be recursive as in (1). According to Mincer the coefficient of determination of the ith regression is given by the following expression: [13]

(9) $$R_i^2 = \cfrac{1}{1 + \cfrac{(1 - R_1^2)\gamma_1^2}{R_1^2\gamma_i^2}(1 + \gamma_1^2 + \cdots + \gamma_{i-1}^2)},$$

where R_i^2 = coefficient of determination of ith regression; and γ_i = coefficient of regression of ith regression. This expression implies that the coefficients of determination will decline with increasing span of forecast whenever $\gamma_i \geq \gamma_{i+1}$; that is, when the coefficients of regression do not increase. Table 4-1 compares the coefficients of determination

[13] See Jacob Mincer, equation (36), p. 103 of this volume, for the derivation.

TABLE 4-1. Comparison Between the Estimated and Predicted Coefficients of Determinations for Regressions of the Error-Learning Model (Durand Data, 1901–55)

Span (1)	Estimated R^2 (adj) (2)	Predicted R^2 (adj) (3)	Span (1)	Estimated R^2 (adj) (2)	Predicted R^2 (adj) (3)
1	.9053	.9053	5	.4004	.4206
2	.7470	.7812	6	.3709	.3345
3	.5819	.6395	7	.4055	.3324
4	.4537	.5154	8	.3289	.2743

Note: Column 2 lists coefficients of determination computed by Meiselman; column 3 lists the ones predicted by equation (9).

that Meiselman found (column 2) with the ones predicted by equation (9). While the expressions for the standard errors of the two sets of statistics are not easily derived to permit an evaluation of the statistical significance of their differences, the figures in the two columns appear to be quite close.[14]

The inference sometimes drawn from Meiselman's declining correlations that the relevance of the expectations hypothesis diminishes with increasing term to maturity, therefore, does not follow.[15]

The consistency of Meiselman's whole set of error-learning equations with a hypothesis of linear extrapolative forecasting strengthens the interpretation of forward rates as expectational magnitudes. Now, we can go further and ask: What is the particular form of the

[14] Formula (9) based on Mincer's equation (33) assumes that the variances of the nonextrapolative components do not change with span. If they decrease with span, predicted R^2 will decline more rapidly than observed R_i^2. Alternatively, nonforecasting components might create the offsetting effect, according to Mincer's equation (33a), if the revision coefficients are declining. In Table 4-1, predicted R^2 do indeed decline somewhat more rapidly than the observed ones.

[15] For example, the following is quoted from Wood [18, p. 165].

It is reasonable to suppose that investors will have fairly firm expectations regarding the level of rates one year from the present and will formulate their decisions on the basis of expectations; whereas expectations of what rates will be several years into the future are likely to be at best hazy and, as a consequence, investors are likely to determine their holdings of one-year relative to, say, eight-year securities to a large extent on the basis of considerations other than expectations of future short rates.

While the point may be correct, it cannot properly be concluded from Meiselman's findings.

extrapolative model that generates Meiselman's revision equations? This question is important because the form of the extrapolation contained in forward rates provides further insights into the expectational behavior in financial markets.

The relationship between the revision variables on the right side of equations (7) and (8) and the current error reveals the relationship between the extrapolative weights, B_i, of equation (1) and Meiselman's regression coefficients, γ_i.

For example, substituting (4) into (7) yields

$$(10) \quad (_{t+2}F_t - {_{t+2}}F_{t-1}) = B_1[B_1(A_t - {_t}F_{t-1})] + B_2(A_t - {_t}F_{t-1})$$

$$+ (_{t+2}E_t - {_{t+2}}E_{t-1})$$

$$= (B_1^2 + B_2)(A_t - {_t}F_{t-1}) + (_{t+2}E_t - {_{t+2}}E_{t-1});$$

and substituting (4) and (7) into (8):

$$(11) \quad (_{t+3}F_t - {_{t+3}}F_{t-1}) = B_1 B_1[B_1(A_t - {_t}F_{t-1})] + B_2(A_t - {_t}F_{t-1})$$

$$+ B_3(A_t - {_t}F_{t-1}) + (_{t+3}E_t - {_{t+3}}E_{t-1})$$

$$= (B_1^3 + B_1 B_2 + B_3)(A_t - {_t}F_{t-1})$$

$$+ (_{t+3}E_t - {_{t+3}}E_{t-1}).$$

Similar expressions for forecasts that span more than three years are analogous to (1) and (11). These expressions produce a system of equations with only one exogenous variable, the current error of forecast. The dependent variable of each of the equations in the system is related to the one exogenous variable directly, as well as through its relationship with the dependent variables of the equations above its own. The expressions for the regression coefficient relating a given revision to the current error includes all the extrapolative weights B_i that are included in the expression for the coefficient of the equation above it plus one additional weight. One can therefore deduce the B_i recursively, in the following manner, denoting Meiselman's coefficients, $\gamma_i i = 1, 8$:

$$(12) \qquad\qquad \gamma_1 = B_1$$

$$\gamma_2 = B_1^2 + B_2$$

$$\gamma_3 = B_1^3 + 2B_1 B_2 + B_3$$

and generally [16]

$$\gamma_i = \sum_{j=1}^{i} \gamma_{i-j} \cdot B_j, \quad \text{where } \gamma_0 = 1.$$

Using Meiselman's reported values of the γ_i we derived the set of B_i according to (12). For example, $B_2 = \gamma_2 - B_1^2$; $B_3 = \gamma_3 - B_1^3 - 2B_1B_2$; and so on for the other values of γ and B not shown here. Table 4-2, column 2, shows the γ_i coefficients, which were recomputed and changed slightly from those Meiselman reported; the B_i coefficients are in column 3. From the derivation of the B_i it is clear that if one of the weights, say B_2, is out of line, the succeeding weight, B_3, will be out of line in the other direction. For example, if B_2 were too high, we would subtract from γ_3 a larger number than we should in order to get B_3; therefore, a high B_2 would lead to a low B_3. If sampling fluctuation knocked one weight out of line, it would set in motion a wiggle that would reverberate down the column of weights. The minus sign attached to B_8 makes little sense in the present context, but it is preceded by a B_7 that is too large and by a B_6 that is too small.

Because of this sampling problem, the weights as raw data do not evince a coherent pattern; yet, when plotted, a pattern may be detected. To glean at least one estimate of the pattern, we plotted on Chart 4-1 the weights, B_i (computed from Meiselman's coefficients shown in Table 4-2, column 3), on semilog paper and drew a smooth curve through the points. The weights read from the smooth curve are in column 5 of Table 4-2. The scatter around the curve in Figure 4-1 is, of course, substantial, and the curve highly subjective. Some may contest the treatment of the extreme point, and, of course, the negative point is meaningless. A partial, though by no means conclusive, test for the validity of this procedure is illustrated in the following experiment.

Working with equations (4), (7), and (8), as well as the equations for the revisions of forecasts of spans 4 through 8, we formed a single independent variable for each equation by multiplying each variable on the right side by the relevant weight and summing the products. For example, in the case of equation (8) we multiplied the first independent variable by .7029, the second by .0318, and the third by .0114,

---

[16] See Mincer, p. 89.

CHART 4-1. Patterns of Smoothed Weights, B_i, for Extrapolation Equation (1)

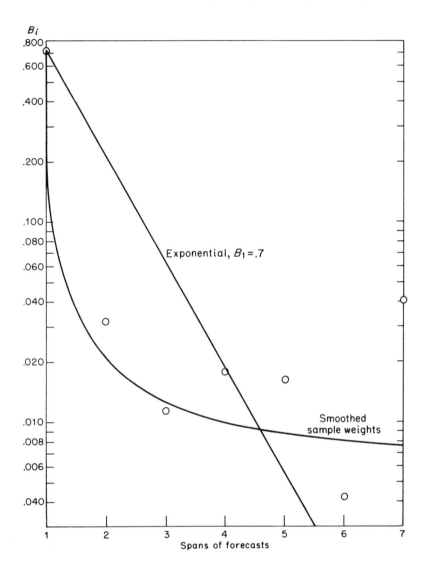

TABLE 4-2. Regression Statistics for Experiments With Estimated Extrapolative Weights

Span of Forecast (1)	γ_i (2)	B_i (Sample) (3)	$R^2_{\bar{B}_i}$ (4)	$\bar{B}_i$ (Smooth) (5)	$R^2_{\bar{B}_i}$ (6)	B_i (Exponential Decline) (7)	$R^2_{\bar{B}_i}(K)$ (8)
1	.7029	.7029	.90526	.7029	.90526	.7000	.90526
2	.5256	.0318	.93545	.0220	.93756	.2100	.90167
3	.4034	.0114	.93421	.0133	.93585	.0630	.89862
4	.3263	.0180	.86998	.0105	.87184	.0189	.86026
5	.2769	.0165	.86353	.0089	.86412	.0057	.87384
6	.2348	.0042	.92688	.0080	.92845	.0017	.92339
7	.2367	.0401	.92430	.0076	.92990	.0005	.91326
8	.2089	−.0016	.87279	.0072	.87801	.0001	.87044

Note: Each set of B_i is used with the same variables in the following set of regressions:

$$(_{t+1}r_1 - _{t+1}r_{t-1}) = A + B_1(R_t - _tr_{t-1})$$
$$(_{t+2}r_t - _{t+2}r_{t-1}) = A + B_1(_{t+1}r_t - _{t+1}r_{t-1}) + B_2(R_t - _tr_{t-1}).$$

In each case the products and variables are summed into one independent variable. There are eight simple regressions for each set of B_i. The R^2 are the coefficients of determination adjusted for degrees of freedom. They are computed for each of the regressions run, with the weights listed in the adjacent column to the left starting from row 1 and continuing down to the row in which the R^2 in question appears. For example, in column 4, .93421 is the R^2 computed from the simple regression the independent variable of which was computed by summing the products of .7029 $(_{t+2}r_t - _{t+2}r_{t-1})$, .0318 $(_{t+1}r_t - _{t+1}r_{t-1})$, and .0114 $(R_t - _tr_{t-1})$. The Durand data were used in this experiment.

the first three weights listed in Table 4-2, column 3. The independent variable of this regression is equal to the linear combination of the variables specified in (8), the constants in the linear combination being the weights. There are eight such regressions, each having one independent variable (formed by the linear combination of the variables listed in the equation) for the corresponding revision of forecast. In one set of eight regressions, we used the weights listed in column 3 and in the other set, the weights listed in column 5. In column 4 we list the adjusted R^2 coefficients of each of the eight sets of regressions, using the empirically estimated weights; column 6 shows the adjusted R^2 coefficients for the smoothed set of weights.

In all but one case, the R^2 coefficients are higher for the smoothed weights; although in no case could the differences appear statistically significant under standard test procedures. Such lack of statistical significance, however, is not too surprising when one considers that the first weight .7029 is almost ten times as large as the sum of all the other weights and, therefore, dominates the linear combination. It is nonetheless interesting to find that relatively small changes in small weights lead to consistently better results, even though only slightly so.

We may tentatively accept the hypothesis that the weights in the extrapolative equation (1) decline in accordance with a smooth curve relating the value of the weight to the period of the lag. The hypothesis allows us to infer the time perspective on the interest rate market. In Figure 4-1, while there is a sharp initial drop between B_1 and B_2, the pattern of decline is much more gradual thereafter; the curve becomes almost horizontal. This pattern implies that interest rates prevailing more than ten years before the time the forecast was made are considered in the forecasts of the future, although the weight attached to these rates is small. Column 7 of Table 4-2 lists the set of geometrically declining weights which produced the best fit in regressions described for the two other sets of weights. Column 8 lists the R^2 coefficients of each of these regressions, which serve as a standard for evaluating the smoothed weights. Here again, in all but one case, the smoothed weights produced a better fit than the geometrically declining weights, although, again, the differences would not appear significant under standard—but inapplicable—test procedures. The relevance of this comparison of weights resides in the fact that they both start from approximately the same place, while the geometrically declining weights indicate a shorter horizon. Therefore, the apparently better fit with smoothed weights provides some evidence that the more distant past is indeed considered in forecasting future rates. In Figure 4-1 the geometrically declining weights are represented by a straight line, since the curves are drawn on semilog paper.

In terms of equation (1), the weights B_i do not depend on the forecast span. As the span changes, the independent variables change, but the weights stay the same. The above analysis does not test whether the weights vary with forecast span. We can evaluate the consequences of this assumption. If the forecast span is not relevant there is no reason for having eight separate regressions. Since the estimate of B_1 is the same, it makes no difference in principle whether this weight is attached to, say, $(A_t - {}_tF_{t-1})$ or $({}_{t+1}F_t - {}_{t+1}F_{t-1})$ so long as the independent variable selected conforms to the appropriate dependent variable.[17] Therefore, we can estimate the B_i with one multiple regression whose first observation is the first observation of equation (4), whose second observation is the first observation of equation (7), whose third observation is the first observation of (8), and, finally, whose ninth observation is the second observation of (4). We can include a dummy variable indicating the span of forecast represented by the particular observation to test the hypothesis that the estimates of the B_i depend upon the independent variable to which they are attached. In other words, we can test the hypothesis that the weights in extrapolative equation (1) vary with the span of forecast by including a dummy variable representing each of the eight equations from which the observations are chosen.

In Table 4-3 we compare the B_i weights, estimated by multiple regression, with those computed from the coefficients γ_i of the error-learning model. The test for the significance of the difference between the two estimates shown there is only illustrative, since it was not possible to estimate the standard errors of both sets of weights. We used our estimates of the standard errors of the B_i from the multiple regression as admittedly poor substitutes for the standard errors of the difference. Unless the correlation between the two sets of estimates is very high and positive, our procedure understates the standard errors of the differences and therefore our t-values are too high. In spite of this, the t-values in column 5 of Table 4-3 show the differences to be statistically significant in only two out of eight cases.

Since there is an exact formula relating the B_i to the γ_i, we can infer either set from estimated values of the other. Having compared the set of B_i inferred from the estimated γ_i with the directly estimated B_i, we will now reverse the process by inferring a set of γ_i from the estimated B_i, reversing the procedure described in (12), and compare this set of γ_i with the set directly estimated from the error-learning model. The results of this comparison are shown in Table 4-4. Once

---

[17] In principle, it is possible to run these regressions directly on the forward and past spot rates, that is, on the eight forecasting equations of the form (1). Since adjacent interest rates are highly correlated, the estimated coefficients would be very unstable. The revisions were used to lessen the multicollinearity problem, on the assumption that the revisions are less intercorrelated than the rates themselves. This assumption is likely to be true since the revisions are less dependent on the over-all level of economic activity.

TABLE 4-3. Comparison Between the Weights Computed With a Multiple Regression and Those Computed From the Coefficients of the Error-Learning Model (Durand Data, 1900–54)

Number of Logs (1)	B_i (Mult. Reg.) (2)	S_{B_i} (3)	B_i (Computed) (4)	t-Value of Difference (5)
1	.7457	.0199	.7029	2.1507
2	.0548	.0248	.0318	0.9274
3	.0347	.0240	.0114	0.9708
4	−.0914	.0192	.0180	−5.6979
5	.0522	.0243	.0165	1.4691
6	.0051	.0258	.0042	0.0349
7	.0412	.0258	.0401	0.0426
8	−.0168	.0260	−.0116	−0.2000

Note: Column 2 lists the weights estimated in the multiple regressions, a few observations of which are as follows:

$$(_{t+1}r_t - {}_{t+1}r_{t-1}) = A + B_1(R_t - {}_tr_{t-1}) + 7 \text{ zero values};$$
$$(_{t+2}r_t - {}_{t+2}r_{t-1}) = A + B_1(_{t+1}r_t - {}_{t+1}r_{t-1}) + B_2(R_t - {}_tr_{t-1})$$
$$+ 6 \text{ zero values};$$
$$(_{t+8}r - {}_{t+8}r_{t-1}) = A + B_1(_{t+7}r_t - {}_{t+7}r_{t-1}) + \cdots + B_8(R_t - {}_tr_{t-1})$$
$$+ \text{ no zero values}.$$

Finally, the ninth observation is of the same form as the first. There is only one multiple regression to compute all the weights. In the first observation the values of the variables 2 to 8 are zero. In the second observation the value of variables 3 to 8 are zero; and so on.

Column 3 lists the standard errors of the coefficients.

Column 4 is the weights implied by the γ_i of the error-learning model.

Column 5 divides the difference between the two estimates of the B_i (cols. 2 and 4) by the standard errors of those estimated by the multiple regression (col. 3). An explanation of this procedure is given in the text.

again, using the same procedure as in Table 4-3, the differences between the two estimates are statistically significant in only two out of eight cases. In this table, while we have estimates of the standard errors of the γ_i computed directly from the error-learning model, we have none for the estimates inferred from the set B_i estimated with the multiple regression. As before, it seems plausible to consider that the significance of the difference between the two estimates of γ_i is overstated in column 5.

The return to normalcy model. Perhaps the most widely recognized phenomenon in expectational economics is the so-called return to normalcy mechanism, whereby people expect a series to move in the direction of its normal level. Any extrapolative model that predicts the value of a series with a moving average of past values of the series,

TABLE 4-4. Comparison Between the Coefficients Inferred From the Directly Estimated Weights and the Coefficients Meiselman Estimated With the Error-Learning Model (Durand Data, 1900–54)

Span of Revision (1)	γ_j (Meiselman) (2)	S_{γ_i} (3)	γ_i (Computed) (4)	t-Value of Difference (5)
1	.7029	.0312	.7457	1.3718
2	.5259	.0419	.6109	2.0286
3	.4033	.0466	.5312	2.7446
4	.3262	.0486	.3641	0.7798
5	.2770	.0459	.2864	0.2048
6	.2349	.0414	.2546	0.4758
7	.2370	.0389	.2477	0.2751
8	.2082	.0401	.2209	0.3167

Note: Column 2 lists the coefficients Meiselman estimated with the error-learning model and column 3 their standard errors. Column 4 is computed from the weights estimated with a multiple regression and listed in column 2 of Table 4-3. The formula for this computation is the same as that shown by (12) in the text, except that now the B_i are known and the γ_i are inferred. Column 5 lists the ratio of the difference of the two estimates of the γ_i to a crude estimate of the standard error of this difference. The estimated standard error is too low because it fails to include the standard error of the M_i inferred from the B_i. Therefore, the t-values listed in column 5 are overestimates.

each past value weighted less than one, will produce forecasts that lie between the extremes of the series and its expected value.[18] Since the estimated weights of the extrapolative model introduced in this study are all less than one, the expectations inherent in the term structure conform with this behavior. This behavior alone, however, does not explain the widely observed manifestation of the expected return to normalcy [see 10] with respect to the term structure; that is, the tendency for yield curves to decline when current short-term rates are high and to increase when they are low. Nor is it clear what the meaning is of the normal rate as distinct from the expected and mean rate.

Algebraically, the return to normalcy hypothesis can be described in the following linear form:

$$(13) \qquad {}_{t+2}F_t - {}_{t+1}F_t = K(A_t - {}_NA_t), \quad K < 0,$$

where, $({}_{t+2}F_t - {}_{t+1}F_t)$ is the change expected at t of the target value, in this case the one period spot rate from $t + 1$ to $t + 2$; A_t is the target,

[18] This idea underlies Hicks' coefficient of expectation when that number is less than one [6, p. 205]. The relevance of the normal rate to the Keynesian liquidity preference function is considered in Section V below.

TABLE 4-5. Statistics Computed From the Regression of the Expected Change of Future Spot Rates on the Level of the Current One-Period Spot Rate (Durand Data, Annual Observations, 1900–54)

Span of Forecast (1)	K (2)	t-Value of K (3)	Constant Term (4)	t-Value of Const. Term (5)	R^2 (adj.) (6)
$_{t+1}r_t - R_t$	−.1627	−7.2109	.6437	7.8584	.4904
$_{t+2}r_t - {}_{t+1}r_t$	−.1264	−11.8510	.4909	12.6817	.7246
$_{t+3}r_t - {}_{t+2}r_t$	−.0997	−17.0387	.3878	18.2505	.8452
$_{t+4}r_t - {}_{t+3}r_t$	−.0741	−12.7946	.2948	14.0311	.7543
$_{t+5}r_t - {}_{t+4}r_t$	−.0737	−8.2939	.3071	9.5246	.5612
$_{t+6}r_t - {}_{t+5}r_t$	−.0475	−7.8774	.1964	8.9637	.5353
$_{t+7}r_t - {}_{t+6}r_t$	−.0332	−6.1131	.1382	7.0177	.4070
$_{t+8}r_t - {}_{t+7}r_t$	−.0361	−8.0801	.1511	9.3173	.5481
$_{t+9}r_t - {}_{t+8}r_t$	−.0250	−4.1018	.0981	4.4308	.2299

Note: The regressions were of the following form $_{t+n}r_t - {}_{t+n-1}r_t = Q + k\ _nR_t + V_n$.

or spot rate, at t; $_NA_t$ is the putative normal value of the series, or normal rate, as of period t; and K is the proportion of the deviation expected to be offset; it is negative to reflect the inverse relation between the expected change and the deviation of the current spot rate from the normal rate.[19]

It is easy to confirm the inverse relation between the slopes of the yield curves and the levels of the one-period spot rates statistically, by running regressions analogous to equation (13).[20] The results of these regressions are listed in Table 4-5. In every case the relation

[19] The expected one-period change in the short-term rate is not quite the same as the average slope between adjacent points of a yield curve, which is a locus of long-term rates rather than forward rates. However, the long-term rates are simply averages of the forward rates. The difference between, say, R_3 and R_2 (using simple interest) is

$$R_3 = \frac{2}{6}(r_1 + r_2 + r_3) - \frac{3}{6}(r_1 + r_2) = \frac{2}{6}r_3 - \frac{(r_1 + r_2)}{6}.$$

$r_3 - r_2$ is therefore only approximately equal to the slope of the yield curve. The notation F and A (forecast and actual) in the following analysis is interchangeable with r and R, forward rate and spot rate, respectively, since the present analysis assumes the forward rates are forecasts.

[20] Since by any definition the normal rate will vary slowly, the use of R_t in place of $(R_t - {}_NR_t)$ will not seriously distort the estimated relationship. The empirical relevance of R_N will be shown presently.

is significantly negative and explains a substantial part of the variation of the expected changes in rates. Table 4-5, of course, is merely a statistical confirmation of the widely recognized relationship described above. Since regressing $(_{t+n}F_t - _{t+n-1}F_t)$ on A_t in place of $(A_t - _nA_t)$ implies a constant normal rate, its magnitude can be inferred by dividing column 2 into column 4 of Table 4-5. The constant term (column 4) is equal to K_nA_t, which, when divided by K, will yield an estimate of the normal rate — approximately 4 per cent. At the expense of elegant phrasing, one may interpret this number as the average normal rate.

Since the normal rate, as yet undefined, is not observable, confirmations of the return to normalcy model's application to the term structure typically substitute A_t for $(A_t - _NA_t)$ in (13), or arbitrarily assign some value or limited number of values to $_NA_t$.[21] Our earlier analysis suggests a different method. Let us define $_NA_t$ in (13) as follows:

(14) $$_NA_t = B_2A_{t-1} + B_3A_{t-2} + \cdots + B_NA_{t-N-1}.$$

In other words

(15) $$_{t+2}F_t - _{t+1}F_t = KA_t - K \left(\sum_{i=1}^{N-1} B_{i+1}A_{t-i} \right).$$

On the hypothesis that (14) is true, we can estimate K as the partial regression coefficient in (15). But we already have an estimate of the partial regression coefficient, K. Recall that equations (2) and (5) above defined $_{t+1}F_t$ and $_{t+2}F_t$, respectively. Substituting (2) into (5)[22] we have:

(16) $$_{t+2}F_t = (B_1^2 + B_2)A_t + (B_1B_2 + B_3)A_{t-1}$$
$$+ \sum_{i=3}^{N} (B_1B_i + B_{i+1})A_{t-i-1},$$

[21] See [14], for example. Van Horne adds a variable he calls "deviation of actual from accustomed level" to Meiselman's formulation of the error-learning model. He divides his sample period into two subperiods. "For each . . . period . . . an arithmetic average of the beginning forward-rate levels is calculated. This average may be thought to represent the accustomed level for the period. The deviation is simply the difference of the actual forward-rate level from the accustomed level and is employed as the second independent variable [in the error-learning equation]." [14, p. 349.]

[22] This procedure is directly analogous to the one used earlier to deduce the extrapolative weights from Meiselman's error-learning model coefficients.

and subtracting (2) from (16) we get:

(17) $_{t+2}F_t - {}_{t+1}F_t = [(B_1^2 + B_2) - B_1]A_t$

$$+ \sum_{i=2}^{N} [B_1B_i + B_{i+1}) - B_i]A_{t-i-1}.$$

The first coefficient on the right of (17) is, therefore, our estimate of K. It will clearly be negative when $B_1 > (B_1^2 + B_2)$. But, according to (12), $B_1 = \gamma_1$ and $(B_1^2 + B_2) = \gamma_2$, where the γ's are Meiselman's error-learning coefficients for the first and second spans, respectively. Therefore, K will be negative when $\gamma_i > \gamma_{i+1}$. In other words, the decline in Meiselman's coefficients as the span of forecast increases is algebraically identical to an inverse relationship between the expected change between any two spans of forecast and the deviation of the current spot rate from the normal rate.

To keep the algebra simple we presented the argument in terms of the first two spans of forecasts. The results for greater spans follow in an identical manner. The decline in the γ_i and, therefore, the fact that $B_1 > (B_1^2 + B_2) > (B_1^3 + 2B_1B_2 + B_3)$ and so forth, implies, as the analysis in the previous section showed, that the extrapolative weights, equation (1), observed for the term structure data, decline drastically from the first weight to the second one and then taper off. In Mincer's terminology, the β coefficients decline in a convex fashion.

It is the convex form of the extrapolation function that ties the decline in Meiselman's coefficients γ_i to the return to normalcy mechanism. For this pattern implies that the weight attached to the current value A_t (a weight, it turns out, that is equal in value to the error-learning coefficient for the same span of forecast) declines for successively greater spans of forecast.[23] Therefore, the subtraction of the shorter- from the longer-span forecast (that is, the expected change) is equivalent to subtracting a larger from a smaller weight attached to A_t—hence the inverse relation.

But if the weight attached to A_t declines with increasing span of forecast, the weights attached to the lagged actual values A_{t-i} must rise, if the sum of the weights for each span of forecast is to equal 1. In other words, as the span increases, the market gives increasing weight to the more distant past and distinguishes less between the more

[23] See Mincer's equation (17), p. 92 of this volume.

TABLE 4-6. Weights for Each Span of Forecast for Equation (12) Implied by the Single Set of Weights Estimated for Equation (1) (Durand Data, Annual Observations, 1916–54)

Span of Forecast (1)	A_t (2)	A_{t-1} (3)	A_{t-2} (4)	A_{t-3} (5)	A_{t-4} (6)	A_{t-5} (7)	A_{t-6} (8)	A_{t-7} (9)
1	.7029	.0220	.0133	.0105	.0089	.0080	.0076	.0072
2	.5161	.0288	.0198	.0163	.0143	.0132	.0125	
3	.3916	.0312	.0231	.0197	.0178	.0166		
4	.3065	.0317	.0247	.0219	.0201			
5	.2472	.0316	.0259	.0233				
6	.2054	.0314	.0265					
7	.1758	.0312						
8	.1547							

Note: Looking down any column we see the weight that a particular variable gets for a particular span of forecast. The weights are computed by taking the set shown in Table 4-1, column 5, which is an estimate of the first eight weights for equation (1) regardless of span of forecast. This single set implies a varying set of weights (one set for each span of forecast) attached only to the independent variables that constitute the current and lagged spot rates. For the second span, for example, equation (1) says $_{t+2}F_t = B_{1(t+1}F_1) + B_2 A_t, \ldots B_{1(t+1}F_t)$ is implicitly equal to $B_1^2 A_t + B_1 B_2 A_{t-1}. \ldots$ To get the figures listed above, we add up all the coefficients attached to the particular variable: first A_t, then A_{t-1}, and so forth.

immediate and the more distant past. Long-span forecasts, therefore, take account of the full history of the series at the expense of the current value and, in this sense, approach what can be called a normal rate. Table 4-6 lists the estimated weights attached to the current and past rates for successive spans of forecast. (The table is triangular only because there was insufficient data to make it otherwise.)

TREASURY DATA

To ascertain whether the results described in the preceding sections were peculiar to the Durand data, we applied the same analysis to data read off the yield curves given in the *Treasury Bulletin.*[24]

Annual rates of return on government securities were read off the yield curves at quarterly intervals from March 1945 to December 1964. It was possible to get a continuous series only by restricting ourselves to not more than five-year maturities; each quarterly observa-

[24] Since Neil Wallace [16] had already read off these yield curves for his study, I simply brought forward the data he supplied.

tion includes the annual rates on one-year, two-year — up to five-year maturities; five rates in all. With five rates we are able to run only three spans of revisions in the context of the error-learning model and infer only three weights of the extrapolation equation (1). It was not possible to smooth so few weights to test for a systematic pattern.

Since the maturities along each yield curve are read at annual intervals, the implied forecasts are also annual. As such, they should not be related to the spot rates observed at quarterly intervals but rather to a four-term moving average of these spot rates. The coefficients obtained in this manner imply a system of weights that can be appropriately applied only to lagged spot rates observed annually instead of to the quarterly observations used in this report. Since the available data span is a period of only nineteen years, the use of annual observations is not feasible. In our work with the error-learning model we have therefore taken the annual forecasts as approximations of the quarterly forecasts. (An experiment justifying this procedure is described in a note to Table 4-10.) In the accuracy analysis described in Section VI we are able to relate the forecasts to a moving average of the spot rates.

Tables 4-7 through 4-10 list the results of applying the earlier analysis to the Treasury data.

Table 4-7, similar to Table 4-1, compares the estimated decline in the coefficients of determination in regressions of the error-learning model with the predicted decline in accordance with equation (9).[25]

TABLE 4-7. Comparison Between the Estimated and Predicted Coefficients of Determination for the Regressions of the Error-Learning Model (Treasury Data, 1946–64)

Span	Estimated R^2 (adj)	Predicted R^2 (adj)
1	.6313	.6313
2	.3838	.3438
3	.2013	.2542

Note: See note to Table 4-1.

[25] The decline in the empirically estimated R^2 is slower than in the predicted decline between the first and second span; this is consistent with the presence of a nonforecasting component in the forward rate. There are obviously too few observations (spans of forecast) to draw any conclusions; in fact, the last observation goes the other way.

Table 4-8, similar to Table 4-2, lists the relevant statistics for the error-learning model regressions. Again, the results are similar to those obtained with the Durand data. When the current error, the independent variable in the error-learning model, is replaced by a linear combination of the prior revisions, the coefficients of determination (column 5, Table 4-8, analogous to column 4 of Table 4-2) do not systematically decline. Table 4-9, like Table 4-3, compares the directly estimated extrapolated weights with those deduced from the error-learning model coefficients. Again, the differences do not appear to be significant. Finally, Table 4-10, like Table 4-4, records the comparison between the directly estimated error-learning model

TABLE 4-8. Error-Learning Model Applied to Interest Rates on Treasury Securities, Quarterly, 1946–64

Span (1)	b (2)	T_b (3)	R^2 adj. (4)	R^2 adj (modified model) (5)
1	.6805	11.3004	.63129	.63129
2	.4552	6.8617	.38376	.80800
3	.3923	4.4332	.20133	.61211

The general formula of the regression is $_{t+n}r_t - {}_{t+n}r_{t-1} = a + b(R_t - {}_t r_{t-1}) + \epsilon$. Column 3 is equal to the regression coefficients b divided by their standard errors.

Column 5 lists the coefficients of determination obtained by altering the independent variable to consist of a linear combination of past revisions plus current error. This column corresponds to column 4 of Table 4-2 for the Durand data.

TABLE 4-9. Comparison Between the Weights, B_i, Estimated With a Multiple Regression and Those Computed From the Coefficients of the Error-Learning Model (Treasury Data, Quarterly, 1946–64)

Span (1)	B_i (mult. reg.) (2)	S_{B_i} (3)	B_i (comp. from γ_i) (4)	t-Value of Difference (5)
1	.6835	.0389	.6805	0.0771
2	.0579	.0451	−.0079	1.4590
3	.1006	.0480	.0826	0.0350

Note: See notes to Table 4-3.

TABLE 4-10. Comparison Between the Coefficients, M_i, Estimated With the Error-Learning Model and Those Computed From the Weights Estimated With a Multiple Regression (Treasury Data, Quarterly, 1946–64)

Span (1)	γ_i (err. learn. mod.) (2)	S_{γ_i} (3)	γ_i (comp. from B_i) (4)	t-Value of Difference (5)
1	.6805	.0602	.6835	0.0498
2	.4522	.0663	.5251	1.0543
3	.3923	.0885	.4991	1.2068

Note: See notes to Table 4-3.

Wallace [15, p. 25] has estimated the coefficients for the error-learning model on the basis of annual forecasts. We have calculated from his estimates the extrapolation weights comparable to those listed in column 4 of Table 4-9. In addition, we have estimated these weights directly with a multiple regression and from these estimates calculated the implied set of coefficients for the error-learning model. Each of these estimates are listed in the following table. At the bottom of the table are references to comparable figures for the quarterly model.

Span (1)	γ_i (err. learn. mod.) (2)	B_i (comp. from γ_i) (3)	B_i (mult. reg.) (4)	γ_i (comp. from B_i) (5)
1	.816	.816	.8116	.8116
2	.621	−.045	−.0480	.6107
3	.499	.029	.0822	.5389

Columns 2 and 5 are analogous to columns 2 and 4, respectively, in the above Table 4-10. Columns 3 and 4 are analogous to columns 4 and 2, respectively, of Table 4-9.

coefficients and those computed from the directly estimated extrapolative weights. As in the case of the Durand data, the differences are not statistically significant. The footnote to Table 4-10 records the tests shown in Tables 4-9 and 4-10, but this time treating the forward rates as annual forecasts. For this experiment, the current error is computed as the difference between the forward rate and a four-term average of the quarterly spot rates to ensure comparability. This more rigorous method strengthens the result.

Table 4-11, comparable to Table 4-5, lists the relevant statistics for the regressions of the expected change in rates on the current spot rate. The return to normalcy mechanism, while present, is not quite as important as in the case of the Durand data. The following are the weights attached to the spot rates for consecutive spans of forecast. (The number of weights shown is limited by the availability of relevant data.)

$$_{t+1}F_t = .6835A_t + .0579A_{t-1} + .1005A_{t-2}$$

$$_{t+2}F_t = .5251A_t + .1403A_{t-1}$$

$$_{t+3}F_t = .4991A_t$$

While limited, the data do indicate a similar pattern to the one described for the Durand data.

CONCLUSION

This section considered three separately conceived models, each of which can be described as a method of forecasting, and each of which is consistent with an expectational interpretation of forward rates. The principal conclusion of the analysis is that the three models are one model looked at from three points of view. The general form is the extrapolative model described by equation (1). This extrapolative model implies a relationship between revisions of forecasts and current errors of forecast, referred to as the error-learning model. It also implies a correlation between expected change in target values and the deviation of the current target value from the normal target value. The return to normalcy phenomenon is indicated by the negative sign of the correlation.

It is essential to distinguish between the specification of the model and the parameters that are estimated for it. While the error-learning model is a particular form of the extrapolative model, its application

TABLE 4-11. Statistics Computed From the Regression of the Expected Change of Future Spot Rates on the Level of the Current One-Period Spot Rate (Treasury Data, Quarterly Observations, 1946–64)

Span of Forecast (1)	K (2)	t-Value of K (3)	Constant Term (4)	t-Value of Const. Term (5)	R^2 (adj.) (6)
$_{t+1}r_t - R_t$	−.0286	−1.1820	.4471	7.1058	.0053
$_{t+2}r_t - {}_{t+1}r_t$	−.0653	−4.5013	.3207	8.5183	.2043
$_{t+3}r_t - {}_{t+2}r_t$	−.0622	−5.8360	.2441	8.8380	.3059
$_{t+4}r_t - {}_{t+3}r_t$	−.0422	−2.0732	.1829	3.4603	.0421

Note: See note to Table 4-7.

to a given set of data need not result in declining revision coefficients (as the span of forecast increase) and, therefore, in a particular pattern of implied extrapolative weights. It is a purely empirical result. Similarly, while the return to normalcy hypothesis is consistent with the extrapolative model, because it can be expressed as a linear transformation of it, there is no necessity in practice that K be negative. The model, equation (13), is a transformation of (1), but the hypothesis that K is negative is subject to an empirical test. This test, however, is redundant once the regression coefficients in the error-learning model are observed to decline; for then the extrapolative function is convex, which implies that the expected change will be inversely related to the current value. Certainly, the results in this study strengthen our confidence that the forward rates contain forecasts since the data were shown to be consistent with several reasonable descriptions of forecasting behavior: error-learning, extrapolation, and return to normalcy. The fact that the coefficients of determination in the regressions of the error-learning model decline with span is consistent with the presence of an autonomous component in the forecasts. This constitutes further evidence in favor of a forecasting interpretation of the term structure.

IV. DECOMPOSITION OF FORECASTS

Section III identified an extrapolative component in forward rates and argued that the term includes something more than mechanical projection. The analysis also pointed to the presence of a nonextrapolative component in forward rates. The present section is concerned with empirically isolating the two components of forward rates.

The following section attempts to isolate the extrapolative component by fitting multiple regressions of the forecasts on the current and past spot rates. The computed values of these regressions measure the part of the forecast that is directly or otherwise related to the current and past spot rates; it does *not* measure the market's actual use of a moving average. The residuals of these regressions measure the autonomous component of the forecasts, the component that is not even indirectly related to the historical pattern of the interest rate series. This estimate of the autonomous component holds, of course, only in the event the forward rates consist entirely of forecasts. Any nonforecasting component — i.e., liquidity premia, errors of measurement, the effects of market disequilibria, and so forth — would also fall out in the residuals. After separating the components we measure their contributions to the accuracy of the forecasts.

The next section utilizes two standard business indicators as possible methods of "autonomous" forecasting, providing a different decomposition of forward rates into the extrapolative and autonomous components. This method drops the assumption of statistical independence between extrapolation and autonomous forecasting. It, therefore, reveals the extent to which the previously estimated extrapolative component can subsume what may be autonomous forecasting. This illustration explains the relatively large extrapolative component found earlier. Indeed, if instead of isolating the autonomous component by first exhausting the extrapolative component of the forecasts, this study had first exhausted the autonomous potential and left the extrapolative component to the residual, there is some chance the proportion between induced and autonomous components would be reversed. The difficulty with this alternate method of decomposing the forecasts lies in this study's inability to specify the relevant autonomous variables. As it stands, the method of decomposition actually used is equivalent to an a priori specification of autonomous variables, each of them bereft of their autoregressive components.

EMPIRICAL DECOMPOSITION

To estimate the induced component of the forecasts we regressed the forward rates, one span at a time, on the current and past spot rates:

$$(18) \qquad _{t+n}F_t = b_1 A_t + b_2 A_{t-1} + \cdots + b_8 A_{t-7} + {}_{t+n}E_t,$$

where, $_{t+n}F_t$ = forecasts made at t referring to $t + n$; $_{t+n}E_t$ = residual term; and A_{t-1} = spot rate lagged i periods. To conserve data we arbitrarily stopped the lagging process after seven lags. To more closely approximate a real forecasting situation, one would fit separate regressions not only for each span of forecast but also for each observation, including, for any given point of forecast, only those spot rates occurring prior to or coeval with the given period. This method, however, would severely limit the sample size, since many observations would be used up in the process of fitting the regressions. More-

over, the method entails a separate weighting scheme for each forecast. We chose, therefore, to run the regressions once for the whole
period.

Another method of estimating the extrapolative component is to
use the weights estimated in our work with the error-learning model.
The procedure used, however, has the advantage of estimating an
autonomous component that is *uncorrelated* with the extrapolative
component, a property required in our definition of autonomous forecasting. It is also a procedure that simulates behavior of forecasters
who, by hypothesis, project the past values of the series into the
future. It is true, of course, that this procedure maximizes the hypothesized *extrapolative* content of the forward rate. While this is a sim-
plification of the expectational analysis, we are imposing an understatement of the importance and, possibly, a misspecification of the
nonextrapolative component in the forward rate.

Each of the n regressions of (18) regresses the forward rate of a
given span on the current and past spot rates. The computed value of
(18) $_{t+n}F_t^*$ is our estimate of the induced component of the forecast
and the residual term, $_{t+n}E_t$, of the autonomous component. We computed this regression for two sets of data: the Durand data, with n
varying from 1 to 9, producing nine regressions; and the Treasury
data, with four regressions. The results of these computations are
shown in Table 4-12.

The figures presented in column 2 of the table indicate that the induced component accounts for a large proportion of the variation of
the forecasts. The decline (as the span of forecast increases) of the
coefficients of determination does not by itself imply that the variance
of the autonomous component is increasing with span.[26] In this study's
samples, however, the variance of the autonomous component increases with increases in the span of forecast.

To ascertain the relative effectiveness of either component in forecasting the future spot rates we have run a set of regressions of the
following form:

$$A_{t+n} = B_1(_{t+n}F_t^*) + B_2(_{t+n}E_t) + U_{t+n},$$

[26] The well-known formula relating the three statistics is $S_E^2 = S_F^2(1 - R^2)$, where S_F^2 is
the variance of the dependent variable, the forward rates in this case.

TABLE 4-12. The Per Cent Variation of the Forward Rates That Is Explained by the Current and Lagged Spot Rates (Durand and Treasury Data)

Span of Forecast (1)	R^2 Adjusted (2)	S_E^2 (3)
Durand: Annual Observations, 1916–54		
Year		
1	.9878	.0346
2	.9735	.0601
3	.9597	.0733
4	.9447	.0798
5	.9196	.0868
6	.9091	.0760
7	.8890	.0748
8	.8727	.0647
9	.8015	.0805
Treasury: Quarterly Observations, 1949–64		
Quarter		
1	.9543	.0377
2	.9314	.0615
3	.9177	.0724
4	.8814	.0839

Note: The general form of the regression is:

$$_{t+n}F_t = B_1A_t + B_2A_{t-1} + \cdots + B_8A_{t-7} + E_n.$$

Column 1 is the value of n; column 2, the adjusted coefficients of determination; and column 3, the squared standard errors of the estimate.

where, A_{t+n} = target rate in $t + n$; $_{t+n}F_t^*$ = induced component of forecast made at t of the spot rate (target) in $t + n$; $_{t+n}E_t$ = autonomous component of the same forecast; and U_{t+n} = residual in the regression. The residual, U_{t+n}, is not the error of forecast except in the special case that $B_1 = B_2 = 1$. The results of this regression allow us to apportion the contribution of the induced and autonomous components of the forecasts to the total accuracy of the forecasts. In particular, we can test the null hypothesis that the autonomous component contributes nothing to the accuracy of the forecasts. In Table 4-13, we show the relevant results of these regressions for the Durand data and the Treasury data.

In the case of the Treasury data, the autonomous component effectively adds to the forecasting accuracy of the induced component in three of the four spans of forecast. Except for the third span the importance of the autonomous component to the accuracy of the forecast increases with span; although it would be rash to generalize this outcome.

The Durand data, however, tell a different story. In column 3 of Table 4-13 we observe a significant relation, aside from the first two spans of forecast, between the autonomous component and the future spot rates, but the relation is inverse. Not only does the autonomous component not contribute to the accuracy of the forecast, it in fact detracts from it.

The reason for this perverse result is not at all clear. It is one thing to show that a component of the forecast does a bad job in the sense that it is unrelated to the target. In such a case we could perhaps pass it off as noise in the data or some other euphemism for our ignorance. But when this component is *systematically* perverse, when it varies inversely with the target, we should at least try to explain it. If the autonomous component consisted entirely or in part of a liquidity premium, would that fact explain its behavior? Why would a liquidity premium be related to a future spot rate except in so far as this spot rate were related to the current spot rate? If it were related to future spot rates, for reasons other than the relation between future and current spot rates, some form of forecasting would be implied. But the liquidity premium component of forward rates is isolated precisely because it is a nonforecasting component. Let us say, then, a liquidity premium is related to future spot rates because both it and future spot rates are related to current spot rates. But recall that the autonomous component is isolated by regressing the forward rates on the current and past spot rates, where the residuals of this regression are the estimates of the autonomous component. By the arithmetic of least squares, the residual term in the regression is necessarily uncorrelated with each of the independent variables, including the current spot rate. The liquidity premium cannot, therefore, be linearly related to the current spot rate and at the same time be included in the autonomous

TABLE 4-13. Selected Statistics From the Regression of the Future Spot Rates on the Induced and Autonomous Components of the Forecasts (Durand and Treasury Data)

Span of Forecast (1)	Partial Correl. Coef. Squared of $_{t+n}F_t^*$ (2)	t-Value of B $_{t+n}F_t^*$ (3)	Partial Correl. Coef. Squared of $_{t+n}E_t$ (4)	t-Value of B $_{t+n}E_t$ (5)	R^2 (adj.) (6)
		Durand: Annually, 1916–54			
Year					
1	.8582	14.3426	.0305	−1.0342	.8505
2	.7374	9.7700	.0746	−1.6556	.7277
3	.6362	7.7108	.1340	−2.2931	.6353
4	.5264	6.1469	.1713	−2.6510	.5432
5	.4563	5.3417	.1810	−2.7419	.4861
6	.3730	4.4973	.2011	−2.9248	.4266
7	.2912	3.7368	.1930	−2.8514	.3582
8	.2484	3.3519	.2014	−2.9285	.3310
9	.2003	2.9178	.2280	−3.1688	.3150
		Treasury: Quarterly, 1949–64 [a]			
Quarter					
1	.7898	13.7063	.0862	2.1715	.7856
2	.3165	4.8115	.0972	2.3195	.3378
3	.4555	6.4676	.0511	1.6410	.4499
4	.4143	5.9483	.1377	2.8256	.4431

Note: The general form of the regression is that shown in the equation on p. 142.
[a] The forecast components were related to a four-term moving average of the quarterly spot rates to make the forecasts and the actuals comparable.

component.[27] For these reasons, the liquidity premium cannot be used in any simple way to explain the perverse behavior of the autonomous component. To the extent that the liquidity premium is a linear function of the current spot rates, it will be included in the induced component and, perhaps for that reason, contribute to the bias in the forecasts that we will describe later.

[27] For a discussion of the view that liquidity premia are linearly related to the current spot rates, see Kessel [8, p. 26].

A possible explanation for the unusual result lies in the sharp decline in rates in the 1930's. The greater the span of forecast, the more effect this decline will have on the results, since there will be more observations in which a forecast made in the 1920's is related to a spot rate in the 1930's. For example, in the case of a one-span forecast, there is a sharp difference between the forecast made in 1929 and the spot prevailing in 1930, while, in the case of a nine-span forecast, the forecasts made from 1921 through 1929 will be matched with spot rates that are unusually low. To the extent that the reversion to normalcy hypothesis is working, the forecasts will move in the same direction though not to the same extent as future spot rates. Since, as we have shown, this hypothesis works through the induced component, only the autonomous component displays the perverse result.

ESTIMATING AUTONOMOUS INDICATORS IN FORWARD RATES

There are many indicators of economic activity that largely share a common historical process, particularly with the interest rate series. In all likelihood, a substantial part of the relationship between the forecasts and the indicators stems from this common historical process. Hence, if we view the indicators as variables used in autonomous forecasting, we must drop the notion of independence between extrapolation and autonomous components. This method of decomposition of forecasts can partition the observed relationship between the forecasts, that is, the forward rates, and the indicators into the part due to a shared historical process and the part that is autonomous.

The coefficients of determination of the forward rates inferred from the Treasury data regressed by span of forecast on the Federal Reserve Board's Index of Industrial Production are .7159, .7806, .8107, and .8176, respectively, for the first four spans of forecast.

To accomplish the partition we have run a set of multiple regressions for each of the four spans of forecast. The forecasts are regressed on their induced component and on the Index of Industrial Production. In other words, we have estimated the following regressions:

$$(19) \qquad\qquad {}_{t+n}F_t = B_1({}_{t+n}F_t^*) + B_2 I + u_n,$$

where ${}_{t+n}F_t^*$ is the column of computed values of equation (18), and I is the Index of Industrial Production. The object is to determine the net contribution of either independent variable (given the other) to the explained variation of $_{t+n}F_t$. Table 4-14 gives the relevant statistics for this experiment.

Comparing columns 2 and 4 of this table we conclude that the relation between the Index of Industrial Production and the forecasts of future rates stems largely from the common historical pattern in the variation of the spot rates and the index. There is, however, a net relation between the index and the forecasts after allowing for the common historical relationship, and this net relation, as seen in column 4, grows with increases in the span of forecast.

The squared partial correlation coefficients between $_{t+n}F_t$ and $_{t+n}F_t^*$, given I, do not reveal the full importance of the induced component in the total forecasts. The figures in column 2 of Table 4-14 are smaller, and necessarily not larger, than the coefficients of determination between $_{t+n}F_t$ and $_{t+n}F_t^*$ listed in column 2 of Table 4-12. The partials associated with $_{t+n}F_t^*$ reveal the net explanatory power of the induced component, given that the common variation between $_{t+n}F_t$ and I is already accounted for. The extent to which I shares in the common variation of $_{t+n}F_t$ and $_{t+n}F_t^*$ is, in effect, deducted from the net contribution of $_{t+n}F_t^*$. This point illustrates an important characteristic of our method of partitioning the forecasts into the induced and autonomous components. Even though the induced component appears to explain a large part of the variation of the forecasts, it may not reveal the extent of the market's reliance on past rates, whether

TABLE 4-14. Regression of Forward Rates on Estimated Induced Component and Index of Industrial Production (Treasury Data, Quarterly, 1949–64)

Span of Forecast (quarters) (1)	Squared Partial Correl. Coef. of F^* (2)	t-Value of Reg. Coef. Attached to F^* (3)	Squared Partial Correl. Coef. of I (4)	t-Value of Reg. Coef. Attached to I (5)	Gross Coef. of Determination (adj.) (6)
1	.8866	21.8365	.0078	.6909	.9667
2	.8075	15.9938	.1049	2.6743	.9564
3	.7343	12.9808	.1947	3.8404	.9480
4	.4705	7.3615	.2394	4.3817	.9003

Note: This table is based on equation (19) in the text.

by extrapolation or other autoregressive models, in making its forecasts. The indicator varies over time in relation to the business cycle in a manner similar to that of the interest rates. Through this common relation, part of the correlation between the forward rates and the indicator will show up in the relation between the forward rates and the past spot rates.

The partials in column 4 of Table 4-14 tell a less ambiguous story. Here we see the influence of the index on the forecasts that is independent of the variation of the past spot rates. The crucial difference between the two sets of partials that underlies the apparent asymmetry of our method resides in the relative ease with which we and others can more or less exhaust the induced variation of the forecasts compared with the difficulty of exhausting the autonomous variation.[28]

To say that the Index of Industrial Production is related to the autonomous component of the forecast does not imply that investors actually consulted this particular indicator. By eliminating variables not related to the forecasts we can reduce the set of possible indicators; but the proper selection among the set of variables that cannot be excluded is not a statistical problem.

We experimented with one other indicator we considered likely to influence the forecasts of future spot rates, namely, an index of industrial stock prices.[29] As before, we regressed the forecasts on their induced component and the indicator. The coefficients of determination of the forecasts regressed on the Index of Industrial Stock Prices are, respectively, .7861, .8595, .8892, and .8889 for the first four spans of forecast. The Index of Industrial Stock Prices is related somewhat more to the forecasts than was the Index of Industrial Production. For the same purpose as before we have run regressions similar to (19), replacing the Index of Industrial Production with the Index of Industrial Stock Prices. The results are shown in Table 4-15.

---

[28] We say more or less because we had to arbitrarily limit the number of lags in the computation of the induced component to seven; we have a limited sample, and we have fit the entire period instead of only the spot rates prevailing in the period prior to the forecast period.

[29] We did not experiment with different indexes for this purpose (or with any other variables) but settled on the Dow Jones Index of Industrial Stock Prices recorded in the *Survey of Current Business*. Whether one indicator is more correlated with the forecasts than another is not crucial in the present context, since our main purpose in this section is to illustrate empirically the proposition that the decomposition of forecasts is a method of analysing market behavior, not a literal description of it.

TABLE 4-15. Regression of Forward Rates on Estimated Induced Component and Index of Industrial Stock Prices (Treasury Data, Quarterly, 1949–64)

Span of Forecast (quarters) (1)	Squared Partial Correl. Coef. of F^* (2)	t-Value of Reg. Coef. Attached to F^* (3)	Squared Partial Correl. Coef. of S (4)	t-Value of Reg. Coef. Attached to S (5)	Gross Coef. of Determination (adj.) (6)
1	.8532	18.8278	.0327	1.4359	.9674
2	.7215	12.5709	.1704	3.5399	.9596
3	.5921	9.4116	.2770	4.8339	.9533
4	.2356	4.3359	.3309	5.4918	.9123

Note: See equation (19) for the general regression underlying this table.

When both indicators are included in the regression as well as the induced component of the forecasts, with the forward rates again serving as the dependent variable, the results are similar to those shown for the indicators taken separately. In Table 4-16, we see that the presence of stock prices in the regression reduces the net contribution of the Index of Industrial Production. The adjusted coefficients of determination shown in Table 4-16 are, in fact, lower than those for

TABLE 4-16. Regression of Forward Rates on Estimated Induced Component, Index of Industrial Production, and Index of Industrial Stock Prices (Treasury Data, Quarterly, 1949–64)

Span of Forecast (quarters) (1)	Squared Partial Correl. Coef. of F^* (2)	t-Value of Reg. Coef. Attached to F^* (3)	Squared Partial Correl. Coef. of S (4)	t-Value of Reg. Coef. Attached to S (5)	Squared Partial Correl. Coef. of I (6)	t-Value of Reg. Coef. Attached to S (7)	Gross Coef. of Determination (adj.) (8)
1	.8545	18.7676	.0343	1.4604	.0094	−.7561	.9673
2	.7211	12.4550	.0733	2.1792	.0002	.1120	.9589
3	.5929	9.3479	.1091	2.7104	.0077	.6830	.9529
4	.2359	4.3044	.1345	3.0541	.0163	.9960	.9122

Note: The general regression underlying this table is as follows:
$$_{t+n}F_t = B_1(_{t+n}F_t^*) + B_2 S + B_3 I + V.$$

the simpler regression in Table 4-15. This experiment concludes the analysis of the relationship between the indicators of economic activity and the decomposition of forecasts.[30]

V. NONFORECASTING COMPONENTS OF FORWARD RATES

LIQUIDITY PREFERENCE

The expression "liquidity preference" appears in the interest rate literature in two distinct contexts, a fact that has led to a certain amount of confusion. One concept of liquidity preference describes the liquidity premium as a component of the forward rates that is added to the expected rate in accordance with the degree of uncertainty with which the expectation is held. The less certain the expectation, the higher the premium. Since the prices of longer-term securities typically vary more than those of shorter maturities, the premium would ordinarily be higher on longer maturities; the greater variation of prices implies a greater variation in the possible holding period yields and, therefore, a greater uncertainty attached to any particular yield. This analysis is applicable, although with varying degrees of importance, whether the security is held to maturity (in which case there is no selling price variation) or is sold in advance of maturity. Even when the security is held to maturity, its value will fluctuate with the price, and the measured wealth of its holder along with it. In many situations — in principle, in all situations — a decline in measured or paper wealth is as significant as a decline in realized or cash equivalent wealth. Where it is not, the price fluctuations are less important. Since long-term securities provide stable income streams and obviate the expense of continual reinvestment, they are preferable to short-term securities in cases in which unrealized capital changes are not important. A positive liquidity premium implies that on balance the reverse is true. Since there are arguments for and against the likelihood of a liquidity premium, its presence is ultimately an empirical question.

In Keynesian literature, the term "liquidity preference" means

[30] For an interesting analysis of the relationship between economic indicators and the forward rates see Wendel [17].

something else. There, the liquidity preference function relates the demand for money to the *level,* not the dispersion, of interest rates. According to Keynesian theory, when this level is low relative to some normal or typical rate, investors expect future rates to be higher, and vice versa. If the interest rate were regarded simply as the opportunity cost of holding money, implying a negatively inclined demand curve for money (as a function of the interest rate), the introduction of this expectational theory justifies hypotheses about its shape [13]. Liquidity preference in this context refers to *expectations* of a change in the level of rates, not to the *risk* of a change in rates. For a given expectation, the liquidity premium due to risk will vary with the certainty with which the expectation is held. When, for example, the current rate is at its normal level, and therefore, according to the expectational theory under review, rates are not expected to change, liquidity premia may still exist and may differ in accordance with the *risk* that the expectation of no change will prove to be wrong. The determinants of this risk (and, therefore, of the liquidity premia) are difficult to specify; but certainly the dispersion of rates in the near past will be a factor in the expected dispersion of future rates.[31]

This notion of an expected return to normalcy is the basis for the controversy some years back over the so-called liquidity trap. In principle, a liquidity trap exists when the level of rates falls so far below normal that investors, expecting an ultimate rise in rates, and

---

[31] It may be that this dispersion is itself a function of the level of rates, a fact that would empirically obscure the distinction between the two concepts of liquidity preference. But, if there is such a relation, it should hold not for the *arithmetic* difference between the level of the current rate and the mean level but for the *absolute* difference, since it is the probability of a turn, whether up or down, that justifies the relation. Therefore, to predict liquidity premia with knowledge of the level of rates alone requires an additional hypothesis that investors' concern over dispersion is asymmetrical. When the level of rates is high and expected to fall, the investor risks a double beating: He accepts a lower rate on longer term securities, whose prices will fall drastically in the event future rates rise instead of fall. This situation could produce a large liquidity premium. However, when the level of the current rate is low and expected to rise, the investor requires a higher rate on longer-term securities in compensation for the expected rise in rates and capital loss. In the event he is wrong and rates actually fall further he is twice blessed — he obtains the higher initial yield plus the unexpected capital gain. Since the investor, in effect, hopes he is wrong, he does not require a liquidity premium to cover this possibility. This asymmetry may account for the often hypothesized positive relation between liquidity premia and the level of rates. On this point see Cagan [1].

therefore decline in prices, are unwilling to hold bonds out of fear that the expected capital loss will wipe out any income they earned from holding bonds instead of money. At this level of rates, the demand for money is said to be infinite. The use of the term "liquidity" in this context implies market forecasting of future rates. In the case of the liquidity trap, the term "liquidity" refers to the investor's preference for holding money rather than bonds because the *expected return* from holding bonds (consisting of interest payment plus the difference between the buying and expected selling prices of the bonds) is too low to compensate him for losing the convenience of storing his wealth in the form of money. Although originally expressed in terms of bonds and money, the concept of liquidity preference can be generalized to mean equalization of *expected* rates of return on all assets. When the level of rates is high, for example, investors, expecting rates to fall (and therefore prices to rise), will accept a lower nominal yield on longer-term securities in expectation of a favorable capital change when the rates fall. This situation is embodied in a declining yield curve. At the same time that the declining yield curve implies the market's forecast of lower rates, it can be said to reflect the market's attempt to equalize expected yields on different maturities. In either case, the shape of the yield curve is a measure of expectations.

Recent writers on the term structure have been aware of the distinction between the two concepts. Wendel [17], for example, distinguishes "regressive forecasting" from "liquidity-hedging," his terms for the expected return to normalcy and the attempt to avoid the dispersion of possible yields around the expected yield, respectively. Kessel [7] ingeniously used the distinction to explain the so-called humped yield curve. After demonstrating to his satisfaction [32] that liquidity premia are positively related to the level of one-period spot rates, Kessel argued that these premia dominate the short part of the yield curve. When the level of rates is high relative to some normal level, however,

[32] According to Kessel, if the bill rate is taken as compensation for eschewing the services of money, then liquidity premia may be viewed as compensation for eschewing the services of money substitutes. Since a three-week bill is closer to a two-week bill than a two-week bill is to money, the premium for holding a three-week bill instead of a two-week bill is less than the premium for holding a two-week bill instead of money. To complete the analogy, Kessel reasoned that liquidity premia should rise with interest rates: The cost of holding two- instead of three-week bills should rise with the cost of holding money instead of two-week bills [8, pp. 25 ff].

future rates are expected to revert toward their normal level, causing the yield curve to decline. This effect, according to Kessel, is most apparent beyond the short part of the curve. The resulting yield curve when the level of rates is high has the familiar humped shape, similar in appearance to a right-skewed frequency distribution. Thus, Kessel's explanation of the humped yield curve clearly requires both a liquidity premium positively related to the level of rates and a convex distribution of extrapolative weights.

ERRORS OF MEASUREMENT

There is little question but that the smoothing of the term structure data into yield curves enhances the autoregressiveness of the data. The use of the raw data in place of readings from the yield curves would result in lower coefficients of determination in the extrapolative regressions, as well as in the error-learning model regressions. Apart from the closeness of fit, the question remains whether the smoothing of data is also responsible for the convex pattern of weights observed earlier and, therefore, for the conclusions that were based on this pattern of weights.

One conclusion of the earlier analysis was that the parameters observed in connection with any one of the three autoregressive models implied the parameters of the other two. It is enough, therefore, to show that the parameters of at least one of the models do not depend on the smoothing of the data in order to release the entire analysis from this constraint.

A study of the actual yield curves reveals that, regardless how faithful the yield curves are to the raw data, there is no tendency for them to alter the direction of rates along a given curve. In October 1959, for example, the level of government rates was relatively high, and the yield curve, as well as the yields themselves, declined with maturity; in April 1963 the level of rates was relatively low, and both the curve and the yields inclined.[33] The same idea materializes in the case of Durand's data [4, "Basic Charts"]. This characteristic of the data motivated the expected return to normalcy model and constitutes evidence of the appropriateness of the model.

Since the inverse relationship between the slope of the yield curve

---

[33] *Treasury Bulletin,* December 1959, p. 54, and June 1963, p. 71, respectively.

and the level of rates is characteristic of the raw data rather than an artifact of the yield curves, the test of the expected return to normalcy model is sound. While the use of the raw data would result in poorer fits and less stable coefficients, it could not abrogate the inverse relationship, which is observable even without regression analysis. The main results of this study, therefore, do not depend on the smoothing of the data. In the case of the Durand data, however, the importance of the extrapolative component is likely to be overstated.

VI. ACCURACY OF THE FORECASTS

THE MEAN SQUARE ERRORS

Several commentators have rejected the expectations hypothesis on the grounds it was implausible for market forecasts to be so bad for so long ([5] and [3]). Meiselman, however, regarded the plausibility criterion as irrelevant, alleging that the expectations hypothesis asserts only that the market *attempts* to forecast future rates, not that it is successful. Between these extremes are those writers who regard the bad forecasting record implied by the term structure as an indication that expectations, while perhaps an important determinant of the term structure, is not the only relevant factor. Within this group, Kessel emphasized the importance of liquidity premia, while Wendel proposed some combination of liquidity preference and hedging.

The presence of liquidity premia would cause an upward bias in the forecasts. However, it does not follow that an upward bias implies the presence of liquidity premia, since the forecasts themselves may be biased. Whatever the cause of the commonly observed tendency for long-term rates to exceed short-term rates, it is useful to separate this effect from the purely random error of forecast. Even when non-forecasting components are not an issue, for example, when the data are explicit forecasts, isolation of a bias in prior forecasts may suggest adjustments of current forecasts to offset the bias. Therefore, instead of simply reporting the mean square error of forecasts, we shall separate the contributions to the error of the bias and the random term.

The mean square error of forecasts, $M = E(A_i - F_i)^2$, can be broken down into the mean error squared $(\bar{A} - \bar{F})^2$, and the mean of the squared deviations of the individual errors from the mean error, or the variance of the errors, $E[(A_i - F_i) - (\bar{A} - \bar{F})]^2$. The purpose of this decomposition is to allow us to distinguish between the systematic errors of forecast, or the bias, and the random errors.[34] A perfect correlation between the actuals and forecasts implies the absence of a random error but does not preclude a consistent bias in the forecasts. The random error, for example, would be unaffected by the existence of a constant liquidity premium that caused the forward rate to consistently overstate the true forecast. In the case where the correlation coefficient was 1, the mean square error of forecast would be zero only in the case where $a = 0$ and $b = 1$ in the regression:

$$(20) \qquad A_{t+n} = a + b(_{t+n}F_t) + u.$$

Since $a = \bar{A} - b\bar{F}$, a would equal the mean bias only in the case where $b = 1$. There are, therefore, two sources of bias: mean bias and bias in the slope, the remaining error being random. It is useful, for this reason, to further decompose the mean square error.

$$(21) \quad M = E(A_i - F_i)^2 = (\bar{A} - \bar{F})^2 + (1 - b_{AF})^2 S_F^2 + (1 - r_{AF}^2)S_A^2,$$

where b is the regression coefficient in (18) and r^2 the coefficient of determination. Following Mincer and Zarnowitz, we combine the first two terms on the right into U_F and call the residual term M_F^1, so that $M_F = U_F + M_F^1$. If the combined term, U_F, is not significantly different from zero, it is not necessary to show the two components of error separately. Since the significance of both the constant term and the regression coefficient of (20) enters into the significance of U_F, it is desirable to test the two terms together.[35]

To evaluate the effectiveness of the forecast it is useful to establish as a criterion a hypothetical set of forecasts that can be generated mechanically, and the effectiveness of which varies with the ease of forecasting any particular series. In general, the ease in forecasting a series is a function not only of the variance of the series but also of the degree of autocorrelation in the series. The more systematically the series varies over time the easier it is to forecast, for reasons that should be apparent from our earlier analysis. However, a series whose

[34] See Jacob Mincer and Victor Zarnowitz, "The Evaluation of Economic Forecasts," and the references therein, in Chapter 1 of this volume.

[35] The formula for this test is given in [7, p. 24].

variation is random with respect to time, unless its range of movement or its variance is very small, is difficult to forecast (assuming no knowledge about the relation between this series and other series).

Many researchers have used the so-called naive models to generate their hypothetical or "benchmark" forecasts. The naive models are simply a class of moving averages relating the current value of some series X to its own lagged values, or

$$(22) \qquad\qquad X_t = \sum_{i=1}^{n} B_i X_{t-i}.$$

The two most common variants of these models are the "no change" and the "same change" models. In the former, B_1 is set to 1 and B_i to 0 for $i > 1$. In the latter, $B_i = 2$, $B_2 = -1$, and $B_i = 0$ for $i > 2$. Other, more complicated, systems of weights have been used. But these methods have in common the fact that the B_i coefficients are chosen without regard to achieving the maximum fit between X_t and ΣX_{t-i}. Since the degree of fit is, in this context, the measure of the effectiveness of the hypothetical forecasts, these methods do not provide the strongest criterion possible for evaluating them.[36]

For reasons analogous to those used to support our method of estimating the induced component of the forecast, an estimation form is required that will exhaust the extrapolative potential of the data. The naive model must provide the sternest criterion possible in evaluating the forecast. To aim for less is to tie the conclusion to the particular naive model chosen and therefore to invite questions of its importance. No set of a priori weights will guarantee the best extrapolation.

In principle, an optimal extrapolation depends on the structure of the series and must be estimated from the data.[37] In practice, this is difficult to accomplish but, as an approximation, we fit one regression for the whole period and use the (squared) standard error of the estimate as the measure of the mean square error of forecast. By regressing the forward rates on the appropriate target values within the sample period for which the benchmark was computed, we computed comparable measures of the errors of forecast of the forward rates and of the

---

[36] While we have no desire to magnify this fine point, it is a fact that some researchers test their models against excessively weak naive models and congratulate themselves unduly on their success.

[37] See Mincer and Zarnowitz, p. 32 ff of this volume.

optimal benchmark. We can say optimal benchmark because the method equates the squared standard error of the estimate, necessarily a minimum, with the mean square error of forecast.

To compute this benchmark we ran, for each span of forecast n, the following multiple regression

$$(23) \qquad A_{t+n} = B_1 A_t + B_2 A_{t-1} + \cdots + B_{i+1} A_{t-i} + W_n,$$

where A_{t+n} is the spot rate at $t + n$ and W_n a random term. Equation (23) measures the maximum amount of the variation of the spot rate that it is possible to explain with the variation of its own lagged values.[38]

We computed the summary statistics M_F, U_F, and M_F^1, described earlier, for both the forward rates and the hypothetical forecasts based on the naive model. We then took ratios of the former statistics to the latter to determine the forecasting effectiveness of the forward rates relative to the moving average forecasts. The presumption is that one forecaster, with knowledge of current and past economic activity and of the relations among the available economic time series, should forecast better than another forecaster with knowledge only of the past behavior of the series being forecast. Table 4-17 shows the relevant results of the simple regressions of the actual values (that is, the forecast targets) on the relevant forward rates for the Durand and the Treasury data. The general form of the regressions is shown in equation (20) above. Table 4-18 decomposes the errors of forecast into three components, as described in equation (21), and relates the components to those of the hypothetical forecasts. If the forward rate had forecast as well as the hypothetical forecasts, the figures in column (8) of Table 4-18 would center on unity. In the case of the Durand data, the ratios are between 1.5 and 2.0; although the corresponding figures for the Treasury data are not far from unity. Comparing columns (7) and (8), especially for the Treasury data of Table 4-18, one can see the extent to which the bias obscures the relation between the forecasts and the future rates. In conclusion, while the forecasts

---

[38] One should take account of the stringency of this criterion in evaluating the empirical results below. However, given the low level of accuracy of the autonomous component of the forecast, described above, it is unlikely the conclusion of the present analysis would change with respect to the Durand data, although perhaps it would with respect to the Treasury data, if a weaker naive model were used.

TABLE 4-17. Relation Between Forecasts and Future Spot Rates

Span of Forecast (1)	b_{AF} (2)	t-Value (b_{AF}) (3)	Intercept (4)	R^2 (adj.) (5)	S_u^2 (6)
		Durand: Annually, 1916–54			
1	1.0397	13.6119	−.4013	.8328	.6170
2	1.0456	8.6671	−.6383	.6670	1.2318
3	1.0318	6.3368	−.7592	.5141	1.7930
4	.8811	4.7555	−.7523	.3688	2.3291
5	.9938	3.8369	−.9016	.2705	2.6919
6	.9473	3.0377	−.8118	.1819	3.0188
7	.8608	2.3785	−.5509	.1118	3.2775
8	.8330	1.9541	−.5341	.0709	3.4287
9	.6167	1.2561	.2368	.0154	3.6332
		Treasury: Quarterly, 1949–64			
1	.8603	13.9589	.0666	.7885	.1627
2	.5467	5.2188	1.0583	.3353	.5114
3	.6416	6.7367	.8176	.4605	.4150
4	.7056	6.5607	.6960	.4471	.4253

Note: Each of the regressions is of the following form: $A_{t+n} = a + b_{(t+n}F_t) + u_n$, $n = 1, 9$.

implied by the Durand data clearly do not evince effective forecasting ability, those implied by the Treasury data do much better, and they deteriorate less rapidly than the naive model.

FORECASTING AND THE TERM STRUCTURE OF INTEREST RATES

This study has explored the importance of extrapolative forecasting as a determinant of the term structure. It has shown not only that an extrapolative model accounts for a large part of the variation of the forward rates but that this model implies a method of making forecasts that is both plausible and consistent with other proposed models. If extrapolation of past spot rates were in fact the *only* method the market used to forecast future rates, then, at best, its forecasts would equal the performance of the naive model. (In this context recall that the naive model used in this study is optimal in view of the method used to evaluate the forecasts.) While the Treasury data reveal some

TABLE 4-18. Comparison Between the Errors of Forecast Due to the Forward Rate Forecasts and the Moving Average Forecasts (Durand Data, Annual Observations, 1916–54)

Span of Fore-cast (1)	$(\bar{A} - \bar{F})^2$ (2)	$(1 - b_{AF})^2 \, S_F^2$ (3)	M_F^1 $(1 - r_{AF}^2)S_A^2$ (4)	M_F (cols. 2 + 3 + 4) (5)	M_A^* (6)	RM (7)	RM^1 (8)
			Durand: Annually, 1916–54				
1	.0626	−.0152	.6170	.6644	.3935	1.6884	1.5679
2	.2087	−.0372	1.2318	1.4033	.8131	1.7258	1.5115
3	.3765	−.0467	1.7930	2.1228	1.1297	1.8790	1.5871
4	.5488	−.0645	2.3291	2.8134	1.5182	1.8531	1.5341
5	.7590	−.0695	2.6919	3.3814	1.7190	1.9670	1.5659
6	.9356	−.0953	3.0188	3.8591	1.8729	2.0604	1.6118
7	1.0396	−.0883	3.2775	4.2288	1.9904	2.1245	1.6466
8	1.1661	−.0747	3.4287	4.5201	1.8147	2.4908	1.8894
9	1.2510	−.0407	3.6332	4.8435	1.8151	2.6684	2.0016
			Treasury: Quarterly, 1949–64				
1	.1341	−.1247	.1627	.1721	.1499	1.1481	1.0854
2	.1009	.0605	.5114	.6728	.4779	1.4078	1.0701
3	.0574	.0379	.4150	.5103	.4013	1.2716	1.0341
4	.0157	.0286	.4253	.4696	.4427	1.0607	0.9607

Note: Columns 2 through 5 are based on equation (19). See text for explanation of symbols. Column 6 is computed from equation (21), where $A_{t+n} = A_{t+n}^* + W_n$. Since there is no bias in the moving average, $M = M^1$.

autonomous forecasting, its extent is too small to compensate for the market's inability to take maximum advantage of the extrapolation. If it is true that extrapolation is the dominant method of forecasting, then the ratios in column 8 of Table 4-18, again referring to the Treasury data, are actually surprisingly close to unity. The fact that the performance of the forward rates improves relative to the naive model as span increases, and actually exceeds the naive model in the fourth span, is consistent with the evidence in Table 4-12, which shows that the importance of the autonomous component increases with span.

Nevertheless, the skimpy evidence of autonomous forecasting is disappointing to those who support a simple expectations hypothesis. It is not possible to ascertain whether the ineffectiveness of the autonomous component is due to a varying liquidity premium, in the absence of a method of accounting separately for the variation of this component.

Another possible source of trouble lies in the greater vulnerability of the forward rates to errors of measuring the long-term rates as the maturity of the latter increases.[39] Such an effect can be visualized as follows: Assume simple interest. Say the one-period spot rate is 3.00 and the two-period, long-term rate 3.01; the implied forward rate is $2(3.01) - 3.00 = 3.02$. Now consider the same numbers for higher maturities: The nine-period long-term rate is 3.00 and the ten-period long-term rate 3.01. In this case, the implied forward rate is $10(3.01) - 9(3.00)$ or 3.10. If either of the two rates in each comparison included a measurement error of one basis point, it would throw off the ten-span forward rate by ten points, but the two-period rate by only two points. We have no way of evaluating the importance of this effect.

In the case of the Durand data, however, the markedly inferior performance of the forward rates compared with that of the naive model is troublesome. The perverse behavior of the autonomous component explains part of this result, but there still remains the inability to make maximum use of the extrapolative potential.

The persistent bias in the forward rate forecasts is another matter. This study has not isolated the source of this bias. There is an undeniable tendency for yield curves to incline; an undeniable tendency for longer maturities to yield more than shorter maturities. Kessel persuasively argues that the source of this bias lies in the presence of a liquidity premium. Since interest rates for most of the postwar period have been low relative to historic levels, the continuing expectation that they would rise also imparts a bias to the forecasts. Whatever the source of the bias, there is little question but that a method of evaluating the forecasts that failed to separate the bias from the random error would cast a shadow over the relevance of forecasting in the determination of the term structure.

VII. SUMMARY AND CONCLUSIONS

This report is an extension of recent attempts to evaluate the hypothesis that yield differentials of securities, differing only by their term to maturity, are determined by market forecasts of future spot rates of

---

[39] This point was made by Van Horne [15].

interest. Since its inception, this hypothesis has appealed to the theorist's urge to summarize in a simple way the vagaries of many groups acting from diverse motives over the whole range of securities. Opponents of the hypothesis, aside from those who argue that the markets for different maturities are independent of each other, think it implausible to suppose that investors make some point estimate of a short-period rate expected to prevail several years later. This criticism, however, is based on an invalid analogy between a market and an individual. The market, like a mean, is an abstraction that may differ from any of the elements participating in it. Horizons differ among the many investor groups, and few may extend over a long period. But the fact remains that yields on nine-year and ten-year securities differ by varying amounts that are unlikely to be explained by variations in the supply of securities. These variations in the yield curve will inspire speculative action whenever their implied forward rates are unusual. The process of ensuring reasonable forward rates is arbitrage rather than speculation, and it lends a certain smoothness to the term structure. The practice of arbitraging along the yield curve implies no unusual horizon, although some investors will look further than others and define reasonableness in a narrower range, at which point arbitrage shades into speculation. There is no great risk in eliminating an implied negative forward rate, but exchanges along the yield curve become more and more speculative as investors attempt to replace one reasonable forward rate with another. How far the observed forward rate must differ from the expected rate before it inspires arbitrage will differ for different investors: Some, obviously, never arbitrage along the yield curve; others, only when the implied forward rates are, perhaps, negative; others will come in for fine adjustments. There is in this process nothing to offend one's sense of reality, even if the more abstract analysis temporarily ignores the market mechanism.

At some point there may be two alternative investments available — a security with n periods left to maturity and one with $n + 1$. The yield differential of the longer security depends on what one-period yield is *expected* in the $(n + 1)$st period. A rise in the one-period yield in $n + 1$ would drive down the price on the longer security at the start of period $n + 1$, in order that buyers of this security in $n + 1$ could get the same yield as that available on a one-period security during the $(n + 1)$st period. The expectation in period t of a fall in the price of the $n + 1$

term security in period $n + 1$ is equivalent to an expectation of a rise in the one-period rate in period $n + 1$. If, on balance, investors act to equalize the yields of the different maturities, then any observed differences in these yields at some point implies particular expectations of future rates (or prices). The link between the equalization of expected holding-period yields and forecasts of future rates, therefore, resides in the fact that a holding-period yield is equal to the sum of the coupon return (if any) and the difference between the known buying and the *expected* selling prices of the security.

The present study is not directly concerned with an evaluation of the expectations hypothesis. Instead, the hypothesis is assumed correct, and the data are evaluated for their implications of how the forecasts are made and for the effectiveness of the forecasts. To consider how the forecasts are made, a dichotomy — one of many possible frames of reference — is proposed that separates the forward rates, regarded for this purpose as forecasts, into the part that is related to the current and past spot rates and the part that is not — the induced and autonomous components, respectively. The induced (or extrapolative) component is most generally expressed as a weighted average of current and past spot rates but is not limited to an extrapolative procedure as the term is generally used. Instead, the induced components collects all possible arrangements of current and past spot rates, as well as the autoregressive components of other variables that are contemporaneously related to the forecasts. Most of the text is devoted to a discussion of this point. The optimal arrangement of the current and past spot rates, as distinct from the arrangement the forecasts are observed to utilize, is used as a standard for evaluating the accuracy of the forecasts.

The study considered the following three variants of the induced component:

(1) the extrapolation model $\quad {}_{t+n}F_t = B_1 A_t + B_2 A_{t-1} + \cdots + B_n A_{t-n-1};$

(2) the error-learning model $\quad {}_{t+n}F_t - {}_{t+n}F_{t-1} = a + B(A_t - {}_t F_{t-1});$

(3) the return to normalcy model $\quad {}_{t+n}F_t - {}_{t+n-1}F_t = K(A_t - {}_n A_t),$
$$k < 0;$$

where, ${}_{t+n}F_t$ = forecast made at t of a target at $t + n$; A_t = actual value at t; and ${}_n A_t$ = normal value at t. The first model says forecasters project some weight of averaged current and past actual values. The second model says forecasters revise their forecasts in accordance with revealed errors of earlier forecasts. The third model says forecasters project a change in target values in the direction of a normal value. All three models are, of course, linear.

Since one linear autoregressive model is naturally a linear transformation of any other linear autoregressive model, the parameters estimated for one such model imply corresponding weights for the others. However, for a given span of forecast, the models need not utilize the same number of past values; more generally, the models may differ in the number of their zero coefficients. This study circumvents the problem of comparability by considering several spans of forecasts, each of which utilizes different values of the series. Therefore, the error-learning model, which utilizes only one lagged value of the series for a given span, will, over several spans, generate a sufficient number of parameters for comparison with an extrapolative model of one span. Since the term structure data incorporate several spans of forecast, they are well suited to the present study.

By establishing algebraically the transformations bridging the extrapolative, error-learning, and return to normalcy models, the study is able to demonstrate the comparability between the parameters directly estimated for any one of the models and those implied by the estimated parameters of the other two. Because of the common derivation of the three models, or of any other linear autoregressive models, it is clearly not possible to select from among them one that can be said to describe the data most adequately. The models are simply alternate methods of describing the induced component.

The algebraic equivalence among the three models, however, does not nullify the value of distinguishing among them, since they each imply different motivations for behavior. It is entirely possible, for example, to obtain a set of parameters for the extrapolative and error-learning models that are plausible but that yield parameters for the return to normality model that contradict the hypothesized expected return to normalcy. While it is not possible to ascertain the precise motivation underlying the forecasts, it is possible to distinguish between the models that do and do not yield parameters that are plausible with respect to their behavioral implications.

Since interest rates are related on a contemporaneous basis with other variables that could conceivably influence the forecasts, the autoregressive structure of interest rates will include part of the autoregressive structure of these other series—the extent of the inclusion being determined by the extent of the contemporaneous correlation. The relative influence of the induced and autonomous components on the forecasts depends, therefore, on which of the two components is measured directly. This study estimated the autonomous component only after exhausting the extrapolative potential of the forecasts, thereby excluding from the autonomous component the autoregressive components of the other variables. It is important to interpret the relative importance of the two components in the light of this method, which clearly exaggerates forecasters' actual reliance on the autoregressive structure of the target series.

With respect to the accuracy of the forecasts, the study showed that the forecasts did not perform as well as the autoregression model. While this result reveals a bad forecasting record, it does not imply that the market is not trying to forecast. This report has shown that moving averages of past rates account for the major part of the variation of the forecasts; the last result implies that these moving averages can themselves stand improvement.

An important part of the accuracy analysis lies in the breakdown of the total mean square error into the part due to bias and the part that is random. The importance of the bias relative to the total mean square error increases, in the case of the Durand data, from about 10 per cent for the one-span forecast to about 25 per cent for the nine-span forecast. For the Treasury data, the ratio is about one-third throughout. The extent of this bias has evoked considerable comment in the literature on the term structure, and its source has been variously explained. For most of the period in which the bias is observed in both sets of data, the one-period spot rates were abnormally low. The mechanism described earlier—the apparent expectation that rates will return toward some central tendency—would also produce a bias in the errors of forecast, especially in the Durand data where the rise in rates expected in the early 1930's failed to materialize for two decades.

The effect of liquidity preference on the term structure is a complex subject that is outside the scope of this report. It is likely that the magnitude of the liquidity premium changes with shifts in the degree of an investor's certainty about future rate movements. If so, the liquidity premia would obscure part of the effectiveness of the true forecasting component of the forward rates. A sequel to this study could very reasonably be based on an analysis of this subject. A clean test for the efficacy of this analysis could be based on the determination whether the removal of properly isolated liquidity premia, so isolated, showed the true forecasting component of the forward rates more clearly.

REFERENCES

[1] Cagan, Phillip, and Guttentag, Jack, eds., *A Study of Interest Rates,* National Bureau of Economic Research, forthcoming.

[2] Conard, Joseph, *Introduction to the Theory of Interest,* California University Press, 1959.

[3] Culbertson, John M., "The Term Structure of Interest Rates," *Quarterly Journal of Economics,* November 1957.

[4] Durand, David, *Basic Yields of Corporate Bonds, 1900–1943,* Technical Paper No. 3, National Bureau of Economic Research, New York, 1942.

[5] Hickman, W. Braddock, "The Term Structure of Interest Rates: An Exploratory Analysis," National Bureau of Economic Research, New York, 1942 (mimeographed).

[6] Hicks, John R., *Value and Capital,* London, 1946.

[7] Johnston, J., *Econometric Methods,* New York, 1963.

[8] Kessel, Reuben, *The Cyclical Movement of the Term Structure of Interest Rates,* National Bureau of Economic Research, 1965.

[9] Macaulay, Frederick R., *The Movement of Interest Rates, Bond Yields and Stock Prices in the United States Since 1856,* National Bureau of Economic Research, New York, 1938.

[10] Malkiel, Burton, "Expectations, Bond Prices, and the Term Structure of Interest Rates," *Quarterly Journal of Economics,* 1957, pp. 197–218.

[11] Meiselman, David, *The Term Structure of Interest Rates,* Englewood Cliffs, New Jersey, 1963.

[12] Theil, Henri, *Economic Forecasts and Policy,* Amsterdam, 1961.

[13] Tobin, James, "Liquidity Preference as Behavior Toward Risk," *Review of Economic Studies,* 1958.

[14] Van Horne, James C., "Interest Rate Risk and the Term Structure of Interest Rates," *Journal of Political Economy,* August 1965, pp. 344–351.

[15] ———, "Liquidity Preference, Interest Rate Risk, and the Term Structure of Interest Rates," doctoral dissertation, Northwestern University, 1965, unpublished.

[16] Wallace, Neil, "The Term Structure of Interest Rates and the Maturity

Composition of the Federal Debt," doctoral dissertation, The University of Chicago, 1964, unpublished.

[17] Wendel, Helmut, "Short Run Interest Rate Expectations in the Government Securities Market," doctoral dissertation, Columbia University, 1966, to be published.

[18] Wood, John H., "Expectations, Errors, and the Term Structure of Interest Rates," *Journal of Political Economy,* February 1963.

FIVE

Consumer Anticipations
and Models of
Durable Goods Demand

F. THOMAS JUSTER

I. INTRODUCTION AND SUMMARY

The contribution of consumer anticipations surveys to models of durable goods demand has been studied since the late 1940's, when data of this kind first appeared. One group of studies [4, 8, 10, 14] has concentrated on analysis of cross-section data, relating differences in anticipations among individual consumer units to differences in purchases during a single time interval. A second group [3, 11, 12, 13] has emphasized time-series analysis, relating average or aggregate anticipations observed at different points of time to the corresponding average or aggregate purchase rates.

The data obtained from anticipations surveys consist of intentions or plans to buy specific consumer products (usually durables, such as automobiles, houses, and major appliances) and general economic attitudes designed to measure the state of optimism or pessimism among

NOTE: Figures in brackets refer to bibliographic references at the end of this essay.

consumers.[1] However, survey data of this sort need not be interpreted literally. For example, intentions can be viewed as one among many dimensions of optimism or as probabilistic statements of future actions, while attitudes can be viewed as the fundamental psychological determinant of behavior or as one among many determinants of intentions.

Surveys of consumer anticipations cover relatively short time spans, and the earliest ones are irregularly spaced within the span covered. Intentions surveys were taken annually by the Survey Research Center at the University of Michigan (SRC) from about 1946 to 1952. After 1952, SRC intentions surveys were conducted several times a year until 1961, and have been on a systematic quarterly basis since. An alternative intentions survey was begun in 1959 by the United States Bureau of the Census and has been available quarterly since its inception.[2] Attitude surveys have been taken since about 1952 by the SRC, at irregular intervals until 1961 and quarterly thereafter. A private survey, covering only buying intentions at first and later including some attitude measures, has been taken by the Albert Sindlinger Co.

[1] Intentions surveys usually ask "Do you expect (plan, intend) to buy X within the next Y months?" Responses are then coded into categories such as, yes-definitely, yes-probably, yes-maybe, and so forth.

The attitude survey conducted by the Survey Research Center at the University of Michigan comprises a set of six questions which yield three-point responses (up, down, no change, or the equivalent) to questions about personal financial attitudes, attitudes towards business conditions, and attitudes towards market conditions. The variables included in the index measure whether people (1) report being better or worse off than a year ago; (2) expect to be better or worse off a year from now; (3) expect business conditions to be better or worse during the next year; (4) expect business conditions to be better or worse during the next five years; (5) think that this is a bad or good time to purchase durable goods; (6) expect prices to be higher or lower next year and view these expectations as "to the good" or "to the bad."

Responses to the component questions are summarized in the form of an index number—per cent reporting up (better, etc.) less per cent reporting down, plus 100. The separate index numbers are then averaged.

An alternative version of the Consumer Attitude Index includes the six measures above plus a measure of intentions to buy new cars during the next twelve months and a measure of intentions to purchase houses during the next twelve months.

In recent years, the SRC Index has been revised to exclude responses to the question about price expectations (no. 6 above). The revised five-question index has roughly the same cyclical movement as the original, but it shows a perceptible upward trend while the other did not.

[2] Both SRC and Census intentions surveys were taken in cooperation with the Federal Reserve Board during their formative years. Differences between the two relate primarily to sample size, sample composition, and regularity of interview. Both have essentially the same design, since the Census survey (QSI) is based on SRC meth-

since the mid-1950's. The lack of sufficient publicly available information makes it difficult to evaluate the Sindlinger data, and the analysis in this paper considers only the SRC and Census surveys.

For consumer anticipations to have demonstrable value in durable goods demand models, it is necessary to show either that anticipations variables make a significant marginal contribution to the explanation of purchases, or that anticipations are about as good as other variables and are in addition less expensive to obtain or more quickly available. This paper examines the question of marginal contribution. It is focused more on the question of the marginal contribution and optimum specification of alternative anticipatory variables than on the question of the marginal contribution of anticipatory variables relative to other variables. The latter question has been extensively examined elsewhere [3, 11, 13] and the present paper adopts the working assumption that the results of these studies are broadly correct.

The test of significant marginal contribution is, of course, appropriate for analysis of both time-series and cross-section data. The empirical analysis in this paper is concerned entirely with time series, although the results of existing cross-section studies are drawn upon as needed.

TIME-SERIES DEMAND MODELS AND CONSUMER ANTICIPATIONS:
A BRIEF REVIEW OF FINDINGS

A number of recent studies have concluded that data on consumer anticipations are an indispensable ingredient in short-run demand models for the household sector, especially for the automobile component which accounts for much of the variability in consumer expenditures. The alternative types of anticipations data have not been found to be equally valuable, however. Consumer attitudes generally play an important role in these models, along with nonsurvey variables like income and durable goods stocks, but consumer buying intentions have tended to be of little or no use.

After examining the relation between durables purchases and a variety of other variables, including past and current income, in-

---

odology. The Census survey is based on a much larger sample and uses an overlapping rotation sequence which retains a large fraction of the sample in the interview group during successive quarters. The rotation sequence is designed to minimize sampling errors while maintaining the representative nature of the panel and automatically producing reinterview data.

come change, the index of industrial production, lagged durable goods purchases, the consumer attitude index, and index of consumer buying intentions, Eva Mueller [11, pp. 915–916] concluded that: "In summary, the analysis indicates that discretionary spending by consumers is determined to a large extent by income *level* and the state of consumer optimism and confidence [as measured by the attitude index]. The index of consumer attitudes does consistently well in the time-series test. Consistency of performance was observed over the entire 10-year time span and regardless of how the forecast equations were formulated . . ." (italics supplied by the author).

Mueller's findings with respect to buying intentions were that: "The predictive performance of buying intentions is much less satisfactory in these time-series regressions [i.e., less satisfactory than attitudes]. . . . When income, attitudes and buying intentions are used jointly to predict durable goods spending . . . the buying intentions term adds virtually nothing to the reliability of the forecast." [11, p. 905.] And, "throughout, the contribution of car buying intentions [to predicting automobile purchases] is negligible when attitude also appear in the equation." [11, p. 913.]

In a study published a short time later, covering the period 1952–62, Friend and Adams came to similar but less clear-cut conclusions about the importance of consumer attitudes, primarily because they found that the influence of attitudes on purchases could, to some degree, be represented by lagged purchases plus deviations from trend in an index of stock prices. "Joint use of lagged purchases and stock price deviations predicts automobile purchases nearly as well as the attitudinal data. The combination of the attitudes data and the stock prices show an improvement in predictive power over the case where either of these variables is used separately." [3, p. 993.]

And "the exclusion from the analysis of the earlier years [1952–56], particularly 1955, greatly reduces the role of attitudinal factors . . . The stock price variable is comparable in its effect to the attitudes, a little better in predicting number of vehicles delivered and a little worse in predicting expenditures." [3, p. 993.]

Friend and Adams come to the same conclusion as Mueller about intentions: "In the prediction of numbers of cars delivered as well as dollar amount of expenditures, . . . buying plans . . . add little or nothing." And again, "buying plans are not useful, and are not shown, although the attitudes continue to make a significant net contribution." [3, p. 993.]

Finally, in a study by Suits and Sparks [13] for the Brookings-SSRC econometric model, the index of consumer attitudes proved to be the most important variable in the automobile-demand equation. An income variable and the stock of automobiles also appear in the model, but buying intentions do not.

THE TIME-SERIES, CROSS-SECTION PARADOX

These time-series results stand in marked contrast to the findings of studies that rely on cross-section evidence to evaluate the role of consumer anticipations. The findings reported in [4, 8, 10, and 14] are representative. All showed buying intention to be strongly related to purchases of durables net of a large number of financial, demographic, and attitude variables, while all experienced great difficulty in detecting significant relationships between attitudes and subsequent purchases. Hence the paradox originally noted by Adams [1]: Attitudes are generally not related to purchases in cross sections, other things being equal, while intentions always are; but attitudes show a stronger relation to purchases in time series than intentions do, and, in fact, the latter seem to have no relation at all when other variables (including attitudes) are held constant.[3]

---

[3] Of the twin facets of the paradox, one is a firmly established empirical generalization (the superior cross-section performance of buying intentions) while the other stands on shakier ground (the superior time-series performance of attitudes). In fact, the opposite conclusion—that intentions have predictive value in time series but attitudes do not—was reached after an examination of a limited amount of data covering an earlier period [12, 15]. These early time-series results, buttressed by cross-section evidence that intentions and purchases were highly correlated, formed the basis for the recommendations made in 1955 by the Consultant Committee on Consumer Survey Statistics [15]. The committee essentially recommended that federal government resources be reallocated in the direction of more emphasis on intentions data and less on attitudes, although they recognized that this judgment was neither universally accepted nor as firmly grounded empirically as would be desirable.

The Consultant Committee recommendations were, in turn, one of the important considerations underlying the subsequent decision of the Federal Reserve Board to reduce its financial support for the SRC attitude studies and extend support to a new consumer survey that concentrated on buying intentions questions, large sample size to reduce sampling error, and regular quarterly interviewing to obtain more frequent measures of consumer anticipations. If the results reported by Mueller and Friend and Jones [3, 11] are correct, and if the cross-section, time-series paradox noted by Adams [1] is real, both the Consultant Committee and the Federal Reserve Board were in error.

The several attempts to resolve the paradox have essentially taken the view that the time-series results are correct and that the problem lies either with misspecification or measurement error in the cross-section analysis. Katona [6, Appendix, pp. 254–256] discusses a number of potential difficulties in the use of cross-section data to test the influence of consumer attitudes on purchases. Adams [1] suggests that differences among households in the interpretation of attitudinal questions are likely to provide enough noise to blur any cross-sectional influence of attitudes. Eliminating this source of noise, by taking differences in the responses of identical households in consecutive surveys as the "true" measure of attitude change, Adams finds some evidence that attitudes are in fact related to purchases in cross sections. The relationship is relatively weak (as measured by, say, explained variance), but there is no a priori reason for it to be strong. Maynes [9], who examines the problem at considerable length, points out several sources of systematic error in measuring the influence of attitudes in cross sections. He argues that the systematic errors could, in conjunction with the purely random sampling errors, easily account for an observed attitudes-purchases correlation of zero in cross sections even though the true correlation were significantly positive.

This line of argument may well be correct, although it should be kept in mind that the supporting evidence consists for the most part of a priori speculation rather than empirical observation. Systematic measurement errors and other sources of statistical noise evidently have only a random influence on time-series observations of mean values, but they might exert a strong influence on cross-sectional relationships. The lack of an observed relation between attitudes and purchases in cross sections, and the highly significant relationship observed in time series, are therefore consistent with this explanation.

THE PARADOX REEXAMINED

Whatever the merits of the Katona, Adams, and Maynes argument that systematic measurement errors explain the failure of attitudes to show up in cross sections, there remains the paradox that buying plans or intentions typically exert a dominant statistical influence on purchases in cross-section analysis but appear to have a weak or nil influence in time series.[4]

[4] In most of the cross-section studies cited earlier, intentions to buy are the most im-

Some possible explanations are that: (1) Intentions are a stable series (like age, for example), and thus have little or no time-series variance. (2) Intentions are highly correlated with purchases in cross sections mainly because they reflect the influence of idiosyncratic circumstances for particular households, and the distribution of such circumstances is, except for random variations, constant over time. Thus intentions may have an important element which behaves randomly over time but is highly correlated with behavior in cross sections, and the other elements may add little or no information to that provided by variables like income and attitudes. (3) Sampling or other measurement errors may be a relatively more serious problem for intentions data in time series than in cross sections, and thus the time-series relation may be obscured by error while the cross-section relation is not. (4) Time-series demand models that use an intentions variable may be improperly specified, and proper specifications might alter the conclusion that no time-series relationship exists.

The first possibility can be dismissed immediately. Intentions have more time-series variance than attitudes or, indeed, than most economic series. The second cannot be tested empirically in any direct way, although there is obviously an important element of truth in the proposition that some part of the cross-section correlation between intentions and purchases is a reflection of idiosyncratic and largely uninteresting differences in household circumstances. The third possibility (time-series measurement errors) is clearly of some relevance. The time-series variable produced by an intentions survey is the proportion of intenders in a sample. This proportion is typically rather small (about 10 per cent), depending on the particular survey question from which the variable is formed. As a consequence, the sampling errors of differences between successive surveys in the proportion of intenders is large relative to the proportion itself, and the sampling error of the difference often exceeds the observed difference. Partly because of its approximately rectangular distribution and partly because it is constructed as an average of several independently measured variables, sampling errors of successive time-series differences

---

portant single variable in the analysis. In this sense they can be said to "dominate," although the proportion of cross-section variance explained by intentions is quite small (from 5 to 20 per cent, usually).

are much smaller, relative to observed differences, for the attitude variable. Kish [7] has compared the sampling errors of time-series differences with the mean observed difference for both attitudes and intentions. His results indicate that relative sampling errors for the two types of surveys (sampling error of the difference divided by mean observed difference) would be equalized only if the sample size were about ten times as large for intentions as for attitudes. Since all the anticipations data analyzed above were drawn from the same sample (SRC), the noise generated by sampling error is much more serious for the intentions data than for attitudes.

It is worth noting that the measurement errors relevant to a cross-section analysis of these two kinds of anticipations data may well contain the opposite bias. The major source of error in measuring cross-sectional influence may not be sampling variability but, in Maynes' terminology, scale compression, anchor point variability among respondents, and interval nonlinearity.[5] It seems likely to me that these types of errors are much more serious for attitudes than for intentions.

The last possibility, specification error, is perhaps the most interesting one. It is argued below that a time-series demand equation which contains the usual intentions variable (the proportion of intenders) in a linear and additive model is likely to be improperly specified. The

---

[5] "Scale compression" refers to the fact that attitude questions are apt to have upper and lower limits which are described qualitatively, e.g., increase or decrease. Thus a respondent who reports that an income increase is expected may not be able to report on subsequent occasions that an even larger increase is expected, or that a given increase is expected with greater certainty. Once a respondent gets to the upper or lower limit of the scale used for a particular question, it is generally not possible for his responses to show further change even though there may in fact be a further change.

"Anchor point variability among respondents" refers to the fact that two respondents may mean quite different things by the statement "I expect to be worse off next year." One may really mean that he expects to be considerably worse off because income will be reduced drastically, while another with the identical response may simply mean that he does not expect any income increase and thinks it likely the prices will rise somewhat. In part, anchor point variability is a scale compression problem in disguise.

The last factor discussed by Maynes, "interval nonlinearity," refers to the possibility that there may be larger real differences between one pair of consecutive points on an attitude scale than between another pair; the customary linear scaling implies equal distance. For example, there may be a bigger difference between those who expect to be worse off and those who expect things to remain the same than between the latter and those who expect to be better off, or vice versa. Interval nonlinearity is more apt to be a problem where the scales are more refined and include varying degrees of being better or worse off.

basic reason is that such an equation implicitly assumes that the purchase rates of intenders and nonintenders (those reporting and not reporting intentions to buy) can be explained by a common set of parameters and independent variables. There is by now a considerable body of evidence which indicates that such an assumption is invalid. The evidence suggests that intenders are simply households whose ex ante purchase probabilities are higher than some undetermined level, while nonintenders are simply those whose ex ante probabilities are lower than the same undetermined level.

Further, the evidence suggests that mean purchase probability in the various intender classes (definite, probable, etc.) is approximately random over time, but that mean probability for nonintenders varies systematically with factors such as income, expectations, and so on. Thus the proportion of intenders can be viewed as a mediocre proxy variable for what an intention survey is really designed to measure — the mean ex ante purchase probability in the population. In the absence of a direct measure of probability, the problem can be managed by a model which specifies that the intender purchase rate is a constant while the nonintender purchase rate has a functional relationship to some specified set of variables.[6]

[6] A direct measure of mean purchase probability is currently being obtained in a new Census Bureau survey which began in July 1966. It is interesting to note that one of the principal conclusions of this paper — that intender and nonintender purchase rates must be treated separately — has a direct carry-over to analysis of the new probability data. Although evidence is inconclusive because so few observations are available (five quarterly measurements) at current writing, it appears that purchase rates in the various probability classes are essentially random provided that the respondent indicated a nonzero probability. For those indicating a purchase probability of zero, the limited evidence we have suggests that purchase rates behave in roughly the same way as did nonintender purchase rates in surveys of buying intentions. That is, the purchase rates of zero probability households appear to vary with factors like income, income change, and consumer attitudes, and hence can be explained with the aid of these or other variables.

Thus the appropriate model for purchase probability data may well be precisely the same as the one that seems optimum for buying intention data: Nonzero probability classes (intenders) should be viewed as having fixed purchase rates, while zero probability households (nonintenders) should be viewed as having purchase rates that need to be explained. A major difference, of course, is that most observed purchases were located in the nonintender class for buying intentions surveys, while just the reverse is true in the probability data. Thus it is much less important to be able to predict the purchase rates of zero probability households than to predict the purchase rate of nonintenders, simply because the first group contributes relatively little to the time-series variance in total purchases while the second contributes relatively much.

PLAN OF THE PAPER

Section II of this paper examines the influence on time-series models of sampling errors in the measurement of buying intentions; several related problems are also discussed. Section III examines the specification problem as it relates to time-series demand models with an intentions variable. Section IV presents updated empirical estimates of the role of both types of consumer anticipations variables in simple time-series models.

SUMMARY AND CONCLUSIONS

Reducing sampling errors by increasing sample size results in a significantly higher time-series correlation between buying intentions and purchases. An empirical measure of the improvement can be obtained by comparing actual purchases with both the Census Bureau's Quarterly Survey of Intentions (QSI, 16,000 households) and the essentially identical survey conducted by the Survey Research Center (1,500 to 3,500 households). Over and above reduction of sampling error, the evidence indicates that adjustment for seasonal variation and the use of weights representing ex ante mean purchase probabilities for various intender categories also improves the time-series correlation between intentions and purchases. The improvement in correlation resulting from the combination of all three factors (reduced sampling error, seasonal adjustment, and weights) is substantial: in round numbers, from 30 to 70 per cent of explained variance in one of the periods tested, and from 10 to 90 per cent during another.

Demand equations involving an intentions variable should specify different purchase rate functions for intenders and nonintenders, since the factors determining purchase rates for these two classes of households appear to differ considerably. In fact, the purchase rate of intenders can be described with reasonable accuracy as a random variable with a fixed mean value. Preliminary empirical tests indicate that best results are obtained from a two-stage estimation procedure: First, the nonintender purchase rate is predicted by regression methods; then the population purchase rate is predicted as a weighted average (the weights themselves being obtained directly from the survey) of nonintender and intender purchase rates.

At the present writing it is not possible to produce a firm generalization about either the relative or joint usefulness of different types of consumer anticipations surveys in time-series prediction models. The most accurate generalization appears to be that surveys of consumer attitudes and of consumer buying intentions both play distinctive and important roles in prediction models. Consumer attitudes appear to be a major determinant of the purchase rates of households classified as nonintenders; intentions data are needed to estimate the relative proportions of various classes of intenders and of nonintenders. These conclusions are based on analysis of Census Bureau Intentions data and Survey Research Center Attitudes data that cover a relatively short time span (1959–66) characterized mainly by a strong upward trend. Examination of similar data for different time periods will not necessarily yield the same conclusions, although the presence of very large sampling errors for intentions data other than the Census QSI series makes it difficult to evaluate periods prior to 1959.

The forecasting record of simple demand models that use consumer anticipations survey variables indicates three things: (1) When used in conjunction with variables like income or income change, the anticipations variables typically exert the dominant influence in the model. (2) Anticipations models generate much more accurate forecasts than autoregressive models. (3) The anticipations models examined in this paper are seriously deficient in a number of important respects.

Models that use consumer attitudes do especially well at predicting major turning points in expenditures on automobiles and other consumer durables. However, most such models seriously underestimated the strength of automobile and durable goods purchases during the 1961–66 expansion.

Models containing both consumer attitudes and consumer buying intentions seem to perform quite well provided a reliable estimate of intentions is available. However, these models cover a relatively short time period mainly characterized by economic expansion, and predictive performance is based largely on evaluation of ex post rather than ex ante forecasts.

II. SAMPLING ERRORS, MEASUREMENT
ERRORS, AND THE TIME-SERIES CORRELATION
BETWEEN PURCHASES AND INTENTIONS

As noted in Section I, buying intentions surveys have been conducted since 1946 by the Survey Research Center (SRC) and since 1959 by the Bureau of the Census (QSI). QSI has been conducted quarterly since its inception, while SRC is available for almost every quarter since 1959. The only substantive difference between the two is their respective sample sizes: roughly 16,000 households for QSI and from about 1,500 to about 3,500 for SRC.[7]

Although the two surveys are essentially identical in design (QSI was originally based on SRC methodology), there appear to be differences in either the coding or interpretation of responses. For example, about 10 per cent of QSI respondents are reported as indicating that they "don't know" about car buying intentions, and an additional 2 per cent or so report that they "don't know" whether they will purchase a new or used car if they do buy. SRC does not publish a response category comparable to the first of these two classes; "don't know" responses in SRC data reflect only indecision about new versus used car intentions. The average percentage of SRC and QSI intenders (those who report they definitely, probably, or might buy) is quite similar for comparable time periods, hence the straightforward intender categories apparently mean roughly the same thing in both series. Thus the interpretative or coding differences come down to the fact that QSI reports a large fraction of households as being uncertain about their buying plans, while SRC apparently classifies similar respondents as nonintenders.

Although QSI and SRC show comparable results on average, there are large differences between the results of single surveys taken at identical time periods; these differences presumably reflect sampling variability. For example, the 1959-II and 1959-IV percentages for twelve-month car-buying intentions are 17.3 and 14.6, respectively, from SRC. But from QSI, comparable percentages are, respectively,

---

[7] The January–February SRC survey has the 3,500 sample size because the intentions data are obtained in conjunction with the Annual Survey of Consumer Finances. All other SRC surveys use the 1,500 sample size.

FIGURE 5-1. Intentions to Buy Automobiles as Reported in Survey Research Center (SRC) and U.S. Census Bureau (QSI) Surveys, 1953–1966

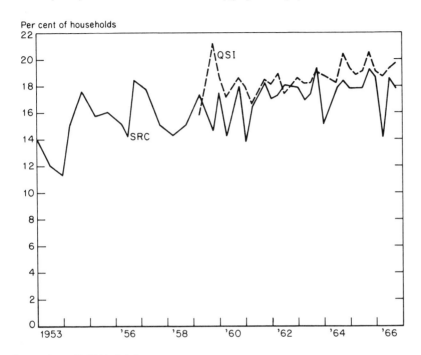

Source: Appendix Table 5-A-1.

15.8 and 21.2 – a reversal of the direction and almost of the extent of change! In 1963-IV the two show virtually identical results (19.3 for SRC and 19.1 for QSI); but for the next quarter, 1964-I, SRC shows a sharp drop to 15.1 while QSI is practically unchanged at 18.8. As can be seen from Figure 5-1, SRC tends to be the more erratic series, although both have a good deal of apparently random variation.

The larger QSI sample not only generates smaller over-all sampling errors, but also facilitates more effective use of the considerable detail which both surveys contain relating to subcategories of intenders.[8] In principal, each intentions subcategory should be weighted by

---

[8] SRC publishes very little detail in its intentions series, especially for surveys where the sample size is about 1,500 cases. In a typical SRC survey there might be from 100 to 150 respondents with some kind of intention to buy a new car within twelve months. Based on Census Bureau data, from fifteen to thirty of these households might report "definite" intentions to buy a new car within six months. The latter figure obviously has a very large relative sampling error.

the mean ex ante purchase probability of respondents in that category. The resulting series would be a more analytically appropriate measure of aggregate buying intentions than the simple sum of all intenders. The purchase rates of various classes of intenders, which can be obtained from reinterview studies, are approximations to the desired probability weight [4].

Finally, the intentions series is clearly in need of adjustment for seasonal variation. Intentions to buy cars — either the sole or the major component of the intentions variable generally used in demand studies — have a marked seasonal high around October when new automobile models are introduced, and this seasonal movement has no counterpart in actual purchases. There appear to be other seasonal variations as well.

From Census Bureau intentions data it is thus possible to construct alternative series which can be viewed as potentially superior to SRC intentions data. Three types of conceptual differences are investigated. First, the influence of pure sampling error can be examined by comparing series which differ only in sample size. Such series are designated QSI-NS (quarterly survey of intentions, not seasonally adjusted), and SRC-NS. Second, the effect of seasonal adjustment can be measured. Here the best comparison presumably involves two Census Bureau series because sampling errors are smaller than in SRC data. Hence the next series is designated QSI-S (quarterly survey of intentions, seasonally adjusted). The third difference involves construction of a weighted series designed to measure the number or proportion of "expected" purchases.[9] This statistic can be represented by the probability of purchase in each category multiplied by the number or proportion of households in the category. If mean purchase probability in any class is independent of the proportion of households in that class, the probability weights should be constant over time. If mean probability is not independent of class size, the weights ought not to be constant, and must be predicted either as a function of class size or of other variables.

---

[9] In the studies analyzed to date (all of which use SRC data), the intentions series consists of all households "definitely" or "probably" intending to buy new or used cars within twelve months plus one-half of those who report that they "might" buy within twelve months. The series therefore involves implicit weights, but these weights lack empirical foundation.

Census Bureau reinterview data (largely unpublished) suggest that the mean probabilities in intender categories, as measured by observed purchase rates, are in fact largely independent of the proportion of intenders. It is clear, however, that nonintender purchase rates are not independent of the proportion of nonintenders. Thus we have constructed an expected purchase series which applies fixed weights to the proportions of various kinds of intenders but eliminates the nonintender group entirely.[10] The weights (which are designed to correspond to the mean ex ante probabilities implied by the new-car purchase rates observed in reinterview studies) are 0.7 for those reporting definite plans to buy new cars within six months, 0.5 for those reporting probable or possible plans to buy new cars within six months, 0.3 for those reporting definite, probable, or possible plans to buy new cars within twelve months but no plans to buy within six months, and 0.2 for those reporting plans to buy used cars within either six or twelve months. These weights are somewhat higher than observed purchase rates due to the presence of regression bias in the observed purchase data [4]. The series is designated QSI-SW$_0$ (seasonally adjusted and weighted buying intentions). An alternative weighted series contains all these components but also includes the class of households reporting that they "don't know" about their car buying intentions. These households are assigned a weight of 0.3, and the series is designated QSI-SW$_3$.

Thus we have five buying-intentions series to be compared: (1) SRC-NS; (2) QSI-NS; (3) QSI-S; (4) QSI-SW$_0$; and (5) QSI-SW$_3$. Differences between the first and second are due entirely to the differential importance of sampling errors. Differences between the second and third are due entirely to the effect of seasonal adjustment. Differences between the third, fourth, and fifth are due to differences in the weights attached to various classes of intenders or to differences in the coverage of intenders.

Comparisons among the series are hampered by the fact that Census Bureau intentions data are not available until 1959. Unfortunately,

---

[10] Other procedures could be used. One could treat all intender categories as separate variables and allow the data to provide the weights. I do not think that this procedure is desirable, given the amount of multicollinearity in the data. Another alternative is to estimate intender and nonintender purchase rates separately and then combine them into an estimate of the over-all purchase rate. This procedure is examined in the next section.

the 1959–66 period cannot be regarded as typical of the economic environment in which survey data are used to predict purchases; since 1959 the U.S. economy has in general been in a period of sustained economic expansion (the 1960–61 recession was very mild, and brief as well). Thus comparisons can be drawn either between QSI and SRC series starting in 1959, or between the SRC series and a QSI series consisting mainly or partly of Census Bureau data, but with a link to SRC data for periods prior to 1959. Although for some purposes the period since 1959 is clearly preferable, for others (the measurement of seasonal adjustment and the separation of trend from cyclical influences) it is not so evident, which is better.

Thus for the present we are left with a choice of evils: We can compare a series which consists entirely of SRC observations with one that consists mainly but not entirely of QSI observations, and these comparisons will cover a period characterized both by large cyclical swings and a long-term upward trend. Alternatively, we can compare a series drawn entirely from QSI with one drawn entirely from SRC but only for a period mainly characterized by an upward trend.

Both types of comparisons are shown in Table 5-1. The series labelled QSI consists of whatever Census data are available plus whatever SRC data are needed because the period includes quarters prior to 1959. Three time periods are examined: 1953 through 1961, the period examined in other recent studies; 1953 through most of 1965, the period available when this analysis was written; and 1959 through most of 1965, the period for which the QSI series consists entirely of Census Bureau data.[11]

---

[11] Only quarters for which SRC data are available have been included in the analysis summarized in Table 5-1. As noted in the text, SRC surveys of either attitudes or intentions were not conducted quarterly until 1962. Hence we have thirty-seven surveys available for analysis between 1953-I and 1965-III (the latest survey for which relevant purchase data were available at writing). One of these (1964-II) has been excluded from all regressions because the comparison between anticipation and action is strongly affected by the automobile strike in the third and fourth quarters of 1964. Although other quarters were also affected by the strike, either anticipation and action were both affected (e.g., 1964-IV and 1965-I) or else actions were only slightly affected on balance (e.g., 1964-III).

Most of the empirical analysis relates anticipations during a particular quarter to purchases in the two *subsequent* quarters; thus 1964-III anticipations are related to purchases during 1964-IV and 1965-I, and for that period the effect of the strike probably balanced out. The quarters used in the analysis are shown below.

Table 5-1 summarizes correlations between automobile purchases (deflated, per household) and the alternative buying intentions series. The variable to be predicted is either deflated per household purchases of automobiles or the ratio of deflated per household automobile purchases to past income.[12] The table shows simple correlations, where the only explanatory variable is buying intentions, and partial correlations, where an income or income change variable is held constant. The basic hypothesis is simply that reduced sampling variability, seasonal adjustment, and appropriate weighting will all tend to increase the correlation between purchases and intentions.

The results are striking. During the 1953–61 period, when the QSI series consists largely of linked SRC data, the differences are quite small and erratic; some of the differences in partial correlation go in the opposite direction from the differences in simple correlations. For the 1953–65 period, where the majority of the observations are drawn from Census Bureau data, sampling error, seasonal adjustment,

1953-I	1956-IV	1960-IV	1963-II
1953-III	1957-II	1961-I	1963-III
1954-I	1957-IV	1961-II	1963-IV
1954-II	1958-II	1961-IV	1964-I
1954-IV	1958-IV	1962-I	1964-III
1955-II	1959-II	1962-II	1964-IV
1955-IV	1959-IV	1962-III	1965-I
1956-II	1960-I	1962-IV	1965-II
1956-III	1960-II	1963-I	1965-III

The following quarters were not used because SRC intentions data were not available:

1953-II	1955-III	1958-I	1960-III
1953-IV	1956-I	1958-III	1961-III
1954-III	1957-I	1959-I	
1955-I	1957-III	1959-III	

In addition, 1964-II was eliminated because of an auto strike in the associated purchase period of 1964-IV.

For some of the quarters labelled "no SRC data," an SRC survey was taken, but it was either a telephone follow-up involving part of the previous quarter's sample or else no intentions data have been published. Only quarters in which the full SRC sample was personally interviewed, and for which both attitudes and intentions data have been published, are used in the analysis.

[12] The dependent variable in equations with buying intentions as the independent variable ought, in principle, to be number of automobile purchases rather than deflated value of purchases, since the intentions survey asks whether a car will or will not be purchased. Deflated purchases will differ from the number of purchases if aver-

and weighting all make a significant difference, although weighting seems to be the most important of the three.[13] For the 1959–65 period—where the comparison is most clear-cut between alternative data sources but where the nature of the period is troublesome—all of the differences are important although the relative amounts of improvement are different for simple and for partial correlations and for equations predicting purchase levels as distinct from the ratio of purchases to income.

The combined effects of all the above differences results in a dramatic improvement, especially for the second and third time periods. The simple r^2 is more than doubled for the second period and the partial r^2 is increased by a factor of at least five. For the third period, the improvement is by a factor of ten or more. In effect, SRC-NS explains almost no variance in the 1959–65 period but QSI-SW$_3$ explains close to 90 per cent of the variance (for simple regressions), and close to 90 per cent of the residual variance when the ratio of purchases to income is dependent. We conclude that the powerful cross-section relationship repeatedly observed between intentions and purchases does in fact show up in time series, and that the paradox noted by Adams [1] is an illusion. Given reasonably small sampling errors, adequate adjustment for seasonal variation, and proper aggregation, intentions

---

age real price per car changes over time, that is, if people upgrade or downgrade their car purchases. In most of the empirical analysis in this paper deflated purchases are used, since there is no reliable series on number of car purchases by households. The available car registrations series includes purchases by business and nonprofit organizations, and registrations lag behind purchases by several weeks on average. The Census Survey of buying intentions contains a series on actual purchases by households. This series is the conceptually appropriate one for the analysis, but there is a great deal of sampling variability in the data even though the sample size is quite large. Therefore, I have preferred for the most part to use the deflated expenditure data. The alternative series are of course highly correlated, and the analysis in this part of the paper is not likely to be very sensitive to the choice of dependent variable. Other investigators have reported that it seems to make little difference, e.g., Mueller [11].

In Section III of the paper, results are presented using an estimate of number of cars purchased by households. The form of the equation for these results requires that number of purchases be used, hence no alternative was possible.

[13] The most important respect in which weighting improves the correlation is in the distinction between new and used car buying intentions. Intentions to buy used cars are erratic in the QSI data. They show little systematic change over the entire period, and car purchases (both new and used) rose strongly. The other elements in the weighting scheme also make a positive contribution.

TABLE 5-1. Correlations Between Automobile Purchases and Alternative Indexes of Intentions

Intentions Variable	Adjusted Simple Correlation Squared, Time Periods			Partial Correlation Squared, Time Periods			Percentage Distribution of Total Improvement in Simple $\bar{r}^2$, Time Periods			
	I (1953–61)	II (1953–65)	III (1959–65)	I (1953–61)	II (1953–65)	III (1959–65)	I (1953–61)	II (1953–65)	III (1959–65)	Average
A: Purchase Levels Dependent [a]										
SRC-NS	.16	.30	.09	.28	.06	(−).00	46.3	10.3	8.9	21.8
QSI-NS	.21	.35	.16	.40	.07	.04	17.1	25.9	33.9	25.6
QSI-S	.23	.46	.44	.42	.11	.07	18.3	49.0	39.9	35.7
QSI-SW$_0$	.25	.66	.77	.37	.32	.12	18.3	14.7	17.3	16.8
QSI-SW$_3$	.27	.72	.91	.41	.40	.23				
B: Ratio of Purchases to Income Dependent [b]										
SRC-NS	.02	.15	.07	.00	.05	.07	7.5	12.3	12.1	10.6
QSI-NS	.02	.18	.17	.06	.15	.45	13.1	21.2	35.2	23.2
QSI-S	.03	.23	.45	.06	.17	.66	73.5	56.6	38.2	56.1
QSI-SW$_0$	.08	.37	.75	.12	.29	.84	5.9	9.8	14.6	10.1
QSI-SW$_3$	.08	.39	.86	.07	.27	.87				

[a] Equations are:

$$M_6 = b_0 + b_1 BI, \text{ and}$$
$$M_6 = b_0 + b_1 Y_{-6} + b_2 BI,$$

where BI is one of the intentions variables, M_6 is deflated per family expenditures on automobiles during the six-month period following the quarter in which the survey was taken, and Y_{-6} is deflated per family income during the six-month period preceding the survey quarter. See Appendix Table 1 for detailed description.

[b] Equations are:

$$M_6/Y_{-6} = b_0 + b_1 BI,$$
$$M_6/Y_{-6} = b_0 + b_1 \Delta Y + b_2 BI,$$

where BI is one of the intentions variables, ΔY is the difference between income in the survey quarter and Y_{-6}, and the other variables are as defined above in note a. See Appendix Table 1 for detailed description.

show a strong association with purchases in time series as well as in cross sections.

The cross-section, time-series paradox referred in principle to the fact that buying intentions showed a significant relationship to purchases in cross sections, holding constant other relevant variables including attitudes, but did not show a significant relation in time series holding these variables constant. The results above show only that the performance of an intentions variable can be greatly improved by reducing sampling errors and adjusting for seasonal variation and weighting, but they do not demonstrate that the improved intentions variable is significantly related to purchases when attitudes are held constant. This question is taken up below. To anticipate the results, the improved intentions variable does, in fact, show a highly significant relation to purchases, holding constant other variables including attitudes.

III. EQUATION SPECIFICATION AND INTENTIONS DATA

A possible inference from the results in Section II is that reduction of sampling errors and measurement errors so improves the time-series relation between intentions and purchases that the problem of forecasting the demand for consumer durables has been largely solved. This conclusion is not warranted, if for no other reason than the trend-dominated character of the period over which intentions and purchases appear to be so closely associated. Hence we turn to the examination of the equation specification problem.

Time-series tests of buying intentions surveys seek to determine whether one or more intentions variables contribute significantly to the explanation or prediction of purchases. Empirical tests have asked whether the proportion of intenders, the usual variable obtained from an intentions survey, has a net association with purchases in a linear and additive model which includes a number of other variables like income, attitudes, the unemployment rate, and so forth. It can be shown that this test gives valid results if, and only if, highly restrictive and empirically unrealistic behavioral assumptions are made.

Less restrictive and empirically justifiable assumptions require equations with somewhat greater flexibility. The argument is developed and preliminary empirical results are presented.

The key to the proper specification of demand equations that use an intentions variable is the recognition that an intentions survey really divides the population of both households and purchases into two compartments — intenders and nonintenders. The fact that the survey further divides intenders into subcompartments is useful but irrelevant to the analysis. Given the basic dichotomy of intender versus nonintender, the variable to be predicted (future purchase rates) can be divided into two components: future purchase rates for intenders and future purchase rates for nonintenders. Defining: p as the proportion of intenders (weighted or unweighted); $1 - p = q$ as the proportion of nonintenders; r as the future purchase rate of intenders; s as the future purchase rate of nonintenders; and x as the future purchase rate in the population as a whole, we have the identity,

$$x \equiv pr + (1 - p)s \equiv pr + qs.$$

The future purchase rate in the population is thus a weighted average of the future purchase rates for households in each of the two compartments, the weights being the proportions of each kind of household. The problem is then to substitute functional relationships for r and s in the above identity; the sizes of p and q are determined by the intentions survey.

A priori it seems that little can be said about the probable determinants of the r and s functions. The basic causes of short-term variations in aggregate purchases of consumer durables are not only complex but are likely to involve factors that are difficult to measure with precision. Purchases of durables may be viewed as an attempt to adjust actual to desired stock. Desired stock is presumably determined by forward looking variables like expected income (including both mean and variance) as well as by other variables such as relative prices, credit terms, asset and debt holdings, family composition, and so forth. Moreover, the speed with which actual stock is adjusted to desired stock may itself be a function rather than a constant; for example, the speed of adjustment may depend on the variance of expected income. It is precisely because of the difficulty of providing an adequate structural explanation of durable goods purchases that surveys of consumer anticipations have come to be widely used in models designed to predict durable goods demand.

The appropriate relationships are even less apparent when we consider variations in intender and nonintender, rather than aggregate, purchase rates. Intenders are, after all, simply households that classify themselves as having some kind of positive buying expectation, while nonintenders are those who fail to provide any positive expectation. Thus one would expect intenders, relative to nonintenders, to have higher average values of any variable that tends to be positively associated with purchases, and lower average values of variables that are negatively associated with purchases. But it does not necessarily follow that even powerful behavioral variables like income or expected income will be determinants of either intender or nonintender purchase rates. A large increase in income may simply shift households from the nonintender to the intender category. As a consequence, average income in *both* categories may remain the same or even decline, and purchase rates in *both* categories could rise, remain the same, or even fall; for the population as a whole, both average income and the purchase rate would evidently rise.

One a priori consideration that is likely to be of some relevance has to do with the question of homogeneity: Is there apt to be a smaller or a larger variance in the distribution of purchase probabilities among intenders than among nonintenders? Since there are several different categories of intenders, and since classification as an intender requires a positive reaction from the respondent rather than the absence of a positive reaction, it is plausible to suppose that the various intender classifications are relatively homogeneous, the nonintender classification, relatively heterogeneous.

With these considerations in mind, let us examine the empirical implications of alternative hypotheses about functional relationships for intender and nonintender purchase rates.

HYPOTHESIS A

A simple but extreme assumption is that the purchase rates of intenders r and nonintenders s are both random variables with means $\bar{R}$, $\bar{S}$ and disturbances d_r, d_s; that is,

$$r = \bar{R} + d_r$$

$$s = \bar{S} + d_s.$$

In such a case we need only the intentions survey to give us optimum predictions; the addition of other data will not improve matters.

(1.0) $\qquad x \equiv pr + qs$

(2.0) $\qquad x \equiv p(\bar{R} + d_r) + q(\bar{S} + d_s)$

$\qquad\qquad \equiv p\bar{R} + q\bar{S} + p(d_r) + q(d_s);$

since $q \equiv 1 - p$,

(2.1) $\qquad x \equiv p(\bar{R} - \bar{S}) + \bar{S} + p(d_r - d_s) + d_s$

$\qquad \hat{x} \equiv p(\bar{R} - \bar{S}) + \bar{S}.$

If equation (2.1) is fitted to data on x and p, we should find that:

(2.2) $\qquad\qquad x = a + bp + u,$

where, $a = \bar{S}$, $b = \bar{R} - \bar{S}$, and $u = p(d_r - d_s) + d_s$.

The variance of the error term depends on the respective variances of d_r and d_s, the size of p, and the correlation between p and both r and s. Since p is a relatively small fraction (.1 to .3), the error variance is likely to be dominated by the variance of d_s.

HYPOTHESIS B-1

A comparable and equally extreme assumption is that the purchase rates of intenders and nonintenders are systematically related to other variables and the relationship is precisely the same for both. For example, where $\bar{Y}_r$, $\bar{Y}_s$ are intender and nonintender mean income, respectively, $\bar{E}_r$, $\bar{E}_s$ are the respective mean expectations, and u_{rs}, u_{sr} are the respective error terms when both purchase rate functions are fitted with identical parameters, we have:

$$r = f(\bar{Y}_r, \bar{E}_r) = a + b\bar{Y}_r + c\bar{E}_r + u_{rs}$$

$$s = f(\bar{Y}_s, \bar{E}_s) = a + b\bar{Y}_s + c\bar{E}_s + u_{sr}.$$

If the mean values of income and expectations for intenders and nonintenders were equal, the survey would be of no value; the purchase rates of intenders and nonintenders would be equal. When the above expressions for r and s are substituted into the definitional equation, the survey variable drops out entirely.

$$(1.0) \qquad\qquad x \equiv pr + qs \equiv pr + (1 - p)s$$

$$(3.0) \quad x = p(a + b\bar{Y}_r + c\bar{E}_r + u_{rs}) + (1 - p)(a + b\bar{Y}_s + c\bar{E}_s + u_{sr}).$$

If $\bar{Y}_r = \bar{Y}_s$ and $\bar{E}_r = \bar{E}_s$,

$$(3.1) \qquad\qquad x = a + b\bar{Y} + c\bar{E} + p(u_{rs} - u_{sr}) + u_{sr},$$

and the error term, u_x, is:

$$u_x = p(u_{rs} - u_{sr}) + u_{sr}.$$

Because of the nature of the intender-nonintender classification, it is quite probable that the mean values of independent variables, such as income and expectations, will in fact be different for intenders and nonintenders. In this case equation (3.1) has two additional terms:

$$bp(\bar{Y}_r - \bar{Y}_s) + cp(\bar{E}_r - \bar{E}_s).$$

These terms obviously vanish if $\bar{Y}_r = \bar{Y}_s$ and $\bar{E}_r = \bar{E}_s$; if, as seems likely, this is not the case, both terms could still be ignored without serious error unless mean income and expectations behaved differently over time for intenders and nonintenders and these differences contribute to the explanation of variance in population purchase rates. Although one cannot demonstrate empirically that either condition holds, it seems reasonable to suppose that omission of the terms in question will not seriously bias the results.

HYPOTHESIS B-2

A more plausible form of the B-1 assumption is to suppose that the regression coefficients in the two functions are the same but that the constant terms differ—an assumption consistent with the empirically observable differences in reinterview purchase rates. If this is so, and if, in addition, a is greater than a' and $u_{rs'}$, $u_{sr'}$ designate the respective error terms where the constant is permitted to vary but the other coefficients are not, we have:

$$r = a + b\bar{Y}_r + c\bar{E}_r + u_{rs'}$$

$$s = a' + b\bar{Y}_s + c\bar{E}_s + u_{sr'}$$

$$(4.0) \quad x = p(a + b\bar{Y}_r + c\bar{E}_r + u_{rs'}) + (1 - p)(a' + b\bar{Y}_s + c\bar{E}_s + u_{sr'})$$

$$(4.1) \quad x = a' + (a - a')p + bY_s + cE_s + p(u_{rs'} - u_{sr'}) + u_{sr'} + [\quad],$$

$$u_x = p(u_{rs'} - u_{sr'}) + u_{sr'}.$$

The expression omitted in brackets in equation (4.1) consists of $bp(\bar{Y}_r - \bar{Y}_s) + cp(\bar{E}_r - \bar{E}_s)$. On the same argument as outlined above, this term probably has no appreciable variance and hence can be ignored.

If B-2 holds, the proper specification for equation (4.1) simply involves adding the survey variable p to the other explanatory variables. This is, in fact, what all existing studies have done. The specification is correct if, and only if, all regression coefficients are the same in both the intender and nonintender purchase-rate functions, the constant terms differ, and the mean income and expectations of the population approximate those of nonintenders.[14]

HYPOTHESIS C-1

A somewhat different approach to the problem is to specify contrasting assumptions for the r and s functions. Both cross-section and time-series evidence suggests that it is not wholly unreasonable to think of r as an approximately random variable, but that s cannot be so viewed. Thus we can usefully examine the implications of assuming that the purchase rate of intenders, r, is a random variable whose value depends on the particular question asked in the survey, while the nonintender purchase rate, s, varies systematically with other known variables.

Let us suppose that s is related to p, $\bar{Y}$, and $\bar{E}$; that is, to the proportion of intenders, income, and expectations, while r is a random variable with mean $\bar{R}$ and disturbance d_r. Then we have, assuming $\bar{Y} = \bar{Y}_s$,

[14] Still a third version of this general assumption is to suppose that the functional relationships for intender and nonintender purchase rates are different; perhaps the relevant variables are different, or perhaps the regression coefficients of common variables are different. The equation gets very involved in this case, particularly if the assumption of equality in mean values between intender and nonintender income, expectations, etc., does not hold, as is likely to be the case. Correct specification then involves a series of terms involving the interaction of the p variable with intender and nonintender income, expectations, etc., in addition to terms involving nonintenders' income, expectations, etc., by themselves. Empirically simpler ways to handle this case are discussed under hypotheses C-1 and C-2.

and $\bar{E} = \bar{E}_s$,

$$r = \bar{R} + d_r$$

$$s = a + bp + c\bar{Y} + d\bar{E} + u_s.$$

Substituting into equation 1.0, we get

(5.0) $x = p\bar{R} + q(a + bp + c\bar{Y} + d\bar{E} + u_s) + pd_r$

(5.1) $x = p\bar{R} + aq + bqp + cq\bar{Y} + dq\bar{E} + qu_s + pd_r.$

Equation (5.1) cannot be fitted without serious bias because the error term $(qu_s + pd_r)$ is correlated with most of the other independent variables $(qp, q\bar{Y}, q\bar{E})$. Most of the bias can be eliminated by dividing through by q.[15]

(5.2) $\dfrac{x}{q} = \dfrac{p\bar{R}}{q} + a + bp + c\bar{Y} + d\bar{E} + u_s + \dfrac{p}{q} d_r.$

Equation (5.2) can be put into a more revealing form by shifting the first term on the right-hand side over to the left.

(5.3) $\dfrac{x - p\bar{R}}{q} = a + bp + c\bar{Y} + d\bar{E} + \left(u_s + \dfrac{p}{q} d_r \right).$

Equation (5.3) is of course nothing more than the original nonintender purchase-rate equation with the error term specified to include any additional error arising from the assumption that d_r is zero. Given the basic definitional relationship, $x \equiv pr + qs$, and substituting $(\bar{R} + d_r)$ for r, we get:

(5.31) $s \equiv \dfrac{x - pr}{q} \equiv \dfrac{x}{q} - \dfrac{p}{q}(\bar{R} + d_r) \equiv \dfrac{x - p\bar{R}}{q} - \dfrac{p}{q} d_r.$

We can think of s as having two components, a predicted value designated $\hat{s}$, and a deviation designated $d_{s'}$. From equation (5.31) we can define $\hat{s} \equiv \dfrac{x - p\bar{R}}{q}$, and $d_{s'} \equiv \dfrac{p}{q} d_r$. The predicted and actual values of s will be the same only if r and $\bar{R}$ are always equal; otherwise they will differ by $\dfrac{p}{q} d_r$.

The implicit model for hypothesis C-1 uses a two-step prediction

[15] Even then, however, the new error term $(u_s + \dfrac{p}{q} d_r)$ is still positively correlated with at least one of the independent variables. Since p/q is small (much less than 0.5), the remaining bias is less serious.

method. First we regress predicted values of s on the relevant independent variables:

(5.4) $$\hat{s} \equiv \frac{x - p\bar{R}}{q} = a + b\bar{Y} + c\bar{E} + u_{\hat{s}}.$$

From this equation we obtain regression estimates of $\hat{s}$, designated s°:

(5.41) $$s^{\circ} = a + b\bar{Y} + c\bar{E}.$$

The latter are then used to obtain estimated values of x from the equation

(5.42) $$\hat{x} = p\bar{R} + qs^{\circ}.$$

The error variance in predictions of x derived from this procedure is somewhat smaller than the error variance in equation (5.4) provided that q is less than unity, since the error term in predictions of x based on equation (5.42) works out to be equal to $u_{\hat{s}}$ (from equation 5.4) multiplied by q.

HYPOTHESIS C-2

Extending this approach one further step yields an equation much like (5.42), with at least as small an error variance. Following the procedure outlined for hypothesis C-1, we have:

(1.0) $$x \equiv pr + qs.$$

Combining (5.31), (5.4), and (5.41), we can write

(5.5) $\quad s \equiv s^{\circ} + u_{\hat{s}} - \dfrac{p}{q} d_r$; rewriting (1.0) and substituting (5.5),

(5.6) $$r \equiv \frac{x - q(s^{\circ} + u_{\hat{s}} - pd_r/q)}{p}.$$

Let us now relax the assumption that the intender purchase rate r, is a random variable with mean $\bar{R}$ and disturbance d_r, and think of r as having an estimated component $\hat{r}$ and an error component $d_{r'}$. The estimated component is the first part of equation (5.6);

(5.71) $$\hat{r} \equiv \frac{x - qs^{\circ}}{p},$$

while the error component is the rest.

(5.72) $$d_{r'} = -\frac{q}{p} u_{\hat{s}} + d_r.$$

The estimated value ($\hat{r}$) in (5.71) may be further divided into a systematic component r° and error component $u_{\hat{r}}$, provided $\hat{r}$ varies systematically with other factors, e.g., $\bar{Y}$ and $\bar{E}$.

(5.73) $$\hat{r} = d + e\bar{Y} + f\bar{E} + u_{\hat{r}}$$

(5.74) $$r^\circ = d + e\bar{Y} + f\bar{E}.$$

Finally, putting all the parts together, we can express the intender purchase rate as

(5.8) $$r = r^\circ + u_{\hat{r}} - \frac{q}{p} u_{\hat{s}} + d_r,$$

and substituting both (5.5) and (5.8) in the definitional equation $x \equiv pr + qs$ gives us:

(5.9) $$x = p\left(r^\circ + u_{\hat{r}} - \frac{q}{p} u_{\hat{s}} + d_r\right) + q\left(s^\circ + u_{\hat{s}} - \frac{p}{q} d_r\right).$$

Using predicted values of both r and s to obtain predicted values for x, we have

(5.91) $$\hat{x} = pr^\circ + qs^\circ,$$

with an error term consisting of

$$u_{\hat{x}} = pr^\circ + pu_{\hat{r}} - qu_{\hat{s}} + pd_r + q_{s^\circ} + qu_{\hat{s}} - pd_r - pr^\circ - qs^\circ;$$

cancelling terms,

$$u_{\hat{x}} = pu_{\hat{r}}.$$

HYPOTHESIS C-3

A symmetrical hypothesis to C-2 uses the same structure but proceeds initially on the assumption that s is a random variable with mean $\bar{s}$ and disturbance d_s. Estimated values ($\hat{r}$) are then regressed on selected independent variables, and the resulting regression estimates (r°) are used to obtain a series of predicted values ($\hat{s}$). The latter is in turn regressed on selected independent variables to obtain s°, and both predicted variables (r° and s°) are used to obtain another estimate of $\hat{x}$. The procedure is completely symmetrical to C-2, and the formulation of the error term is predictably symmetrical as $u_{\hat{x}} = qu_{\hat{s}}$.

There is a good deal of cross-section evidence, both theoretical and empirical, that bears on the question of which set of assumptions is likely to hold. Elsewhere [4] I developed the notion that responses to intentions surveys reflect an underlying continuous distribution of purchase probabilities. Thus intenders (nonintenders) are simply households with relatively high (low) mean ex ante purchase probabilities. The extensive empirical evidence examined in [4] suggests that the probability density functions for groups of households classified by an attribute like income level are apt to be roughly symmetrical in the high-probability part of the function where relatively few households are located. The functions cannot be symmetrical throughout if the mean values differ, as would be true for a classification based on income, but the lack of symmetry appears to show up primarily in the low-probability part of the distribution where the bulk of households are located. Thus intenders with high incomes do not necessarily have higher mean probabilities and purchase rates than intenders with low incomes, although mean probabilities and purchase rates among *nonintenders* clearly differ with income class. Similar results are obtained for other classifications associated with purchase rate differences. Intenders reporting that their automobiles "need to be replaced" do not always have higher mean probabilities and purchase rates than other intenders; but among nonintenders, reported replacement need is a powerful discriminator of purchase rates.

Moreover, empirical tests of the probability hypothesis [5] not only indicate that this hypothesis is a useful way to interpret intentions data, but are consistent with the assumption that shifts over time in the probability-density functions are likely to be roughly parallel at the high end of the scale but not at the low end. In general the distributions are shaped like an inverse J; the type of distributions that seem to be typical are shown in Figure 5-2. These portray cross-section differences, where the j subscripts refer to low-income and the h subscripts to high-income families.

Taking a probability of 0.5 as the dividing line between intenders and nonintenders, and denoting x_h and x_j as the mean probability for high- and low-income families, it is often true that the mean probabilities for intenders (r_h, r_j) are independent of income, but it is never true that mean probabilities for nonintenders (s_h, s_j) are independent of income. Although the empirical results bearing on this question all relate to cross sections, the potential application of the analysis to time series is clear: high and low income could readily be income at

FIGURE 5-2. Illustrative Distributions of Purchase Probabilities for High- and Low-Income Respondents

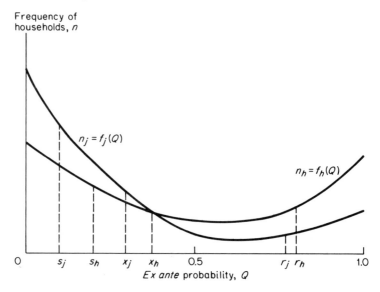

time t and $t + n$. These considerations all suggest that hypotheses C-1 and C-2 are likely to be the equation forms with minimum errors.

EMPIRICAL RESULTS

Preliminary regression estimates showed pronounced serial correlation in the residuals for practically all equations tested, indicating either incomplete or improper specification of the model. Since the main focus of this paper is on the forecasting role of expectational variables in the context of relatively simple standard models, we decided to improve the fit by incorporating the autoregressive structure of the disturbances into the model. Hence lagged dependent variables were introduced into all equations. In a number of equations both one- and two-period lag terms proved to be useful.[16]

[16] There is no simple interpretation of what lagged dependent variables represent in a regression model. One possibility is that they stand for the influence of variables that should be included in the model but have been omitted. Another is that they stand for the influence of lagged values of the independent variables. If the true lag structure happens to take the form of geometrically declining weights for successive past values of all the independent variables, the appropriate specification is to add the lagged dependent variable to the right-hand side of the equation. If the lag structure is more complicated—say, the weights rise to a peak and then decline—the addition of one- and two-period lagged dependent variables may be the appropriate form.

An additional reason for the introduction of lagged values of the dependent variable is that a purely autoregressive model provides a benchmark against which to measure the explanatory power of the substantive part of the model. It was noted earlier that the period covered by the Census intentions survey is largely dominated by a strong cyclical upswing, and that such a period cannot constitute a very satisfactory test for alternative demand models involving different anticipatory variables. One characteristic of such a period is that it can be rather fully explained by an autoregressive model. Asking whether alternative anticipations variables add significantly to the explanation provided by an autoregressive model is thus a much more satisfactory test than asking whether anticipatory variables explain significant amounts of the total variance.

To the several hypotheses outlined above we therefore add one more: A naive or autoregressive model does as well as any of the substantive ones. Designating this hypotheses as N, putting the appropriate lag structure into the equations corresponding to the alternative A . . . C_2 hypotheses, and representing expectations by the SRC index of consumer attitudes (A) and unspecified variables by Z, Z_1, Z_2 . . . , we have:

Hypothesis

N: $\qquad x_t = b_0 + b_1 x_{t-1} + b_2 x_{t-2} + u_{x_t}$

A: (2.2) $\quad x_t = b_0 + b_1 p + b_2 x_{t-1} + b_3 x_{t-2} + u_{x_t}$

B-1: (3.1) $\quad x_t = b_0 + b_1 Y + b_2 A + b_3 x_{t-1} + b_4 x_{t-2} + u_{x_t}$

B-2: (4.1) $\quad x_t = b_0 + b_1 Y + b_2 A + b_3 p + b_4 x_{t-1} + b_5 x_{t-2} + u_{x_t}$

C-1: $\qquad \hat{r}_t = \bar{R}$

$$(5.4) \quad \hat{s}_t \equiv \frac{x_t - p_t \bar{R}}{q_t} = b_0 + b_1 Y + b_2 A + b_3 Z + h_4 \hat{s}_{t-1} + b_5 \hat{s}_{t-2} + u_{\hat{s}_t}$$

$$(5.42)\ \hat{x}_t = p_t \bar{R} + q_t s_t^\circ$$

For our purposes, it is not necessary to choose between these alternative interpretations. Putting the autoregressive structure of the disturbances to use by adding one or more lagged dependent variable to the equation will optimize the forecasting accuracy of the model whether or not these terms stand for omitted variables or for a distributed lag structure. If one were interested in the size of the parameters, however, it would be necessary to specify an interpretation.

C-2: (5.4) $\hat{s}_t = \dfrac{x_t - p_t \bar{R}}{q_t} = b_0 + b_1 Y + b_2 A + b_3 Z + b_4 \hat{s}_{t-1} + b_5 \hat{s}_{t-2} + u_{\hat{s}_t}$

(5.73) $\hat{r}_t \equiv \dfrac{x_t - q_t s_t^{\circ}}{p_t} = b_4 + b_5 Z_1 + b_6 Z_2 + u_{\hat{r}_t}$

(5.91) $\hat{x}_t = p_t r_t^{\circ} + q_t s_t^{\circ}$

The above equations are fitted to estimates of new automobile purchase rates obtained by dividing personal consumption expenditures on automobiles by the average retail price of new automobiles. Both survey variables are measured during the first quarter of the purchase period, while income is measured as the average for the survey quarter and the two prior quarters. The dependent variables — the population purchase rate for new automobiles (x) and the purchase rate for nonintenders (s) — are measured for alternative time spans involving six, nine, or twelve months.

After some experimentation with the earliest available Census intentions data (1959-I), it was decided to fit regressions over the period 1960-I through 1967-III. The first two Census surveys appear to be markedly out of line with the others, which can plausibly be attributed to the fact that both interviewers and respondents must be "broken-in" to any new survey vehicle. The 1959-III and 1959-IV surveys cannot be used because one of the lagged dependent variables for these quarters must be estimated from 1959-II data. The most recent survey variables included in the regressions are for 1966-IV; one of the dependent variables for that quarter covers the latest period for which purchase data are available (1967-III) at current writing.

The results are summarized in panels 1 through 5 of Table 5-2. The autoregressive equation in panel 1 indicates that the test period is relatively easy to explain statistically: Most of the variance in purchase rates is due to the prolonged upward movement from 1961 through the first part of 1966. Panels 2, 3, and 4 clearly contradict all of the extreme hypothesis outlined above. The naive hypothesis (panel 1) is contradicted by the fact that both survey variables contribute significantly to explained variance (panels 2, 3, or 4). Hypothesis A, that both intender (r) and nonintender (s) purchase rates are random and hence that other variables are of no value, is contradicted by the finding that the index of consumer attitudes has a significant partial correlation with purchases, holding constant the proportion of in-

TABLE 5-2. Tests of Alternative Hypotheses About Equation Specification for Demand Models With a Buying Intentions Variable

Dependent Variable	Independent Variables (t ratios)	Regression Statistics [a]		
		R^2	SE	DW
	Panel 1. Naive Model: Autoregressive Equation			
$x_6 =$	$1.35 + 1.144x_{-1} - 0.252x_{-2}$	.890	0.46	1.45
	$\quad\quad(5.8)\quad\quad(1.3)$			
$x_9 =$	$0.96 + 1.350x_{-1} - 0.426x_{-2}$	.937	0.34	1.77
	$\quad\quad(7.7)\quad\quad(2.5)$			
$x_{12} =$	$0.80 + 1.477x_{-1} - 0.542x_{-2}$	.955	0.28	1.91
	$\quad\quad(8.7)\quad\quad(3.2)$			
	Panel 2. Hypothesis A: r, s Random Variables			
$x_6 =$	$-1.72 + 0.820x_{-1} - 0.405x_{-2} + 0.320p^*$	.946	0.32	1.75
	$\quad\quad(5.4)\quad\quad(2.9)\quad\quad(5.1)$			
$x_9 =$	$-0.95 + 1.024x_{-1} - 0.470x_{-2} + 0.232p^*$	.957	0.28	2.22
	$\quad\quad(5.9)\quad\quad(3.3)\quad\quad(3.5)$			
$x_{12} =$	$-0.68 + 1.262x_{-1} - 0.663x_{-2} + 0.202p^*$	.966	0.24	2.01
	$\quad\quad(7.7)\quad\quad(4.4)\quad\quad(3.0)$			
	Panel 3. Hypothesis B-1: r, s Functions Have Identical Parameters			
$x_6 =$	$-9.34 + 0.726x_{-1} - 0.187x_{-2} + 0.100A + 0.076Y_e$	.932	0.36	1.48
	$\quad\quad(3.9)\quad\quad(1.1)\quad\quad(4.1)\quad\quad(2.0)$			
$x_9 =$	$-6.96 + 0.982x_{-1} - 0.352x_{-2} + 0.077A + 0.058Y_e$	.954	0.29	1.46
	$\quad\quad(5.2)\quad\quad(1.9)\quad\quad(3.2)\quad\quad(1.8)$			
$x_{12} =$	$-3.04 + 1.254x_{-1} - 0.447x_{-2} + 0.042A + 0.019Y_e$	.957	0.27	1.73
	$\quad\quad(5.9)\quad\quad(2.1)\quad\quad(1.6)\quad\quad(0.6)$			
	Panel 4. Hypothesis B-2: r, s Functions Differ Only in Their Respective Constant Terms			
$x_6 =$	$-5.91 + 0.668x_{-1} - 0.240x_{-2} + 0.057A + 0.267p^*$	.960	0.28	1.79
	$\quad\quad(4.8)\quad\quad(1.8)\quad\quad(3.0)\quad\quad(4.7)$			
$x_9 =$	$-5.58 + 0.722x_{-1} - 0.252x_{-2} + 0.058A + 0.233p^*$	.971	0.23	1.93
	$\quad\quad(4.3)\quad\quad(1.9)\quad\quad(3.4)\quad\quad(4.2)$			
$x_{12} =$	$-4.57 + 0.945x_{-1} - 0.480x_{-2} + 0.047A + 0.235p^*$	.974	0.21	1.92
	$\quad\quad(5.2)\quad\quad(3.3)\quad\quad(2.8)\quad\quad(3.9)$			
	Panel 5. Hypothesis C-1: r Function Random, s Function Systematic			
$\hat{s}_6 =$	$-10.96 + 0.332s_{-1} + 0.095A + 0.176p^*_{-1}$	.864	0.28 [b]	1.15
	$\quad\quad(2.8)\quad\quad(4.0)\quad\quad(3.3)$			
$\hat{s}_9 =$	$-12.28 + 0.249s_{-1} + 0.112A + 0.180p^*_{-1}$	.895	0.24 [b]	1.08
	$\quad\quad(2.0)\quad\quad(4.8)\quad\quad(3.8)$			
$\hat{s}_{12} =$	$-10.12 + 0.376s_{-1} + 0.103A + 0.112p^*_{-1}$	.872	0.25 [b]	1.09
	$\quad\quad(2.2)\quad\quad(3.4)\quad\quad(2.1)$			

[a] The DW statistic is biased towards a value of 2.0 because lagged dependent variables have been included in the model. The presence of serially correlated residuals cannot therefore be gauged by the usual tests. R^2 and SE values are adjusted for degrees of freedom. All equations are fitted with a dummy (1,0) variable to represent the influence of the automobile strike in 1964-IV. The dummy usually has a significant t ratio.

Variables are as follows (more complete definitions and basic data are in Appendix Table 2): x_6, x_9, x_{12} = six-month, nine-month, and twelve-month purchase rate for new automobiles, based on estimates of consumer expenditures for new cars and the estimated average retail price. A = SRC index of consumer attitudes, 1956 = 100. p^* = weighted Census Bureau intentions to buy cars, the weights being rough *a priori* approximations to mean ex ante purchase probability for different classes of intenders. Y_e = per family real disposable income, averaged for the survey quarter and the preceding six months. $\hat{s}_6, \hat{s}_9, \hat{s}_{12}$ = the estimated purchase rate of nonintenders. Estimates are based on the assumption that intender purchase rates are constant at the levels implied by the weights used in construction of the p series.

[b] Estimated from x equation: $\hat{x} = p\bar{r} + qs^\circ$, where x is the predicted values of x, p and q are the proportions of intenders and nonintenders in the survey, $\bar{r}$ is the fixed purchase rate of intenders, and s° is the predicted value of s from the equations in panel 5.

tenders (panel 4). Hypothesis B-1, that both r and s functions have identical parameters and hence that the intentions variable is of no value, is also contradicted by the results in panel 4; intentions clearly have a significant partial correlation with purchases.[17]

The next hypothesis, B-2, which states that the r and s functions are identical except for a difference in the value of the constant term, is not clearly contradicted by any of the evidence. The p^* coefficient (which should be roughly equal to the difference between intender and nonintender purchase rates) has about the right order of magnitude, and the fits are quite good for all purchase periods.

These equations essentially say that automobile purchase rates can be explained by the autoregressive structure of the data and by the two survey variables A and p^*. Income does not appear in the equation, apparently because the lagged dependent variables swallow up its trend effect while the survey variables pick off its cyclical movements.

Tests of hypothesis C-1, given in the last panel, show results that are about on a par with tests of B-2. For the nonintender purchase rate function, the dependent variable is estimated from the observed population purchase rate on the assumption that intender purchase rates are constant. This estimated variable is best explained by the index of consumer attitudes (A) and lagged buying intentions (p^*_{-1}). It should be noted that lagged rather than current buying intentions play a role in the s equation: Current intentions add nothing to the explanation of variance. A possible explanation is that changes in the desired level of automobile stocks constitute a kind of "social disease" which infects intenders first and nonintenders subsequently. Intenders are, after all, simply those who have reported an awareness that they are likely to purchase a car. Thus they may differ from nonintenders, among other reasons, partly because they react more quickly to the same economic stimuli which eventually will cause reactions throughout the population.

Although the proportion of explained variance in the nonintender purchase rate equations is markedly lower than in panels where popula-

---

[17] Although income is not included as one of the independent variables in the panel 4 regressions, it would make no difference to the results; income has a t ratio of less than unity in the panel 4 equation, apparently being redundant to a combination of the lagged dependent variable and buying intentions.

tion purchase rates are the dependent variable, the standard error of population purchase rate prediction based on these nonintender equations is just about the same as in the best of the direct estimates. The standard error calculations in panel 5 are not the standard errors applicable to the equations shown in that panel. Rather, they are the standard errors applicable to the x equations, which correspond to, and are estimated from, the s equations.

On the whole, however, the purchase rate functions in panel 5 are not very satisfactory. They provide no evidence to support the a priori argument that hypothesis C-1 is a better description of reality than, say, hypothesis B-2. I have not found any sensible way to rectify the shortcoming of these nonintender equations, although it is easy to add variables which provide much better fits in the s equation as well as substantially smaller standard errors in the x equations derived from them. For example, the inclusion of income in the panel 5 equations produces a marked increase in explained variance and reduction in standard error. However, income enters with a negative sign whether it is measured with a lag (expected income) or contemporaneously (actual income). I can think of no reasonable explanation for the empirical finding that income exerts a negative effect on nonintender purchase rates. Expected income might well have this effect, since it could easily be standing for unexpected income change. However, not only expected but also actual income have strongly significant and negative regression coefficients in these equations, and the inclusion of both, which provides a measure of unexpected income change, yields a negative coefficient for expected income and either an additional negative coefficient for actual income or a coefficient of approximately zero.

Tests of hypothesis C-2 (the assumption that a random r variable is an oversimplification and that r is functionally related to other variables), were inconclusive. If variations in intender purchase rates are not in fact random but can be explained, C-2 should yield better estimates of the population purchase rate than C-1. But neither income, the index of consumer attitudes, the weighted proportion of intenders, nor the lagged dependent variable prove to have any association at all with "predicted" intender purchase rates. For the limited number of independent variables against which predicted values of r were regressed, the adjusted R^2 was always 0: the series of predicted r values appears to be wholly random.[18] This result is consistent either with hypothesis C-1 (that the r and s functions are quite different, r being random and s systematically related to other variables) or with hypothesis B-2 (that the r and s functions are identical except for the constant). If the latter happens to be the case, the s function specified by hypothesis C-1 will pick up all of the systematic variation in r as well as in s, leaving no systematic variation in r to be explained.

Although the evidence does not give any clear advantage to either the B-2 or C-1 hypotheses, the structure of the underlying model seems to me more satisfactory for the latter. Both provide very close fits to the observed purchase rate. In fact, the fit of B-2 is so good that I do not view the inability of C-1 to improve the fit as constituting strong evidence against it. Hence, I conclude that, although improper specification arising out of differences in intender and nonintender purchase rate functions has not (during the 1959–67 period) adversely affected the fit of equations that include an intentions variable and has not, therefore, been a source of error in measuring the time-series contribution of intentions surveys, nonetheless, this type of specification error is probably characteristic of demand models incorporating an intentions variable. It is more accurate, in my judgment, to treat intender purchase rates as a random variable with a fixed mean value than as being determined by the parameters and variables in the nonintender purchase rate function. And nonintender purchase rates, in turn, appear to be most accurately described as a function of the consumer attitude index and lagged buying intentions. Thus, both types of anticipatory surveys are essential ingredients in demand models. Intentions surveys provide data on the proportions of various classes of intenders (to whom fixed purchase rates can be applied) and the proportion of nonintenders. Attitude surveys provide the data needed to estimate the purchase rate of nonintenders.

It should be noted that the above analysis can readily be applied

---

[18] If the predicted r variable from equation (5.73) is a random variable, then the variance of predicted r is equal to the variance of the error term in that equation, u_r, the constant is equal to the mean value of predicted r, and the regression coefficients of all independent variables are zero. If this is the case, it can easily be shown that the error term for equation (5.91) $pu_{\hat{r}}$ is precisely the same as the error term for equation (5.42) $qu_{\hat{s}}$.

to a new body of survey data which measures subjective purchase probabilities directly rather than intentions or plans to purchase. The basic structure of the C-1 equation specifies a distinction in the time-series variability of purchase rates in two subgroups of households — those who have so classified themselves that their purchase rates can be presumed largely or wholly independent of other factors, and those who have not. The first group is taken to comprise intenders in the above analysis, but could equally well be viewed as comprising households reporting purchase probabilities in excess of some specified level. The second group is taken to comprise nonintenders in the above analysis but could evidently be viewed as comprising those with purchase probabilities at or below some specified level. In short, high-probability households may have stable purchase rates that do not need to (and cannot be) explained, while low- or zero-probability households may have purchase rates that vary systematically with other factors and hence do need to be explained. There would of course be differences between the proportions of the population in the two groups depending on whether intentions or probabilities were the basis for the classification, but the general principle seems applicable to either basis of classification.

DEFLATION BIAS

A second type of specification error arises from the use of deflated per capita (or per household) expenditures as the variable to be explained in a model of durable goods demand. In most such models [e.g., those in 3, 10, 13] the influence of both price and population movements are ordinarily removed from both dependent and independent variables, since otherwise common trends are likely to be imposed on both. But the resulting model seems clearly misspecified.

For simplicity of both analysis and empirical testing, we deal only with demand for a single product — automobiles. We can define: M_t as the rate of consumer expenditures on new automobiles, V_t as the average unit price of new automobiles, S as unit sales to consumers of new automobiles, P_a as the price index of new automobiles, and H as the number of households in the population. Dropping the time subscripts for convenience, M can be expressed as SV. Deflated per household expenditure, M^*, can be expressed as $\frac{M}{HP_a}$. Thus,

$$M^* = \frac{M}{HP_a} = \frac{SV}{HP_a} = \frac{S}{H}\left(\frac{V}{P_a}\right).$$

The first of the two terms on the right hand side is the purchase rate, denoted as x, while the second is the real price per unit, denoted as V^*.

$$x = \frac{S}{H}$$

$$V^* = \frac{V}{P_a};$$

hence,

$$M^* = xV^*.$$

Demand models seeking to explain M^* evidently should be structured in terms of a multiplicative relation involving the two component variables, x and V^*. The only exception arises when either x or V^* are best described as random variables with constant mean values. In that case, the appropriate M^* equation is simply a linear transformation of the function for the component which contains systematic variation. That is, if

$$x = f(Z) \quad \text{and} \quad V^* = \bar{V}^* + u,$$

$$M^* = \bar{V}^* f(Z) = f'(Z),$$

where the x and M^* functions differ only by a multiplicative constant.

Thus we have alternative demand models for M^*: we can write either

(1) $M^* = f(Z_1)$,   where
       $M^* = xV^*$,   or

(2) $M^* = f(Z_2) \cdot f(Z_3)$,

where

(2.1) $x = f(Z_2)$,

(2.2) $V^* = f(Z_3)$.

Let us look first at empirical estimates of equations 2.1 and 2.2, the two components of real expenditures per family. Regressing both x and V^* on a common set of parameters indicates that the relevant independent variables are entirely different. The numbers below the regression coefficients are t ratios; the independent variables are weighted buying intentions (p^*), the index of consumer attitudes (A), real per family disposal income in the recent past (Y_e), and a dummy variable (D) reflecting the shift of purchases (between the last quarter of 1964 and the first half of 1965) induced by the automobile strike in late 1964. The R^2 and standard error (SE) values are both adjusted for degrees of freedom.

$$(2.10) \quad x = 4.15p^* + 1.03A + 0.23Y_e + 3.50D - 108, \quad R^2 = 0.942$$
$$ (5.0) \quad\;\; (4.4) \quad\;\; (0.6) \quad\;\; (1.5) \qquad\qquad SE = 3.27$$
$$ DW = 1.27$$

$$(2.20) \quad V^* = 0.17p^* - 0.18A + 3.07Y_e + 100, \qquad R^2 = 0.964$$
$$ (0.2) \quad\; (-0.9) \quad\; (9.7) \qquad\qquad\quad SE = 2.94$$
$$ DW = 0.87$$

The survey variables p^* and A dominate the purchase rate equation, while income dominates the real price per unit equation. A look at the x and V^* series indicates that changes in unit purchase rates are the dominant cyclical component in the expenditure series, while changes in real price per car (= increased quality per unit) are dominantly a secular influence. The cyclical movements in purchase rates are captured by the survey variables p^* and A, while the secular movements in real price per unit are captured by income. It will come as no surprise that regressing real expenditures on the same variables shows all three to be highly significant.

$$(1.0) \quad M^* = 11.7p^* + 2.97A + 4.81Y_e + 15.5D - 576, \quad R^2 = 0.966$$
$$ (4.4) \quad\;\; (4.0) \quad\;\; (4.3) \quad\;\; (2.1) \qquad\qquad SE = 10.5$$
$$ DW = 1.10$$

The "best" x, V^* and M^* functions are slightly different from the ones just summarized. Introduction of a distributed lag structure considerably improves the fit and seems plausible on a priori grounds; all independent variables continue to be highly significant with the exception of Y_e in the M^* equation. The best fitting lag structure usually but not always involves geometrically declining weights.

$$(2.11) \quad x = 2.32p^* + 0.59A + 3.41D + 0.72x_{-1} \qquad R^2 = 0.972$$
$$ (4.3) \quad\;\; (3.6) \quad\;\; (2.2) \quad\;\; (4.4) \qquad\qquad SE = 2.27$$
$$ -0.25x_{-2} - 56. \qquad\qquad\qquad\qquad\quad DW = 2.01$$
$$ (1.9)$$

Alternatively,

$$(2.12) \quad x = 2.18p^* + 0.80A - 0.58A_{-1} + 2.90D \qquad R^2 = 0.976$$
$$ (4.4) \quad\;\; (4.5) \quad\;\; (2.2) \quad\;\; (2.0) \qquad SE = 2.10$$
$$ + 0.87x_{-1} - 0.30x_{-2} - 30. \qquad\qquad DW = 2.26$$
$$ (5.2) \qquad (2.4)$$

$$(2.21) \quad V^* = 1.61Y_e + 0.52V^*_{-1} + 34. \qquad\qquad R^2 = 0.980$$
$$ (4.8) \qquad\;\; (4.6) \qquad\qquad\qquad SE = 2.19$$
$$ DW = 1.86$$

$$(1.1) \quad M^* = 7.8p^* + 2.08A + 1.33Y_e + 16.1D \qquad R^2 = 0.982$$
$$ (3.7) \quad\;\; (3.6) \quad\;\; (1.2) \quad\;\; (3.0) \qquad SE = 7.7$$
$$ + 0.48M^*_{-1} - 319. \qquad\qquad\qquad DW = 1.73$$
$$ (4.7)$$

As before, the "best" x and V^* equations indicate quite different roles for the two survey variables and for income. The survey variables dominate the purchase rate equation, and income does not even appear; income would have a small negative coefficient in equation (2.11) and a t ratio of less than unity. For the real price equation, in contrast, neither survey variable appears and income is the only significant variable other than the lag term.

The analysis suggests that equation $2[M^* = f(Z_2) \cdot f(Z_3)]$ should give a better empirical fit than equation $1[M^* = f(Z_1)]$. The "best" estimate of the latter (equation 1.1) has a very close relationship to actual expenditures and there is limited room for possible improvement in fit. Equation (2) says that the appropriate form of the M^* equation is a multiplicative version of the underlying x and V^* equations. If both equations have constant terms, as they do, proper specification would involve all of the independent variables that appear in either the x or V^* equations plus all the possible cross-product terms involving variables that appear in either. Selecting equation (2.10) for x and (2.20) for V^*, for example, implies fitting an M^* equation with sixteen terms and comparing its characteristics to those of equation (1.0). If the x and V^* equations are more complicated, as in equations (2.11) and (2.21), there are even more terms in the multiplicative equation. Given the limited number of truly independent observations available in a time series with autoregressive characteristics, it was judged inadvisable to estimate an equation with that many variables.

The tabulation below compares adjusted R^2 values and incremental F ratios for two additive M^* equations and several versions of the associated multiplicative equation. I did not conduct systematic tests to determine the maximum obtainable adjusted R^2 for the multiplicative equations, but simply experimented with a limited number of equations involving different terms of the sort that should appear in the latter equation. Since all the multiplicative equations actually estimated are missing most of the relevant cross-product terms, the regression coefficients are highly unstable and are often implausible. What matters, however is whether any of the independent variables implied by the multiplicative equation contribute significantly to the explanation of variance in M^*, and the F ratio is a measure of this contribution. The results suggest that the multiplicative relation is in fact superior; some of the F ratios shown in the tabulation below are highly significant.

Equation Type and Independent Variables	R^2	SE	DW	F Ratio [a]
Additive (1.0)				
$M^* = f(p^*, A, Y_e, D)$	.966	10.5	1.10	—
Multiplicative (2.10 × 2.20)				
$M^* = f(p^*, A, Y_e, D, p^*Y_e)$	.973	9.4	1.00	6.4 [b]
$M^* = f(p^*, A, Y_e, D, p^*Y_e, AY_e)$	.972	9.5	1.03	3.5
Additive (1.1)				
$M^* = g(p^*, A, Y_e, D, M^*_{-1})$	.982	7.7	1.73	—
Multiplicative (2.11 × 2.21)				
$M^* = g(p^*, A, Y_e, D, x_{-1}, x_{-2}, V^*_{-1})$	.983	7.4	2.17	1.9
$M^* = g(p^*, A, Y_e, D, x_{-1}, x_{-2}, V^*_{-1}, p^*Y_e)$	.989	6.0	2.38	5.9 [c]
$M^* = g(p^*, A, Y_e, D, x_{-1}, V^*_{-1}, p^*Y_e)$	.990	5.8	2.37	9.2 [c]

[a] F ratio for incremental explained variance, multiplicative equation relative to associated additive equation.
[b] F ratio significantly different from unity at 5 per cent level
[c] F ratio significantly different from unity at 1 per cent level.

Hence I conclude, tentatively, that a multiplicative relation

$$M^* = f(Z_2) \cdot f(Z_3), \quad \text{where}$$

$$x = f(Z_2) \quad \text{and} \quad V^* = f(Z_3),$$

is the appropriate specification for a deflated expenditure equation.

IV. AN APPRAISAL OF SOME EXISTING
TIME-SERIES MODELS

This section examines a number of relatively simple demand models that make use of consumer anticipations data, focusing mainly on an examination of forecasting accuracy. Models similar to some of the ones examined here were originally fitted to data covering the 1950's and the early 1960's. For these, an ex ante measure of forecast accuracy can be generated by extrapolating the model beyond the original period of fit. Next, the stability of the parameters in the various models can be examined by comparing parameter estimates for different periods of fit. Finally, the forecasts generated by the substantive (anticipations) models can be compared with a realistic benchmark — forecasts from autoregressive models which use only lagged values of the dependent variable.

The purpose of this excursion into forecast models is not to bestow praise on "winners" or cast blame at "losers," although one objective is certainly to find out if being a "winner" is a serially correlated property of forecast models. More important aims are to examine the stability of the parameters of alternative models, to find out if the models contain any information about the future other than some extrapolative element of the variable to be forecast, and to measure the consistency and importance of the apparent contribution of consumer survey data.

All the models examined below have a relatively simple structure. The dependent variables all measure expenditures during the six months after the survey quarter, that is, the quarter in which the survey data are obtained. Independent variables are per household deflated disposable income during the six months prior to a survey quarter (Y_{-6}), the difference between income of the survey quarter and past income (ΔY), the SRC index of consumer attitudes (A) and a buying intentions variable (p^*) that is a spliced series consisting of weighted Census Bureau QSI data from 1959 to date and essentially unweighted SRC intentions data before 1959. A lagged dependent variable is included in some models. Alternative dependent variables are deflated per household expenditures on automobiles and parts during the six months after the survey quarter (M_6), deflated per household expenditures on total durables during the six months after the survey quarter (D_6), and the two ratios M_6/Y_{-6} and D_6/Y_{-6}. The denominators of the last two variables use past rather than contemporaneous income, both because it was desirable to have all variables predetermined except for expenditures and because it also seemed desirable to eliminate the possible causal association running from expenditures in a given period to disposable income of the same period.

The models are fitted to a number of different time spans. One of the most extensive recent investigations of the role of consumer anticipations in durable goods demand models is Eva Mueller's 1963 study, which estimated relationships from surveys covering the 1953–61 period; since the dependent variable (purchases) extends two quarters beyond the last survey quarter, Mueller's data actually go through the second quarter of 1962. Other recent studies (Friend and Adams and the Suits chapter in the Brookings-SSRC model) use the 1953–62 period. Hence, we start with the fit period 1953–61 and generate forecasts for the period 1962–67. Other fit periods are obtained by adding additional quarters to the original 1953–61 span. Parameters are also estimated for periods constructed by removing observations from the beginning of the fit period and simultaneously adding an equal number of observations to the end; the extrapolation periods are the same as for spans in which all observations are retained. This second set of parameters is designed to get a better measure of the influence of the buying intentions variable, which, as indicated above, is a spliced series.[19]

Table 5-3 summarizes the parameter estimates for alternative forms of two simple demand models. Equation (1) is the model found to be optimum by Mueller [11] after investigation of a large number of po-

[19] From Section II we know that the part of the p^* series based on SRC data is subject to much larger sampling and other measurement errors than the part based on Census QSI data. Hence, we have a more accurate measure of intentions for the period from 1959 to date than for 1953–58, and dropping observations in the latter period should tend to improve the usefulness of the intentions variable.

It should be noted that the procedure of dropping pre-1959 observations does not provide a really satisfactory test of the role of buying intention in time-series models. The 1960's, the period for which Census intentions data are available, has been trend-dominated until quite recently, while the 1950's showed virtually no trend in durables purchases from 1953 onward but contained large cyclical fluctuations.

TABLE 5-3. Regression Statistics for Alternative Prediction Models and Fit Periods, 1953-67

Fit Periods	Regression coefficients (t ratios)					DW		$\bar{R}^2$		$\overline{SE}$ (billions of dollars)		Forecast Error	
	Equation 1		Equation 2										
	Y_{-6} [a]	A	Y_{-6} [a]	A	p^*	Eq. 1	Eq. 2	Eq. 1	Eq. 2	Eq. 1	Eq. 2	Eq. 1	Eq. 2
			A: M_6 Dependent										
1953-II–1962-II	.061 (2.8)	.323 (4.7)	.032 (1.3)	.250 (3.5)	.101 (2.2)	1.47	1.72	.505	.588	1.38	1.26	2.90	3.18
1953-II–1962-III	.076 (5.3)	.341 (5.8)	.049 (2.8)	.275 (4.5)	.098 (2.3)	1.44	1.62	.671	.720	1.29	1.19	2.27	2.37
1953-II–1964-III	.092 (7.9)	.358 (6.2)	.059 (3.6)	.280 (4.7)	.110 (2.7)	1.30	1.51	.759	.802	1.29	1.17	1.26	1.66
1953-II–1966-I	.101 (12.2)	.378 (7.3)	.071 (5.3)	.312 (5.8)	.105 (2.7)	1.35	1.46	.890	.907	1.24	1.14	1.05	1.19
1953-II–1967-II	.103 (18.6)	.346 (8.0)	.078 (7.5)	.280 (6.0)	.099 (2.7)	1.29	1.38	.918	.930	1.19	1.10	—	—
			B: M_6/Y_{-6} Dependent										
1953-II–1962-II	.078 (2.5)	.071 (3.1)	.075 (2.5)	.064 (3.0)	.023 (2.0)	1.46	1.51	.622	.676	1.24	1.16	2.57	1.49
1953-II–1963-III	.072 (2.4)	.077 (3.6)	.070 (2.6)	.064 (3.3)	.025 (2.8)	1.32	1.47	.609	.694	1.24	1.09	2.82	1.55
1953-II–1964-III	.089 (3.2)	.072 (3.4)	.071 (3.0)	.062 (3.4)	.028 (3.8)	1.16	1.46	.616	.741	1.27	1.04	3.01	1.69
1953-II–1966-I	.081 (3.0)	.093 (4.2)	.054 (2.5)	.069 (4.0)	.032 (5.1)	1.16	1.55	.674	.813	1.40	1.06	3.77	1.90
1953-II–1967-II	.086 (3.0)	.069 (3.0)	.045 (2.2)	.056 (3.6)	.038 (7.0)	0.77	1.44	.550	.802	1.66	1.11	—	—

C: M_6 Dependent, Earliest Data Dropped as Fit Period Is Extended													
	(2.8)	(4.7)	(1.3)	(3.5)	(2.2)								
1953-II–1962-II	.061	.323	.032	.250	.101	1.47	1.72	.505	.588	1.38	1.26	2.90	3.18
	(3.8)	(5.6)	(2.4)	(4.5)	(1.6)								
1955-III–1963-III	.076	.326	.055	.280	.088	1.61	1.53	.651	.677	1.20	1.15	2.29	2.18
	(6.1)	(4.0)	(4.5)	(2.9)	(1.7)								
1957-I–1964-III	.117	.286	.097	.221	.083	1.34	1.42	.840	.855	1.01	0.96	0.85	0.71
	(8.0)	(1.3)	(1.7)	(2.3)	(3.9)								
1959-III–1966-I	.156	.152	.052	.202	.258	1.29	1.32	.942	.967	0.86	0.65	3.18	0.90
	(17.9)	(7.2)	(6.1)	(4.5)	(5.1)								
1961-II–1967-II	.116	.328	.066	.186	.230	1.08	2.45	.949	.978	0.78	0.52	–	–
D: M_6/Y_{-6} Dependent, Earliest Data Dropped as Fit Period Is Extended													
	(2.5)	(3.1)	(2.5)	(3.0)	(2.0)								
1953-II–1962-II	.078	.071	.075	.064	.023	1.46	1.51	.622	.676	1.24	1.16	2.57	1.49
	(1.7)	(4.0)	(2.2)	(3.3)	(2.2)								
1955-III–1963-III	.054	.082	.065	.066	.029	1.63	1.65	.633	.697	1.16	1.06	2.81	1.46
	(1.7)	(3.9)	(3.1)	(1.3)	(4.0)								
1957-I–1964-III	.051	.096	.070	.032	.043	1.24	1.48	.650	.804	1.11	0.83	2.77	1.28
	(0.3)	(4.9)	(1.1)	(1.4)	(7.4)								
1959-III–1966-I	.011	.168	.018	.035	.068	1.72	1.14	.704	.922	1.27	0.65	4.34	1.01
	(0.4)	(2.4)	(0.7)	(4.4)	(12.5)								
1961-II–1967-II	.016	.086	−.009	.054	.066	0.28	2.16	.349	.929	1.67	0.56	–	–

(continued)

TABLE 5-3 (concluded)

Fit Periods	Equation 1 Y_{-6}[a]	Equation 1 A	Equation 2 Y_{-6}[a]	Equation 2 A	Equation 2 p^*	DW Eq. 1	DW Eq. 2	$\bar{R}^2$ Eq. 1	$\bar{R}^2$ Eq. 2	$\overline{SE}$ Eq. 1	$\overline{SE}$ Eq. 2	Forecast Error Eq. 1	Forecast Error Eq. 2
										(billions of dollars)			
E: D_6 Dependent Variable													
1953-II–1962-II	.138 (5.3)	.415 (5.0)	.114 (3.7)	.354 (3.9)	.084 (1.4)	1.32	1.36	.644	.662	1.65	1.61	6.93	7.17
1953-II–1963-III	.164 (9.2)	.448 (6.1)	.142 (6.1)	.394 (4.8)	.080 (1.4)	1.27	1.27	.806	.814	1.61	1.58	6.04	6.13
1953-II–1964-III	.207 (11.6)	.498 (5.6)	.172 (6.4)	.417 (4.3)	.115 (1.7)	0.86	0.92	.841	.852	1.97	1.91	3.09	3.61
1953-II–1966-I	.228 (17.7)	.556 (6.9)	.200 (8.9)	.494 (5.5)	.098 (1.5)	0.92	0.89	.932	.934	1.94	1.90	2.12	2.39
1953-II–1967-II	.239 (27.4)	.492 (7.2)	.218 (12.4)	.437 (5.5)	.084 (1.4)	0.86	0.81	.956	.957	1.88	1.86	—	—
F: D_6/Y_{-6} Dependent Variable													
1953-II–1962-II	.105 (2.9)	.089 (3.4)	.102 (2.9)	.082 (3.2)	.019 (1.5)	1.40	1.36	.679	.698	1.43	1.39	6.25	5.14
1953-II–1963-III	.096 (2.5)	.100 (3.7)	.093 (2.7)	.085 (3.4)	.029 (2.4)	1.10	1.20	.627	.690	1.55	1.41	7.01	5.25
1953-II–1964-III	.154 (3.4)	.085 (2.5)	.124 (3.4)	.067 (2.4)	.047 (4.1)	0.75	1.01	.571	.728	2.01	1.60	6.96	4.27
1953-II–1966-I	.166 (3.6)	.126 (3.3)	.114 (3.4)	.081 (3.0)	.061 (6.0)	0.82	1.16	.650	.830	2.41	1.68	8.61	4.71
1953-II–1967-I	.186 (3.3)	.074 (1.6)	.100 (2.9)	.047 (1.7)	.081 (8.4)	0.43	0.99	.458	.809	3.27	1.94	—	—

G: D_6 Dependent, Earliest Data Dropped as Fit Period Is Extended

Period													
1953-II–1962-II	.138 (5.3)	.415 (5.0)	.114 (3.7)	.354 (3.9)	.084 (1.4)	1.32	.644	1.36	.662	1.65	1.61	6.93	7.17
1955-III–1963-III	.181 (7.6)	.438 (6.4)	.172 (5.9)	.418 (5.3)	.039 (0.6)	1.45	.802	1.37	.794	1.42	1.45	5.18	5.13
1957-I–1964-III	.288 (9.6)	.322 (2.9)	.267 (7.6)	.254 (2.0)	.087 (1.1)	0.84	.897	0.87	.899	1.56	1.55	1.73	1.58
1959-III–1966-I	.335 (11.2)	.154 (0.9)	.220 (4.0)	.209 (1.3)	.286 (2.4)	0.94	.965	1.00	.972	1.32	1.18	5.11	1.38
1961-II–1967-II	.270 (24.4)	.458 (5.9)	.188 (9.6)	.224 (3.0)	.376 (4.6)	0.97	.969	1.81	.985	1.34	0.94	—	—

H: D_6/Y_{-6} Dependent, Earliest Data Dropped as Fit Period Is Extended

Period													
1953-II–1962-II	.105 (2.9)	.089 (3.4)	.102 (2.9)	.082 (3.2)	.019 (1.5)	1.40	.679	1.36	.698	1.43	1.39	6.25	5.14
1955-II–1963-II	.075 (2.0)	.106 (4.2)	.089 (2.4)	.087 (3.5)	.032 (2.0)	1.29	.668	1.35	.711	1.43	1.33	6.08	4.48
1957-I–1964-III	.115 (2.1)	.129 (2.8)	.154 (3.7)	.005 (0.1)	.083 (4.3)	.72	.576	1.05	.776	2.08	1.51	6.48	3.02
1959-III–1966-I	.064 (1.1)	.272 (4.5)	.076 (3.0)	.027 (0.7)	.125 (9.0)	1.46	.721	1.43	.946	2.23	.98	9.58	1.83
1961-II–1967-II	.100 (1.1)	.085 (1.1)	.042 (1.8)	.014 (0.7)	.145 (15.9)	.17	.211	2.59	.945	3.58	.94	—	—

(Table notes are on following page)

tential explanatory variables. Equation (2) is the same model with the spliced buying intentions variable included. A slightly different version of both models is also estimated. The dependent variable (either automobile or total durable expenditure) is put in the form of a ratio to past income, and an additional independent variable (past change in income) is used. Separate regressions are estimated for automobiles and for total durable goods expenditures, and data are shown for alternative sets of five sequential fit periods. Reading vertically, the columns indicate the change in regression coefficients, standard errors, etc., as the fit period is altered either by adding observation or by both adding and dropping observations simultaneously.

One of the first things to note is that the parameter estimates of equation (1) in the 1953–61 period are by no means the same as originally estimated in [11] simply because the basic income and expenditure data have been revised. For example, the Y_{-6} variable had a t ratio of less than unity in the Mueller study, but shows a t ratio of almost three in Table 5-3. Mueller also found that buying intentions (SRC series) did not add significantly to the explanation of variance in

---

Notes to Table 5-3

Variables are defined as follows:

M_6 deflated per household expenditures on automobiles and parts (*Survey of Current Business* definitions) during the six months following the survey quarter.

D_6 deflated per household expenditures on durable goods (*Survey of Current Business* definitions) during the six months following the survey quarter.

Y_{-6} deflated per household disposable income during the six months prior to the survey quarter.

A index of consumer attitudes as prepared by the Survey Research Center, University of Michigan: The measure of A used above does not include the two buying intentions components.

p^* weighted seasonally adjusted intentions to buy automobiles, based on Census Bureau data for the period 1959–67 and on SRC (largely unweighted) data for periods prior to 1959.

A more complete description of the basic data is contained in the Data Appendix.

General Note: Period shown covers the *purchase* period included in the equation. The survey data cover a slightly earlier period since the equations are designed to be forecasting equations. For the first fit period 1953-II–1962-II, for example, the surveys cover the period 1953-I–1961-IV; the 1953-I survey is used to predict purchases during 1953-II and -III while the 1961-IV survey is used to predict purchases during 1962-I and -II. Not all quarters are used in the regressions because the survey variables are not always available.

All estimates of $\overline{SE}$ and RMS are in billions of 1958 dollars. Where the dependent variable has the form of a ratio to past income (M_6/Y_{-6}), the $\overline{SE}$ and RMS are converted to billions by multiplying the computed values by the average value of Y_{-6} during the fit period (for $\overline{SE}$) and forecast period (for RMS), respectively. This is not precisely the same as converting each residual to billions and then reestimating the $\overline{SE}$ and RMS, but the resulting error is small.

The root-mean-square error is for the period covering the end of the fit period up to 1967-II. For the first fit period there are nineteen forecast or extrapolation periods; for the second, fifteen extrapolations; for the third, ten; and for the fourth, five extrapolations.

[a] In equations where the ratio of expenditures to income is the dependent variable, ΔY rather than Y_{-6} is used. ΔY is the difference between Y (deflated per household disposable income during the survey quarter) and Y_{-6}.

either automobile or durable goods purchases. Using the spliced p^* series to measure intentions, Table 5-3 shows a significant partial correlation between intentions and purchases of automobiles, holding income level and attitudes constant, although the association between intentions and durable goods purchases is not significant at conventional levels.

Three general points stand out clearly from the data. First, the regression coefficient of all variables in both equations is a function of the time span included in the fit period. Simply extending the fit period beyond 1961-IV by adding additional quarters ordinarily results in higher regression coefficients for all three independent variables when purchase levels are dependent, and in higher coefficients for both survey variables when the ratio of purchases to past income is dependent. Second, both attitudes and buying intentions generally make a significant contribution to the explanation of variance in either automobile or durable goods purchases during all of the fit periods examined, although the relative importance of the two survey variables depends both on the time span and on the form of the dependent variable. Third, the partial correlation between buying intentions and purchases increases strongly as the fit period is extended, especially when pre-1959 observations are dropped as additional quarters are added and when the dependent variable is in ratio form. In fact, when both these conditions are met (panels D and H), the buying intentions variable tends to dominate both the automobile and durable goods purchase equation.

The instability of the regression coefficients when alternative fit periods are used suggests that these models are apt to provide unreliable forecasts. That this is indeed the case is demonstrated by Figure 5-3, which shows the successive forecasts made by the simplest of the above models fitted to alternative periods. The top panel has forecasts of expenditures for automobiles, the lower panel forecasts of total durable goods expenditures. The dashed line shows actual purchases. The solid line for 1953-I–1961-IV shows regression estimates of purchases for the original period of fit. Starting with the solid black dots, both panels show extrapolations beyond alternative fit periods. Thus we have an extrapolation period running from 1962-I through 1966-IV (which covers purchases through 1967-II), a somewhat shorter extrapolation period beginning with 1963-I and also going to

FIGURE 5-3. Predicted and Actual Expenditures for Automobiles (Panel A) and Total Durable Goods (Panel B), Alternative Fit Periods and Forecast Periods

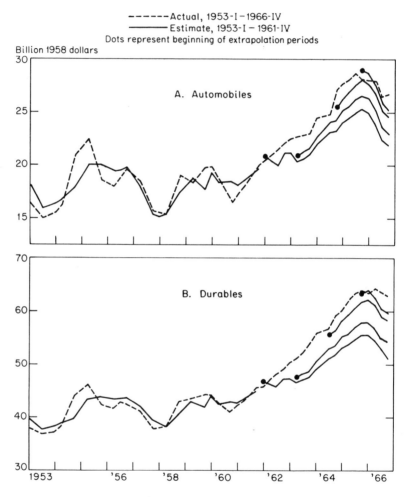

Equations are: Panel A: $M_6 = b_0 + b_1 Y_{-6} + b_2 A$
                  Panel B: $D_6 = b_0 + b_1 Y_{-6} + b_2 A$
Source: Appendix Table 5-A-3.

1966-IV, and two additional and shorter extrapolation periods. Each set of extrapolations is based on a regression fitted to all data up to the point where the extrapolation begins.

The extrapolations have two characteristics: (1) all, with the possible exception of the last extrapolation in the top panel, consistently underpredict purchase levels; (2) for any given extrapolation period, the forecast value is less far below the actual value when the forecast is based on a more up-to-date fit period. That is, reestimating the parameters of the regression will reduce, but will not eliminate, a persistent tendency towards underprediction.

The reason for the systematic underprediction in Figure 5-3 is apparent from examination of Figure 5-4, which shows the contribution of each independent variable to the predicted value of the dependent variable for two of the time spans shown in Table 5-3. The extrapolation period runs from the beginning of 1962 through 1966. In general, the dependent variable (expenditures six months ahead) rises consistently from the beginning of 1962 up through about the third quarter of 1965, and then declines. Of the two independent variables, the first (income) rises steadily and fairly rapidly during the period when expenditures are rising, but the income coefficient in the regression does not have sufficient weight to pull predicted expenditures up unless the second (attitudes) also shows a consistent and rapid improvement. However, during the first two years of the extrapolation period, 1962-I–1964-I, the attitude index essentially moves sideways with some gentle upward tilt. Thus, by 1964, a substantial gap had developed between actual and predicted expenditures and the gap is never fully overcome by reestimating parameters.[20]

Virtually all the equations which use expenditure level as the dependent variable and any combination of the three independent varia-

---

[20] It is, incidentally, quite clear from Figure 5-4 that cyclical turning points in automobile purchases are, on the whole, well reproduced by the equation, due almost entirely to the contribution of the consumer attitudes variable. However, the relative strengths of cyclical upturns or downturns is not well foreshadowed. The equation yields serious underpredictions of the strength of the expansion from 1962 on, and one can see evidence that the attitude index is an erratic predictor of the strength of contractions. For example, the brief decline from 1960 to 1961 is barely reflected in attitudes, but the fairly modest rate of decline from 1966 on appears to be seriously overstated by the decline in attitudes. For identification of turning points in the automobile expenditure series, however, the attitude variable has quite a good record.

FIGURE 5-4. Components of Predicted Value for Automobile Expenditures, Alternative Fit Periods and Forecast Periods

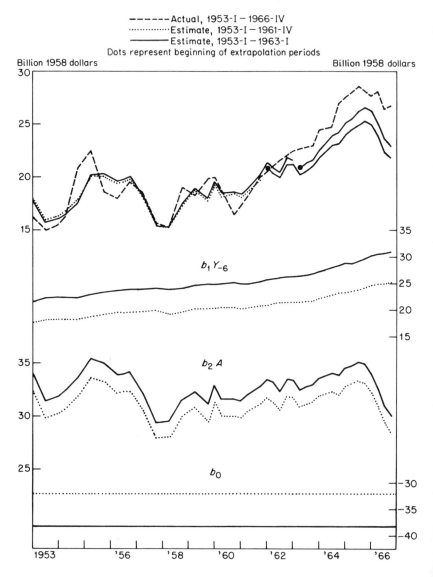

Equation is: $M_6 = b_0 + b_1 Y_{-6} + b_2$
Source: Appendix Table 5-A-3.

bles shown in Table 5-3 show this same pattern. That is, they all consistently underpredict the strength of the 1962–66 expansion. The tendency towards underprediction is somewhat less pronounced for models that drop off pre-1959 observations as additional post-1962 ones are added, largely because those models give relatively more weight to the intentions variable (which rose more or less consistently from 1961-I to 1965-III) and relatively less to attitudes (which rose during 1961 and after 1964).

It is interesting to note that the equation form which uses ratio of expenditures to past income appears to give systematically better predictions during most of the extrapolation period. Figure 5-5 shows two sets of extrapolation-period and fit-period residuals. The top panel has residuals from equation (2) with the level of automobile purchases dependent; the lower panel has residuals from a comparable equation with the ratio of automobile purchases to income dependent. The last line in each panel shows residuals using the entire 1953–67 span as the fit period, while the first two lines show residuals for shorter fit periods and their associated extrapolation periods.

Extrapolations based on the level equations systematically underpredict purchases, and the underpredictions are consistently worse the further the base period from the extrapolation period. Although the residuals from equations that use the ratio of expenditure to past income as the dependent variable are not small, they do not systematically deteriorate to the same extent as the others do. Yet, if one were to look at the fit-period statistics for both equations, it would be difficult to see any reasons why predictions should be based on the equation in the lower panel rather than on the one in the upper panel. The standard errors are quite comparable if put into the same units, the extent of serial correlation is about the same, and the coefficients are just as plausible.

One possible explanation for the finding that durable goods demand models with the ratio of expenditures to income as the dependent variable give better predictions than comparable models with expenditure level dependent is that the first equation is more accurately specified. In Section III it was found that the correct specification for a demand model with deflated per household expenditures as the dependent variable was a multiplicative relation involving purchase rate and real price per unit. If income is a determinant of real price and the

FIGURE 5-5. Residuals from Automobile Expenditure Regressions, Alternative Equation Forms and Time Spans

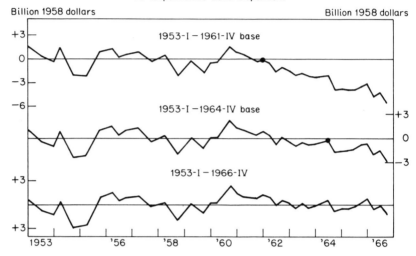

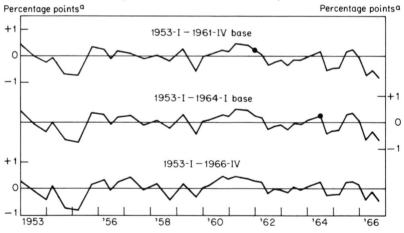

[a] One percentage point in the M_6/Y_{-6} ratio is roughly equal to 3.5 billion 1958 dollars.

Equations are: Panel A: $M_6 = b_0 + b_1 Y_{-6} + b_2 A + b_3 p^*$
                     Panel B: $M_6/Y_{-6} = b_0 + b_1 \Delta Y + b_2 A + b_3 p^*$

Source: Appendix Table 5-A-3.

anticipatory variables are determinants of purchase rate, a properly specified real expenditure equation should have $p*Y$ and AY as independent variables. But regressing the expenditure–income ratio on the survey variables is equivalent to the introduction of the cross-product terms $p*Y$ and AY into a real expenditure equation, as can be seen below.

$$M_6/Y_{-6} = b_0 + b_1\Delta Y + b_2 p^* + b_3 A + u;$$

therefore,

$$M_6 = b_0 Y_{-6} + b_1 \Delta Y Y_{-6} + b_2 p^* Y_{-6} + b_3 A Y_{-6} + u Y_{-6}$$

DISTRIBUTED LAG EQUATIONS

Evidence presented above in Section III indicated that introduction of a lagged dependent variable resulted in considerable improvement in the fit for most of the equations tested. Let us interpret this result as suggesting the presence of a distributed lag structure in the relation between independent and dependent variables. This interpretation seems reasonable, since the demand for durable goods basically constitutes an attempt to equate actual with desired stocks, and desired stocks are quite likely to be a function of past as well as current values of the explanatory factors.

Table 5-4 summarizes the results of putting the model in distributed lag form. It is assumed that the weights for lagged values of the independent variables decline geometrically, hence that a simple Koyck transformation provides the appropriate lag structure. Regression statistics covering two fit periods, presence and absence of a lag structure, and all four of the dependent variables used above are summarized.

Introduction of a lag structure considerably improves the results. All independent variables continue to show a significant association with automobile or durable goods expenditures, and the standard errors are substantially reduced. The estimated mean lag generally runs between one and two quarters, suggesting that past values of the independent variables have appreciable effects for three or four quarters, which seems reasonable a priori.

The distributed lag equations fit the data somewhat better for automobiles than for total durables. As can be seen from Figures 5-6 and 5-7, the over-all fit is quite good for both, but almost all the turning

TABLE 5-4. Comparison of Anticipations Models With and Without Distributed Lag Adjustment Process

Dependent Variable and Fit Period	Regression Coefficients and t Ratios					$\bar{R}^2$	SE	DW
	Y_{-6}	ΔY	A	p^*	Lagged Dep. Var.			
M_6								
1953-II–1962-II	.032(1.3)		.250(3.5)	.101(2.2)	—	.588	1.26	1.72
1953-II–1962-II	.008(0.4)		.109(1.4)	.063(1.5)	.532(2.8)	.700	1.08	2.10
1953-II–1967-II	.078(7.5)		.280(6.0)	.099(2.7)	—	.930	1.10	1.38
1953-II–1967-II	.026(2.0)		.121(2.5)	.062(2.1)	.590(4.9)	.957	.87	2.01
D_6								
1953-II–1962-II	.114(3.7)		.354(3.9)	.084(1.4)	—	.662	1.61	1.36
1953-II–1962-II	.037(0.9)		.114(0.9)	.068(1.3)	.546(2.5)	.738	1.42	1.60
1953-II–1967-II	.218(12.4)		.437(5.5)	.084(1.4)	—	.957	1.86	.81
1953-II–1967-II	.041(1.5)		.100(1.4)	.074(1.8)	.765(6.9)	.981	1.23	1.88
M_6/Y_{-6}								
1953-II–1962-II		.075(2.5)	.064(3.0)	.023(2.0)	—	.676	1.16	1.51
1953-II–1962-II		.053(1.9)	.032(1.3)	.016(1.5)	.417(2.3)	.738	1.04	1.91
1953-II–1967-II		.045(2.2)	.056(3.6)	.038(7.0)	—	.802	1.11	1.44
1953-II–1967-II		.026(1.5)	.027(1.9)	.019(3.0)	.511(4.4)	.869	.90	1.94
D_6/Y_{-6}								
1953-II–1962-II		.102(2.9)	.082(3.2)	.019(1.5)	—	.698	1.39	1.36
1953-II–1962-II		.080(2.0)	.052(1.5)	.017(1.3)	.265(1.3)	.707	1.37	1.51
1953-II–1967-II		.100(2.9)	.047(1.7)	.081(8.4)	—	.809	1.94	.99
1953-II–1967-II		.039(1.6)	.011(0.6)	.032(3.3)	.644(6.8)	.914	1.30	1.55

Note: t ratios are in parentheses.

Variables are as described earlier in the notes to Table 5-1. The lagged dependent variable used above overlaps the dependent variable by one quarter; if the dependent variable covers the period 1961-III and -IV, for example, the lagged dependent variables would cover the period 1961-II and -III.

The period shown covers the *purchase* period included in the equation. The survey data cover a slightly earlier period since the equations are designed to be forecasting equations. For the first fit period, 1953-II–1962-II, for example, the surveys cover the period 1953-I–1961-IV; the 1953-I survey is used to predict purchases during 1953-II and -III while the 1961-IV survey is used to predict purchases during 1962-I and -II. Not all quarters are used in the regressions because the survey variables are not always obtainable.

Estimates of SE are in billions of 1958 dollars. Where the dependent variable has the form of a ratio to past income (M_6/Y_{-6}), the SE are converted to billions by multiplying the computed values by the average value of Y_{-6}. This is not precisely the same as converting each residual to billions and then reestimating the SE, but the resulting error is small.

The Durban and Watson statistic is biased towards 2.0 in equations with a lagged dependent variable, hence does not constitute an adequate test for the presence of serial correlation in the residuals.

FIGURE 5-6. Predicted and Actual Expenditures on Automobiles, Distributed
Lag Equation

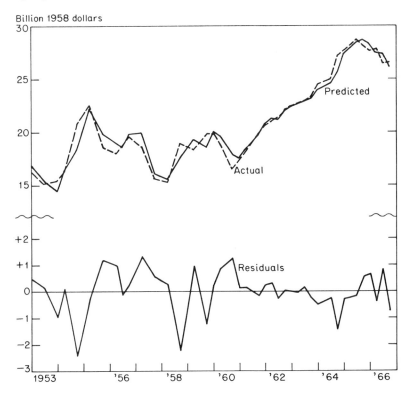

Equation is: $M_6 = b_0 + b_1 Y_{-6} + b_2 A + b_3 p^* + b_4 (M_6)_{-1}$
Source: Appendix Table 5-A-3.

points in the durable goods series are missed by the fitted regression
line. Moreover, the adjustment coefficient for total durables in the
distributed lag equation may be on the high side. According to Table
5 4, the adjustment process implied by the coefficient of the lag term is
considerably more gradual and extends further back in time for total
durables than for automobiles. Since the most important independent
variables (p^* and A) reflect consumer *decisions* about expenditures
rather than the factors that influence decisions, one would have thought
that the total durables equation should show shorter average lags than
the automobile equation. But the data indicate just the reverse, possibly
because the coefficient of the lagged dependent variable reflects habit

FIGURE 5-7. Predicted and Actual Expenditures on Durables, Distributed
Lag Equation

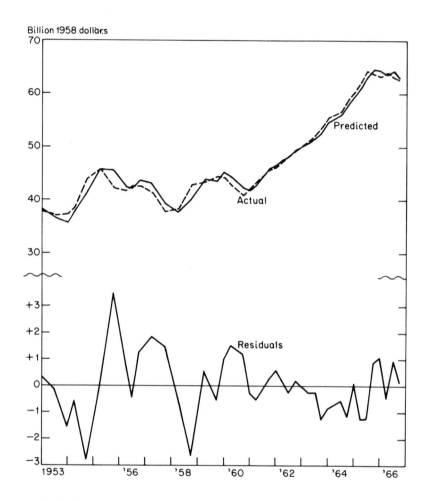

Equation is: $D_6 = b_0 + b_1 Y_{-6} + b_2 A + b_3 p^* + b_4 (D_6)_{-1}$
Source: Appendix Table 5-A-3.

persistence and the highly autoregressive nature of total durables expenditures rather than incomplete adjustment to change.

COMPARISON WITH AUTOREGRESSION MODELS

Although the regression estimates considered above indicate that one can get quite good fits with anticipations variables in quarterly time series, the relevant question is whether these models are markedly superior in forecasting performance to naive models. For this comparison, we use an autoregressive naive model consisting of up to eight lagged values of the dependent variable. The autoregressive model is constrained in the same way as the anticipations models, in that we use only those lagged dependent variables that would have been available at the forecast date (the survey quarter). Each of the expenditure variables is regressed against successive lagged dependent variables in the respective base periods; the process is stopped arbitrarily when additional lagged values fail to improve the adjusted R^2. Thus, each of the autoregressive models could contain different numbers of lagged dependent variables, although in general the optimum number of lags was about the same in all periods. Autoregressive models of automobile expenditures generally showed a maximum adjusted R^2 after three lagged values had been used, while for total durables expenditures, adjusted R^2 was maximized after seven or eight lags.

The anticipations models used for this test are the ones analyzed above in Table 5-3. In equations where the level of durable goods expenditures is the dependent variable, explanatory factors include income level and either one or both of the survey variables A and p^*. Where the ratio of durable goods expenditures to income is the dependent variable, explanatory variables are income change and one or both of the survey variables. Lagged values of the dependent variable do not appear as explanatory factors in any of the anticipations models. With rare exceptions, the lagged dependent variable failed to improve the statistical fit in any of the anticipations equations during any of the base periods tested. The apparent inconsistency between the results here and in the preceding section of the paper is due to the fact that the models under discussion here are pure forecast models; the values of all independent variables must be known prior to the start of the time period covered by the dependent variable. The distributed lag equations discussed earlier did not impose this constraint. As a consequence, the first lag term available for the pure forecast model is actually the third lag term in the series.[21]

Both autoregressive and anticipations models are estimated for the same set of base periods as are shown in Table 5-3, and for the same set of dependent variables. Table 5-5 summarizes the root mean square forecast errors for the three anticipations models and the autoregressive model, using alternative extrapolation periods and dependent variables. The first set of four extrapolation periods is constructed by simply adding quarters to the 1953–61 fit period, while the second set is constructed by simultaneously adding and dropping quarters at the end and the beginning, respectively, of the 1953–61 period. As noted above, the anticipations models include, besides the survey variable shown in Table 5-5, either income level (when expenditure level is dependent) or income change (when the expenditure–income ratio is dependent).

There are only a few cases in which any of the anticipations models is outperformed by the autoregressive model, although the margin of superiority varies considerably. In general, the comparative advantage of the anticipations model is somewhat stronger for automobile than for total durable regressions. The anticipations model is also generally superior for extrapolation shown in the right-hand side of Table 5-5 where beginning period observations are dropped as additional quarters are added. Relatively speaking, the worst performance of the anticipations models is in prediction of total durables purchases with the ratio of purchases to income dependent and with all data retained for successive extrapolation. Here, the prediction errors in the autoregressive equation average about the same size as in each of the three anticipations models, and none of the latter is consistently superior to the autoregressive model. The best performance of the anticipations model, again relatively speaking, is for automobile regressions with the ratio of expenditures to income dependent

---

[21] The forecast model predicts durable goods expenditures during the two quarters subsequent to the quarter in which the anticipations survey or surveys are taken. Thus, a survey taken in 1967-I would be used to forecast expenditures during 1967-II and 1967-III. A dependent variable lagged one quarter would thus consist of expenditure during 1967-I and 1967-II, one lagged two quarters would include expenditures during 1966-IV and 1967-I, and so forth. At the survey date of 1967-I, the latest known expenditure data would be expenditures during 1966-III and 1966-IV, that is, the third in the above series of dependent variable lags.

and with observations in the early part of the fit period dropped as additional quarters are added. Here, autoregressive model errors are at least twice as high, and in the last few extrapolation periods four to five times as high, as in the best anticipations model.

The contrast between automobile and total durables expenditures models can be clearly seen in Figures 5-8 and 5-9. The top panel of each figure plots extrapolation errors from models in which parameters are reestimated every four or five quarters; all data are re-

FIGURE 5-8. Residuals From Anticipations and Autoregressive Models of Automobile Expenditures

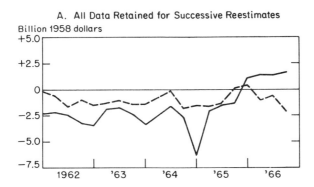

Equations are: Panel A: $M_6 = b_0 + b_1 Y_{-6} + b_2 A + b_3 p^*$
                 Panel B: $M_6 = b_0 + b_1 (M_6)_{-3} + b_2 (M_6)_{-4} + \cdots$
Source: Appendix Table 5-A-3.

TABLE 5-5. Comparison of Extrapolation Errors for Autoregressive and Anticipations Models, Alternative Prediction Periods, Fit Periods, and Forms of Dependent Variable, 1953-II–1967-II

| | Beginning Quarters for Fit Period (F) and Extrapolation Period (E) | | | | | | | |
Equation Form	1 F 1953-II E 1962-III	2 F 1953-II E 1963-IV	3 F 1953-II E 1964-IV	4 F 1953-II E 1966-II	1 F 1953-II E 1962-III	2a F 1955-III E 1963-IV	3a F 1957-I E 1964-IV	4a F 1959-III E 1966-II
	A: Prediction Errors [a] for Expenditures on Automobiles, Billions of 1958 Dollars							
M_6 dependent								
Autoregressive	5.16	3.94	2.76	1.51	5.16	6.58	3.52	4.78
Anticipations, using								
A	2.90	2.27	1.26	1.05	2.90	2.29	0.85	3.18
p^*	5.13	3.35	2.70	1.02	5.13	3.16	1.74	2.27
A, p^*	3.18	2.37	1.66	1.19	3.18	2.18	0.71	0.90
M_6/Y_{-6} dependent								
Autoregressive	3.01	3.09	2.76	1.22	3.01	3.84	3.02	4.19
Anticipations, using								
A	2.57	2.82	3.01	3.77	2.57	2.81	2.77	4.34
p^*	1.42	1.43	1.68	1.37	1.42	1.40	1.29	1.50
A, p^*	1.49	1.55	1.69	1.90	1.49	1.46	1.28	1.01

B: Prediction Errors [a] for Expenditures on Total Durables, Billions of 1958 Dollars

D_6 dependent								
Autoregressive	9.12	5.82	3.31	4.31	9.12	3.58	7.12	7.22
Anticipations, using								
A	6.93	6.04	3.09	2.12	6.93	5.18	1.73	5.11
p^*	9.92	7.54	5.17	1.70	9.92	6.59	2.98	3.88
A, p^*	7.17	6.13	3.61	2.39	7.17	5.13	1.58	1.38
D_6/Y_{-6} dependent								
Autoregressive	5.59	5.99	3.72	4.34	5.59	3.73	6.24	6.65
Anticipations, using								
A	6.25	7.01	6.96	8.61	6.25	6.08	6.48	9.58
p^*	4.77	4.59	4.06	3.60	4.77	3.39	2.98	1.57
A, p^*	5.14	5.27	4.27	4.71	5.14	4.48	3.02	1.83

[a] Prediction errors are defined as the root mean square error of the extrapolation. Errors for equations where the dependent variable is the ratio of expenditures to past income (M_6/Y_{-6}, D_6/Y_{-6}) are converted to billions of 1958 dollars by multiplying the computed RMS error by the average level of Y_{-6} during the prediction period. As indicated above in the notes to Table 5-4, the resulting inaccuracy (the correct procedure is to convert each error first and then average) is quite small.

FIGURE 5-9. Residuals From Anticipations and Autoregressive Models of Durables Expenditures

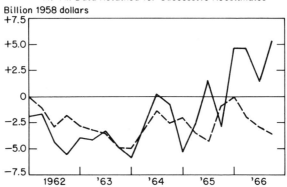

A. All Data Retained for Successive Reestimates

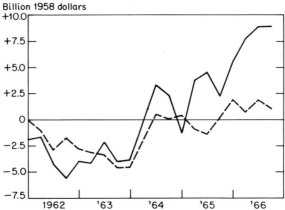

B. Earliest Data Dropped for Successive Reestimates

Equations are: Panel A: $D_6 = b_0 + b_1 Y_{-6} + b_2 A + b_3 p^*$
                 Panel B: $D_6 = b_0 + b_1 (D_6)_{-3} + b_2 (D_6)_{-4} + \cdots$
Source: Appendix Table 5-A-3.

tained with each reestimation. The bottom panel follows the same procedure except that beginning period observations are dropped with successive reestimation, so that the fit period continually moves forward in time. Figure 5-8 has prediction errors for automobile expenditures, Figure 5-9 prediction errors for total durables expenditures. The anticipations model in both these figures uses all three independent variables, that is, Y_{-6}, A, and p^*.

For automobiles, both upper and lower panels clearly show that the anticipations model out-performs the autoregressive model in virtually every quarter of the extrapolation period. Both the margin of superiority of the anticipations model as well as the absolute size of its forecast errors are improved in the lower panel where older data are dropped. In Figure 5-9, in contrast, the upper panel shows no clear advantage to either anticipations or autoregressive models, although the former actually has a somewhat lower mean error. The anticipations model shows a small but marked advantage in the lower panel during virtually the entire period, especially toward the latter part where the autoregressive model goes completely off the track.

On the whole, this examination of anticipatory demand models brings out two clear-cut conclusions. First, the anticipations series themselves are strong cyclical indicators; both consumer attitudes and consumer buying intentions have cyclical turning points which precede those in durable goods and automobile expenditures by about six months. The attitude index appears to be a bit better at reflecting turning points than buying intentions, partly because the series itself is considerably smoother; however, the random component of the buying intentions series appears to be considerably reduced since the initiation of the large sample Census Bureau survey in 1959.

Although both anticipations series contain pronounced cyclical movements, only buying intentions appear to have a distinct trend component. This factor works to the comparative disadvantage of the attitude variable in regression models, since all of the trend influences on durable goods expenditures must be picked up by other variables. This difference in ability to measure trends is very probably the explanation for the results obtained in Section III, where it was found that the attitude index was comparatively more useful in predicting changes in the purchase rate of nonintenders than in predicting changes in the population purchase rate. The first variable (nonintender purchase rates) appears to be trendless; the secular movement in the proportion of total purchasers in the population apparently shows up as a secular increase in the proportion of intenders rather than as an increase in purchase rates for either intenders or nonintenders.

Whether the anticipations variables are more accurate predictors of cyclical movements in durables expenditures than variables like unemployment rate, average weekly hours, and so forth, is a purely empirical question. We have not examined this question here, although other studies which have done so, e.g. [11], found that attitudes were a more useful variable than other candidates for the cyclical role. However, the question has not been answered in a definitive way and clearly warrants further investigation.

REFERENCES

[1] Adams, F. Gerard, "Prediction with Consumer Attitudes: The Time Series-Cross Section Paradox," *The Review of Economics and Statistics,* November 1965.

[2] Byrnes, James, "An Experiment in the Measure of Consumer Intentions to Purchase," *Proceedings of the Business and Economic Statistics Section, the American Statistical Association,* May 1965.

[3] Friend, Irwin and F. Gerard Adams, "The Predictive Ability of Consumer Attitudes, Stock Prices, and Non-Attitudinal Variables," *Journal of the American Statistical Association,* December 1964.

[4] Juster, F. Thomas, *Anticipations and Purchases: An Analysis of Consumer Behavior,* Princeton University Press for NBER, 1964.

[5] ———, "Consumer Buying Intentions and Purchase Probability: An Experiment in Survey Design," *Journal of the American Statistical Association,* September 1966.

[6] Katona, George, *The Powerful Consumer,* New York, 1964, Appendix B.

[7] Kish, Leslie, "Variances For Indexes From Complex Samples," *Proceedings of the Social Statistics Section, American Statistical Assn.,* 1962, pp. 190–199.

[8] Klein, Lawrence R. and John B. Lansing, "Decisions to Purchase Consumer Durable Goods," *Journal of Marketing,* October 1955.

[9] Maynes, E. Scott, "Consumer Attitudes and Buying Intentions: Retrospect and Prospect," September 1966, mimeographed.

[10] Mueller, Eva, "Effects of Consumer Attitudes on Purchases," *American Economic Review,* December 1957.

[11] ———, "Ten Years of Consumer Attitude Surveys: Their Forecasting

Record," *Journal of the American Statistical Association,* December 1963.

[12] Okun, Arthur, "The Value of Anticipations Data in Forecasting National Product," in *The Quality and Economic Significance of Anticipations Data,* Princeton University Press for NBER, 1960.

[13] Suits, Daniel B., and Gordon R. Sparks, "Consumption Regressions with Quarterly Data," in the *Brookings Quarterly Econometric Model of the United States,* edited by J. S. Duesenberry, G. Fromm, L. R. Klein, and E. Kuh, Amsterdam, 1965.

[14] Tobin, James, "On the Predictive Value of Consumer Intentions and Attitudes," *Review of Economics and Statistics,* February 1959.

[15] U.S. Congress, Joint Economic Committee, *Reports of the Federal Reserve Consultant Committee on Economic Statistics,* 1955.

V. DATA APPENDIX

TABLE 5-A-1

Survey Quarter	Y_{-6} ($ bills.) (1)	M_6 ($ bills.) (2)	ΔY ($ bills.) (3)	1956 = 100 A (4)
1953-I	251.9	14.5	5.3	100.0
III	258.4	12.5	0.1	92.3
1954-I	258.3	13.5	−2.4	93.6
II	257.0	14.2	−1.7	95.1
IV	255.9	18.3	3.4	98.7
1955-II	259.9	19.7	7.3	104.2
IV	268.9	15.8	5.1	102.6
1956-II	273.7	15.1	2.6	99.3
III	274.8	15.3	1.8	99.8
IV	276.5	15.9	2.2	100.3
1957-II	278.4	15.5	2.4	94.4
IV	281.3	12.1	−2.7	86.0
1958-II	277.4	12.3	−0.8	86.5
IV	279.8	15.4	4.4	92.7
1959-II	285.4	14.9	6.0	95.1
IV	290.4	16.2	−0.8	91.1
1960-I	289.5	16.0	0.4	96.7
II	289.8	15.2	2.8	92.9
IV	292.9	13.3	−0.9	92.8
1961-I	292.6	14.2	−0.5	92.4
II	292.1	14.8	3.6	94.4
IV	297.3	16.3	5.6	96.4
1962-I	300.9	16.7	3.3	98.7
II	303.6	16.8	2.8	96.8
III	305.3	17.5	1.0	95.0
IV	306.4	18.2	1.3	
1963-I	307.0	18.4	2.1	98.3
II	308.4	18.5	2.3	95.4
III	309.9	18.9	3.2	96.2
IV	311.9	19.4	4.2	96.9
1964-I	314.6	20.1	6.6	99.0
III	324.5	20.4	5.5	100.2
IV	328.9	22.1	3.9	99.4
1965-I	331.4	22.4	4.7	101.5
II	334.5	23.2	2.8	102.2
III	336.7	23.5	7.7	103.2

	Per Cent of Households Reporting Intentions to Buy Automobiles				Weighted Per Cent of Households Reporting Intentions to Buy Automobiles	
Basic SRC (5)	Un-weighted QSI (6)	SRC-NS (7)	QSI-NS (8)	QSI-S (9)	QSI-SW$_0$ (10)	QSI-SW$_3$ (11)
14.1	n.a.	15.2	15.2	15.1	4.29	7.00
12.0	n.a.	12.9	12.9	13.5	3.79	6.16
11.3	n.a.	12.2	12.2	12.2	3.44	5.62
15.0	n.a.	16.2	16.2	16.6	4.70	7.69
17.6	n.a.	19.0	19.0	17.9	4.90	7.99
15.7	n.a.	16.9	16.9	17.3	4.93	8.04
16.0	n.a.	17.2	17.2	16.2	4.46	7.25
15.1	n.a.	16.3	16.3	16.7	4.74	7.74
14.2	n.a.	15.3	15.3	16.0	4.48	7.30
18.5	n.a.	19.9	19.9	18.7	5.08	8.38
17.7	n.a.	19.1	19.1	19.6	5.56	9.07
15.1	n.a.	16.3	16.3	15.3	4.20	6.86
14.3	n.a.	15.4	15.4	15.8	4.49	7.30
15.1	n.a.	16.3	16.3	15.3	4.20	6.86
17.3	15.8	18.6	15.8	16.2	4.30	7.08
14.6	21.2	15.7	21.2	20.0	5.57	8.17
17.5	18.7	18.8	18.7	18.6	4.95	8.25
14.2	17.1	15.3	17.1	17.5	4.67	7.78
17.9	18.6	19.3	18.6	17.5	4.61	7.61
13.8	17.9	14.9	17.9	17.8	4.89	7.80
16.4	16.6	17.7	16.6	17.0	4.59	7.70
18.3	18.5	19.7	18.5	17.4	4.73	8.07
17.1	18.1	18.4	18.1	18.0	5.05	8.14
17.4	18.9	18.7	18.9	19.4	5.33	8.64
18.1	17.4	19.5	17.4	18.1	5.01	8.30
17.9	18.6	19.3	18.6	18.5	5.19	8.46
16.9	18.2	18.2	18.2	18.7	5.41	9.00
17.4	18.2	18.7	18.2	19.0	5.43	9.12
19.3	19.1	20.8	19.1	18.0	5.15	8.85
15.1	18.8	16.3	18.8	18.7	5.40	9.08
17.8	18.3	19.2	18.3	19.1	5.64	9.14
18.3	20.4	19.7	20.4	19.2	5.73	9.74
17.8	19.4	19.2	19.4	19.3	5.79	9.57
n.a.	18.8	18.6	18.8	19.3	5.89	9.77
17.8	19.1	19.2	19.1	19.9	5.97	9.89

(Table notes are on following pages)

NOTES TO TABLE 5-A-1

GENERAL NOTE: The income and expenditure data used in Table 5-A-1 are formed from series in the *Survey of Current Business* (*SCB*). All variables are in constant (1954) dollars and are deflated by an index of the number of families. After 1964, data for disposable income and durables purchases are available only in 1958 constant dollars; these series were converted to a base 1954 = 100. The deflation for the number of families is based on an index (1954 = 100) constructed from a series interpolated from the *Statistical Abstract of the U.S.* The index is as follows:

1953-I	98.5	1958-II	105.8	1963-I	113.2
1953-III	99.0	1958-IV	106.3	1963-II	113.5
1954-I	99.4	1959-II	107.1	1963-III	113.8
1954-II	99.8	1959-IV	108.1	1963-IV	114.1
1954-IV	100.6	1960-I	108.4	1964-I	114.4
1955-II	101.6	1960-II	108.8	1964-III	114.9
1955-IV	102.7	1960-IV	109.4	1964-IV	115.1
1956-II	103.6	1961-I	109.8	1965-I	115.4
1956-III	104.0	1961-II	110.2	1965-II	115.7
1956-IV	104.4	1961-IV	111.0	1965-III	116.7
1957-II	104.9	1962-I	111.5		
1957-IV	105.3	1962-II	111.9		
		1962-III	112.4		
		1962-IV	112.8		

Column 1: Y_{-6} is average disposable income in 1954 dollars for the six months preceding the survey quarter, deflated by the index of families.

Column 2: M_6 is the average expenditure on automobiles and parts in 1954 dollars for the six months after the survey quarter, deflated by the index of families. The *Survey of Current Business* quarterly series for automobile expenditure in current prices was deflated by the Consumer Price Index for new automobiles, 1954 = 100, as reported in the quarterly releases of the Bureau of Labor Statistics.

Substantive revisions of the series in the August 1965 *SCB* are taken into account: data are made comparable with the original series by using the average ratio of an overlap period.

Column 3: ΔY is the difference between disposable income in the survey quarter and disposable income in the six months preceding the survey. Data are in 1954 prices deflated by an index of families.

Column 4: A is the SRC Index of Consumer Attitudes, based on responses to a battery of questions about the household's financial condition and prospects and about general business and product market conditions; the fall of 1956 is taken as 100. See [11] for a complete description. In the 1966 *Survey of Consumer Finances,* the 1959-IV index is shown as 91.4. This revised figure was unavailable at the time the regressions were run.

Prior to August 1963 the published index averaged the responses to six questions. One question, on attitudes towards expected price changes, was deleted from the index in August 1963 and in all subsequent quarters. Thus the A series used here is a composite based on six questions during the 1953-I 1963-II period and on five questions thereafter. The 1966 *Survey of Consumer Finances* describes the modification introduced in August of 1963, and gives data for the five question index back to 1953.

Column 5: SRC automobile buying intentions. The series measures the proportion of families intending to buy automobiles in the next twelve months, and includes those who reported that they would or probably would buy, plus one-half of those who said they might buy. Prior to 1961 the published series counts all "might buy" responses. The early data were made comparable by adjustment factors which were available for the period 1956–60; prior to 1956 an average adjustment factor was used. The data for 1964-III and -IV are not quite comparable to the others because of differences in sample composition. Basic data for these quarters are linked on the assumptions that families with income under $5,000 would behave in the same way as others, and also increased by 1 per cent to compensate for the bias arising from the fact that the entire sample had been interviewed in previous surveys. These data and the estimated factors were obtained directly from the Survey Research Center. In Figure 5-1, this series is plotted through 1966-IV. The data are as follows:

	Basic SRC
1965-IV	19.3
1966-I	18.6
1966-II	14.1
1966-III	18.6
1966-IV	17.9

Column 6: Census Bureau series, unweighted percentage of all families reporting an intention to buy new or used automobiles in the next twelve months; basic data from *Consumer Buying Indicators,* U.S. Census Bureau Series P-65, various issues. In Figure 5-1, this series is plotted through 1966-IV. The data are as follows:

	Unweighted QSI
1965-IV	20.5
1966-I	19.1
1966-II	18.7
1966-III	19.3
1966-IV	19.7

Column 7: SRC-NS is col. 5 ratioed to the level of col. 6 by the average ratio during an overlap period. The figure for 1965-II, for which no reliable survey data are available, is interpolated; it is assumed that the seasonally adjusted series is unchanged from 1965-I to 1965-II. Regressions that include data through 1964-IV only were run before these SRC data were available. For the 1964-III-IV quarters, QSI-NS was used.

Column 8: QSI-NS is col. 6 with a link to col. 7 to provide data for the period before 1959.

Column 9: QSI-S is col. 8 seasonally adjusted by the following seasonal factors calculated from col. 6: $Q_1 = 100.4$, $Q_2 = 97.5$, $Q_3 = 95.9$, $Q_4 = 106.2$.

Column 10: QSI-SW$_0$ is a weighted series based on Census Bureau data with a link to col. 5 to provide data for the period before 1959. The following weights are assigned to the various intended categories: definitely planning to buy a new automobile within the next 6 months = .7; probably or may buy a new automobile within the next 6 months = .5; intending to buy a new automobile within 12 months but not within 6 months = .3; intending to buy a used automobile within 12 months = .2; does not know about 12 month intention or does not know about 6 months intention = 0. The weighted series is seasonally adjusted by factors estimated from the Census Bureau part of the series. The seasonal factors are as follows: $Q_1 = 99.4$, $Q_2 = 96.3$, $Q_3 = 95.8$, $Q_4 = 108.5$.

Column 11: QSI-SW$_{3C}$ is an alternative weighted Census Bureau series; the weights and construction are the same as in col. 10 except that the "don't know" categories are given a weight of .3. As before, the series is linked back to col. 5 to provide data for the period before 1959. The pre-1959 part of the series is seasonally adjusted as in col. 10. The 1959–65 part is seasonally adjusted by slightly different factors, estimated from the 1959–65 part of the series. The latter seasonal factors are: $Q_1 = 101.1$, $Q_2 = 98.3$, $Q_3 = 95.8$, $Q_4 = 104.8$.

TABLE 5-A-2

Survey Quarter	Y_e (1958 dollars) (1)	M (1958 dollars) (2)	Percentage of Households			
			x (3)	x_6 (4)	x_9 (5)	x_{12} (6)
1959-I	6,368	304	10.41	10.68	10.80	10.41
II	6,422	321	10.95	11.00	10.41	10.63
III	6,430	325	11.04	10.14	10.53	10.74
IV	6,429	279	9.24	10.28	10.64	10.78
1960-I	6,411	326	11.31	11.34	11.29	11.10
II	6,429	325	11.36	11.28	11.03	10.63
III	6,440	324	11.20	10.87	10.39	10.21
IV	6,422	299	10.53	9.99	9.88	9.93
1961-I	6,405	268	9.45	9.56	9.72	9.90
II	6,419	272	9.66	9.86	10.04	10.36
III	6,472	285	10.06	10.24	10.59	10.79
IV	6,549	299	10.41	10.86	11.03	11.20
1962-I	6,604	324	11.30	11.35	11.46	11.60
II	6,658	331	11.39	11.55	11.69	11.85
III	6,687	339	11.70	11.85	12.01	12.10
IV	6,721	351	11.99	12.16	12.23	12.26
1963-I	6,758	363	12.33	12.35	12.35	12.37
II	6,797	363	12.37	12.36	12.38	12.47
III	6,848	369	12.35	12.39	12.51	12.61
IV	6,899	370	12.42	12.59	12.69	12.81
1964-I	6,985	381	12.76	12.83	12.94	12.69
II	7,094	384	12.90	13.04	12.67	13.16
III	7,206	398	13.17	12.56	13.24	13.43
IV	7,288	354	11.94	13.28	13.52	13.70
1965-I	7,342	451	14.62	14.31	14.28	14.27
II	7,390	430	14.00	14.12	14.15	14.28
III	7,491	443	14.23	14.23	14.00	14.00
IV	7,613	446	14.23	14.45	13.93	13.76
1966-I	7,727	469	14.67	13.78	13.60	13.48
II	7,771	416	12.89	13.06	13.08	12.76
III	7,803	433	13.24	13.18	12.71	12.69
IV	7,843	422	13.12	12.45	12.51	12.32

V (current dollars) (7)	V* (1958 dollars) (8)	P_a (9)	House-holds (millions) (10)	A (1956 = 100) (11)	Percentage of Households	
					p (12)	q (13)
3,012	2,919	103.2	51.36	93.9*	23.2	76.4
3,041	2,935	103.6	51.66	95.1	22.8	77.1
3,049	2,943	103.6	52.00	93.1	24.3	75.6
3,082	3,019	102.1	52.35	91.1	25.6	74.4
2,953	2,887	102.3	52.69	96.7	25.4	74.8
2,928	2,862	102.3	52.91	92.9	24.9	74.8
2,909	2,892	100.6	53.08	92.8*	24.1	75.3
2,854	2,837	100.6	53.24	92.8	24.0	75.4
2,852	2,832	100.7	53.41	92.4	24.3	74.9
2,873	2,814	102.1	53.66	94.4	24.3	75.3
2,892	2,838	101.9	53.96	95.4*	25.7	74.5
2,939	2,867	102.5	54.26	96.4	25.5	74.6
2,921	2,872	101.7	54.55	98.7	25.7	74.4
2,951	2,905	101.6	54.74	96.8	26.9	72.8
2,959	2,895	102.2	54.88	95.0	26.1	74.2
2,987	2,926	102.1	55.01	98.6	26.8	73.5
2,985	2,941	101.5	55.14	98.3	26.9	73.4
2,995	2,936	102.0	55.32	95.4	27.9	72.9
3,019	2,989	101.0	55.53	96.2	28.7	72.5
3,034	2,977	101.9	55.73	96.9	27.9	73.2
3,040	2,983	101.9	55.93	99.0	28.9	72.3
3,035	2,981	101.8	56.21	98.1	29.3	71.9
3,064	3,025	101.3	56.52	100.2	28.8	72.3
2,991	2,961	101.0	56.83	99.4	30.5	71.1
3,123	3,086	101.2	57.15	101.5	30.5	71.3
3,087	3,075	100.4	57.39	102.2	30.3	71.5
3,075	3,112	98.8	57.60	103.2	31.1	71.2
3,111	3,136	99.2	57.81	102.6	30.2	71.6
3,126	3,196	97.8	58.02	99.8	30.3	71.7
3,157	3,225	97.9	58.22	95.8	29.7	71.8
3,195	3,274	97.6	58.41	91.1	30.7	71.4
3,187	3,213	99.2	58.59	88.3	29.0	72.5

(Table notes are on following page)

NOTES TO TABLE 5-A-2

Source, by column

Column 1: Y_e is disposable income per family in constant (1958) dollars, averaged for the survey quarter and the two preceding quarters. Data for the period up to 1963-IV are obtained from *The National Income and Product Accounts of the U.S., 1929–1965,* a supplement to the *Survey of Current Business.* Later periods are obtained from various issues of the *Survey of Current Business.*

Column 2: M is personal consumption expenditures for automobiles per household in constant (1958) dollars. Data are obtained from Table 1.16 in the *Survey of Current Business.*

Column 3: x is the portion of households purchasing new automobiles during the survey quarter, expressed as an annual rate of purchase. Since it is obtained from seasonally adjusted data on expenditures for automobiles and average retail prices paid for automobiles, x is also a seasonally adjusted series.

Column 4: x_6 is the new automobile purchase rate averaged for the survey quarter and the following quarter, expressed as an annual rate.

Column 5: x_9 is the new automobile purchase rate averaged for the survey quarter and the two following quarters, expressed as an annual rate.

Column 6: x_{12} is the new automobile purchase rate for the survey quarter and the three quarters following, expressed as an annual rate.

The three variables above (x_6, x_9, x_{12}) are simply moving averages of the x series in column 3.

Column 7: V is the average retail price of new automobiles in current dollars. The data were obtained directly from the Office of Business Economics, U.S. Department of Commerce. The prices reflect not only pure price changes but also changes in the mix of models, differences in optional equipment from one year to the next, and so forth. The series is adjusted for seasonal variation in trade-in margins.

Column 8: V^* is column 7 deflated by an index of new automobile prices.

Column 9: P_a is a new automobile price deflator derived from Tables 1.15 and 1.16 of the *Survey of Current Business.*

Column 10: The number of families in the U.S. population is derived from annual series given in *Current Population Reports,* Series P-20; quarterly figures are estimated by straight-line interpolation of the annual figures.

Column 11: A is the SRC Attitude Index, 1956 = 100. This index is identical to the one in Table 5-A-1, except that values have been interpolated (indicated by asterisk) for quarters in which no SRC survey was taken and for which the index is therefore not obtainable.

Column 12: p is an estimate of the average probability of purchase by those reporting some kind of intention to buy a new or used car in the Census Bureau's Quarterly Survey of Intentions. Probability weights are assigned to the various classes of intenders reported in the QSI, the weights being estimated from the purchase rates observed in reinterview studies. The derivation of the p series is such that it can be expressed as a weighted proportion of intenders divided by the average weight in a base period; hence p and the series labeled QSI-SW$_{3V}$ are identical except for a multiplicative constant. The latter series is shown in Table 5-A-3.

Column 13: q is 1 minus the proportion of intenders in the Census Bureau's Quarterly Survey of Intentions. It is obtained by subtracting from unity the proportion of the population reporting any kind of six-month intention to buy, any kind of twelve-month intention to buy, and "don't know" about twelve-month buying intentions.

TABLE 5-A-3

	Y_{-6} (1)	M_6 (2)	D_6 (3)	ΔY (4)	A (5)	QSI-SW$_{3V}$ (6)
1953-I	288.8	16.4	37.8	4.7	100.0	7.00
III	295.3	15.1	36.9	0.1	92.3	6.16
1954-I	294.9	15.5	37.2	−1.0	93.6	5.62
II	294.2	16.2	38.3	−2.2	95.1	7.69
IV	293.1	20.8	44.0	6.5	98.7	7.99
1955-II	300.6	22.6	45.8	6.7	104.2	8.04
IV	309.4	18.6	42.2	4.8	102.6	7.25
1956-II	314.2	18.0	41.6	1.0	99.3	7.74
III	314.7	18.8	42.6	0.5	99.8	7.30
IV	315.2	19.6	42.5	3.6	100.3	8.38
1957-II	318.4	18.6	41.2	0.7	94.4	9.07
IV	319.7	15.6	37.7	−1.3	86.0	6.86
1958-II	316.6	15.3	38.1	−1.8	86.5	7.30
IV	317.9	19.0	42.9	6.5	92.7	6.86
1959-II	325.7	18.4	43.4	5.6	95.1	7.27
IV	329.5	19.8	44.4	−.4	91.1	8.16
1960-I	328.4	19.9	44.1	2.8	96.7	8.10
II	330.2	18.8	42.9	2.4	92.9	7.92
IV	332.4	16.5	40.9	−3.7	92.8	7.63
1961-I	330.3	17.4	42.1	−.4	92.4	7.75
II	329.3	18.1	43.4	5.0	94.4	7.74
IV	336.3	20.0	45.6	7.1	96.4	8.11
1962-I	340.8	20.6	46.2	3.9	98.7	8.18
IV	344.1	21.0	47.3	3.2	96.8	8.56
III	346.0	21.5	48.3	1.6	95.0	8.30
IV	347.5	22.1	49.2	1.3	98.6	8.55
1963-I	348.2	22.5	50.1	3.6	98.3	8.56
II	350.3	22.7	51.1	2.6	95.4	8.87
III	352.4	22.9	52.2	4.3	96.2	9.13
IV	354.8	23.4	54.0	5.9	96.9	8.87
1964-I	358.7	24.5	55.6	8.0	99.0	9.20
III	370.8	24.9	56.8	8.2	100.2	9.18
IV	376.9	27.2	59.2	3.9	99.4	9.71
1965-I	379.9	27.7	60.1	4.7	101.5	9.70
II	382.7	28.1	62.3	5.3	102.2	9.66
III	386.3	28.6	64.4	12.6	103.2	9.91
IV	393.5	28.1	63.9	11.1	102.6	9.63
1966-I	401.8	27.6	63.4	5.8	99.8	9.64
II	406.1	27.9	64.2	0	95.8	9.46
III	406.9	26.5	63.2	2.0	91.1	9.79
IV	411.0	26.7	62.7	2.0	88.3	9.25

(Table notes are on following page)

NOTES TO TABLE 5-A-3

Column 1: The Y_{-6} series is conceptually identical to that in column 1 of Table 5–A-1; its differences are that it (a) covers a slightly longer time period, (b) is in 1958 rather than in 1954 dollars, and (c) uses the revised data that began to appear with the August 1965 revision of the NIP Accounts.

Column 2: M_6 is average expenditure on automobiles and parts in 1958 dollars for the six months after the survey quarter, deflated by an index of families. The same procedures followed in derivation of the M_6 series in Table 5–A-1 were followed in this series except that revised income and product data (August 1965 issue of the *SCB*) were used.

Column 3: D_6 is average expenditures for total durable goods in 1958 prices for the six months after the survey quarter, deflated by an index of families.

Column 4: ΔY is the difference between disposable income in the survey quarter and average disposable income in the six months preceding the survey. Data are in 1958 prices deflated by an index of families.

Column 5: A is identical to the series in column 4, Table 5–A-1, extended forward to 1966-IV.

Column 6: QSI-SW$_{3V}$ is the same weighted series as in column 11 of Table 5–A-1 except for the seasonal adjustment. Data in this column have seasonal adjustment factors which vary through time. The difference between the contant seasonal adjustment in Table 5–A-1 and the variable seasonal in this table shows up mainly over the period 1959 through 1963 in quarters I and II. The estimated seasonal adjustment factor for the first quarter declines from 103.7 in the first quarter of 1959 to 99.9 in the first quarter of 1963, while for the second quarter the estimated seasonal rises from 95.7 in the second quarter of 1959 to 99.7 in the second quarter of 1963. Since 1963, the estimated seasonal adjustment factors show only small and apparently random variation. The seasonal factors estimated for 1966 are as follows: first quarter, 100.0; second quarter, 99.2; third quarter, 95.6; fourth quarter, 105.4.

INDEX